DIONYSUS IN PARIS

DIONYSUS IN PARIS

A Guide to Contemporary French Theater

by WALLACE FOWLIE

MERIDIAN BOOKS, INC. *New York*

WALLACE FOWLIE

*Wallace Fowlie was born in Brookline, Massachusetts, in
1908. Educated at Harvard, he completed his doctoral
dissertation on the French religious thinker Ernest Psichari.
A frequent visitor to France and a widely acknowledged
authority on French literature, Mr. Fowlie has taught
at Harvard, Yale, the University of Chicago, and, at
present, at Bennington College. He is the author of many
works of criticism, among them* MALLARMÉ, DE VILLON
À PÉGUY, CLOWNS AND ANGELS, RIMBAUD, *and a parallel
to the present work,* A GUIDE TO CONTEMPORARY FRENCH
LITERATURE *(Meridian Books, M48); a volume of auto-
biography,* PANTOMIME; *and the following translations:*
SIXTY POEMS OF SCÈVE, MID-CENTURY FRENCH POETS,
JOURNALS OF JEAN COCTEAU, *St.-John Perse's* SEAMARKS,
and Claudel's A POET BEFORE THE CROSS.

A MERIDIAN BOOKS ORIGINAL
Published by Meridian Books, Inc. April 1960
First printing March 1960

Contents

Foreword

I have referred to too many plays and too many playwrights in the course of this relatively brief study. And
yet many other plays and playwrights have been omitted,
on various grounds, sometimes other than those of the
mere exigencies of space. I have not discussed the lighter
type of play, that of Roussin and Achard, for example,
because my principal concern has been the evolution of
the serious play—that approaching a form of tragedy in
our day. A certain number of successful playwrights, Jules
Romains and Salacrou among others, are neglected because the "literary" qualities of their craft seem less striking than the art of those playwrights I have selected.
Michel de Ghelderode, a gifted and prolific playwright,
I have omitted on the grounds that his tradition is more
Flemish than French.

In the past, the greatest dramatists have been the
greatest poets: Sophocles, Shakespeare, Racine. The modern theater in every country will inevitably be measured
by theirs. This is especially true in France, where the
playwright learns that in his tradition the poet is interested not in the exploits of the hero but in his sufferings.
During the past thirty years, a new literary theater has
been created in France where the combined themes of

human greatness and human defeat have been explored in a variety of literary styles. This study proposes to look at them not long after the time when they were first conceived, and to consider them as examples of that rigorous social art called theater, where the imagination of the director and the technical skill of the actor are so vital.

WALLACE FOWLIE

October 1959

I. INTRODUCTIONS

1. French Theater Today: Traditions and Achievements

During the past quarter of a century, the theater in France has recaptured a prestige comparable to that which once existed at the time of Louis XIV and which was associated with the achievements of Racine and Molière. If there seems to be no one playwright equal to Racine or Molière, there is an abundance of new plays, an undiminishing variety of skillful directors, many examples each season of brilliant acting, and above all an unflagging critical enthusiasm on the part of theatergoers, which have assured prosperity to the various kinds of theater in Paris and maintained what can perhaps best be called a kind of nobility in the dramatic art form.

This prestige of nobility comes about whenever the theater for a given community is more than the theater, whenever a new play, or a new production of an old play, affects the daily life of a city, when the ideas generated during the performance continue afterwards to affect the thinking of the spectators and hence modify their existence to some extent. This is precisely what has happened in our time. The theater has been reintegrated into so many lives in the metropolis that it counts as a social and spiritual force. After a new Jouvet production, for example, a new Dullin production, a new Barrault production, ideas circulated around the Athénée, the Atelier, or the Marigny, and from those centers spread throughout the city and the country, as possibly ideas once circulated around the Acropolis. The discussions for and against certain ideas of the play would not in time be quite so important as the new lesson in sensibility the play afforded, the new modifications of instincts and understanding which came about through that collaboration of playwright, director, and actors we call a theatrical performance.

Throughout the history of the theater, in every country, the same phenomenon seems to take place at those moments when it is vital and meaningful. The same gods descend upon the earth who were participants in the very distant, very mysterious origins of the theater. It would seem—and this surely applies to recent years in Paris— that the eloquence of human speech is revitalized and even resanctified. New formulas are discovered, in the particular literary art of playwriting, for the oldest and most persistent enigmas of mankind. By these enigmas we mean the relationships existing between men and the obscure forces of destiny which at times appear beneficent and at other times deadly and inimical. At the great moments of the theater—Athens at the time of Sophocles, Elizabethan London, Versailles in the seventeenth century —the problems of justice and political order, the physical and metaphysical experiences of love and death, are given new forms and propounded once again in new solutions.

When Jouvet devised the first production of a Giraudoux play (*La Guerre de Troie n'aura pas lieu*, for example), when Dullin devised the first production of *Les Mouches* of Jean-Paul Sartre, these men, in their very art of directing a new play at a moment of political tension—the first at the time of the Spanish Civil War, and the second, during the German occupation of Paris—preceded all the literary critics of these plays, and provided not only a luminous interpretation of a difficult text, but at the same time countless evenings of intellectual satisfaction and aesthetic happiness for a large number of spectators. Our most vivid memories of the theater are paradoxically those of serious and even tragic plays that were brilliantly staged and acted. The all-pervasive mystery of the theater is its ability, in its most transcendent instances, so to present and transform the most bitter and tragic stories of human fate, that we experience at the end of the evening, and thereafter in our memory of that evening, a joyous elation, an exaltation in our new understanding of the ways of man and the powers that beset him. We remember, if we had the good fortune to see them, the feverish eyes of Jean Vilar as Richard II, the poignant expression on the face of Ludmilla Pitoëff as Saint Joan, the cajoling, unctuous gestures of Ledoux as Tartuffe. We soon realize that those parts which upset us the most, enchanted us the most. When on a summer evening, in the court of the Palais des Papes at Avignon, Gérard Philipe played Rodrigue, he created for the thousands of spectators watching him an experience of beauty, of vibrant youthfulness and nobility, of emotion, such as *Le Cid* has perhaps never provided since it was first performed in 1636.

One of the principal characteristics of the French theater, both of the subsidized state theaters and the privately owned independent theater companies, is the custom of alternating new plays and revivals of the so-called classical plays, those especially of Corneille, Racine, and Molière, to which have been added a few eighteenth- and nineteenth-century plays, of Marivaux, Beaumarchais, and Musset, for example. When a Frenchman attends the theater, it is often to rediscover and enjoy for perhaps the tenth or twentieth time a text with which he is perfectly familiar. The average theatergoing Frenchman has a wider, more varied, and more permanent heritage of plays than the average theatergoer of other countries. He has therefore developed what is often called a "classical" taste, namely the pleasure of rediscovery and re-evaluating the familiar. A fairly extensive number of plays, representing a very high standard of dramaturgy, form a set of criteria in terms of which the Frenchman will judge any new play. His familiarity with Racine and Molière supplements his innate tendencies and makes of him a harsh, articulate theater critic. New plays that are weak in structure and language disappear quickly in Paris. Only the strongest of them are able to stand this proximity to the classical plays that inhabit all the French theaters, at least as ghosts when they are not being actively performed.

The French attend a performance of *Phèdre* or *Le Malade imaginaire* or a Marivaux comedy in somewhat the same spirit that an opera-lover attends *La Traviata* or *Carmen,* and even in the spirit in which a baseball fan attends a World Series game. The Molière text is always the same, and the score of a Verdi opera remains the same, and the pitcher and catcher are inevitably in their same posts at every baseball game. One attends these three spectacles in order to watch and enjoy and judge a performance, to witness the histrionics of a fixed form. The performance of an actor playing *Le Malade imaginaire,* of the soprano singing Violetta, and of a pitcher in a specific game, is never the same as that of any other actor, soprano, or pitcher. The theatergoer of classical taste prefers not to be held or disturbed by a new plot, a new situation. When he is actually attending a new play, he will instinctively search for the original myth of which the new play is a mere contemporary expression.

There are three kinds of literary theater in Paris, which, for some time now, have maintained rather strict characteristics and styles. The government-subsidized theaters form one category: the Comédie-Française had, until recently (see page 35), two houses, the Salle Richelieu and the Salle Luxembourg. This is the museum theater, official, consecrated, traditional, maintaining a large classical repertory and cautiously admitting newer plays that usually have been tested in other theaters. Despite constant internal storms and political upheavals, the troupe, highly trained, performs admirably and still provides France with a standard of acting and theatrical skill. The more recently created Théâtre National Populaire is also state-subsidized, on a far smaller budget than the Comédie-Française, and is at the moment housed in the vast Palais de Chaillot. The repertory is smaller and contains more foreign plays. The company was created to bring important drama to large, popular audiences.

The second type of theater is privately owned, catering to the middle and wealthy classes, and known by the art and temperament and peculiarities of a director. Jean-Louis Barrault and his wife Madeleine Renaud founded a company that occupied the Marigny Theatre for several years, and that at the present time is using the large and less attractive Théâtre Sarah-Bernhardt (see page 35 for recent changes). Jouvet's company at the Athénée, and Dullin's at the Atelier, were once good examples of this kind of serious independent theater, which regularly performed new plays alternating with new experimental productions of older plays. Here the director is the real star. Copeau and his company at the Vieux-Colombier were the prototype. These companies are fairly small, and the actors and actresses become so well known that they become stars too and attract a faithful following. Edwige Feuillère and Maria Casarès, for example, have become famous in Barrault's theater, in their performances of Claudel and Camus plays. The principal protagonists in Racine's tragedies are women, and partly because of those enviable parts, the serious French theater had always been dominated by actresses. The English critic Kenneth Tynan has with some justification called the French theater a matriarchy.

At the Comédie-Française the honors are perhaps more evenly divided between men and women, between heroes and heroines, but in the smaller independent companies the great actress dominates. The regime of Sarah Bernhardt did not end with her death. There are countless examples between the time of Racine and today of playwrights composing their plays for an actress they admire and love. The world of the French theater is in this respect the microcosm of French civilization, where woman is perhaps more loved and worshipped than in any other. In France the supremacy of woman's virtue and influence is an important although subtle factor. During the generation immediately preceding the years with which we are concerned, the popular so-called bourgeois play turned almost exclusively on the subject of adultery. Woman was the deceiver and man was the cuckold. Woman was presented as a power unto herself and man as the semifarcical character who is tricked.

The male audience in France can always find a kind of revenge for this state of affairs in the music halls, such as Le Casino de Paris and Les Folies Bergères, where the nude female figure is spectacularly and abundantly shown, and where the skits demonstrate the more humorous aspects of love both conjugal and adulterous. But this form is hardly literary theater and should not be included in our categories.

The avant-garde theater is the third and final grouping, which, during these recent years, has played a more important part than ever before in the life and evolution of the French theater. These are the often ludicrously small theaters, "pocket theaters" as they are called, where new experimental plays are performed on precariously small budgets and with the always imminent threat of having to close. During the past ten or fifteen years, the number of successes, both literary and commercial, almost warrants the use of the new term *Ecole de Paris*. Pichette, Beckett, Ionesco, Adamov, Schehadé, and Ghelderode are writing new types of plays, so opposed to the successes of the first part of the century that it is possible to see in their work a renaissance of the theater, a promise of renewed vitality, and the cause of the gradual forming of an enthusiastic public. The success of this recent crop of experimental plays is paradoxical because, of all the arts, the theater is the slowest to evolve. Already during the 1940's the very marked commercial successes of Sartre and Anouilh and Montherlant threw into disrepute the older fixed formulas of the thesis play and the adultery play of Bernstein and Becque. But in the 1950's, the successes of Ghelderode, Beckett, and Ionesco made the Bernstein play the product of an era that is over.

This evolution in the theater, which in reality is a renovation, is the result of many forces and changes, each one of which will have to be studied in detail. The art of certain directors and the particular kind of training to which they submitted their actors stand out prominently. Jacques Copeau is of course the most eminent figure. Close in importance to him are the four directors whose major contribution was made between the two wars, and who are known collectively as the Cartel: Jouvet, Dullin, Baty, and Pitoëff. These four directors, in their respective theaters, knew both successes and failures. In the gradually expanding prestige that their efforts were bringing to the Paris stage the type of play they chose to direct helped to form literary taste. They were quick to perceive and utilize the influences that were being felt in all domains of literature, the growing awareness, for example, of Freud and Proust and Pirandello. The drama of adultery, or the well-made play, so popular before the First World War, was slow to die, but a few new plays, far more sincere and simple in tone, with a deeper sense of human reality, began attracting attention, plays such as *Martine* of Jean-Jacques Bernard, and *Le Paquebot Tenacity* of Vildrac. Jules Romains's *Knock*, with Louis Jouvet, was such a resounding success in 1923, probably because it was so far removed from the already worn-out theme of adultery in the bourgeois class. During the thirties and forties, when such professional playwrights as Lenormand (*La Vie est un songe*) and

Salacrou (*L'Inconnue d'Arras*) provided new plays with great regularity, a number of highly competent and highly esteemed writers, poets and novelists especially, became known as playwrights and brought the prestige of literary creation to the theater: Giraudoux, Claudel, Cocteau, Montherlant, Gide, Mauriac, Sartre, Julien Green.

The case of Jean Anouilh, who has always been exclusively a playwright, was the exception, because his plays, more than those of Salacrou and Lenormand, seemed destined to survive. The novelists and poets—Claudel, Cocteau, Montherlant—wrote their plays in a new kind of language, both strong and lyric, which had not been heard for a long time. They brought a seriousness to their work and a focus on political and religious themes. Sartre's *Les Mains sales*, for example, *Dialogues des Carmélites* of Bernanos, and *Bacchus* of Cocteau, emphasized themes that had been absent from the French theater. The stringent law of conformity, which is necessary for immediate success in the theater—and which may also be detrimental to its vitality—seemed to have been broken by the emergence of the new type of supremely literary playwright.

These men chose for their plays ambitious, profound, and well-tested subjects. They favored classical mythological themes and thus renewed the Greek tradition of Racine's tragedies. Precisely because of Racine, these subjects are better known to a contemporary audience in France than in other countries. Cocteau's *La Machine infernale* is on the story of Oedipus, Giraudoux's *La Guerre de Troie* is on Hector and the theme of war, Anouilh's *Antigone* is his interpretation of the Sophocles tragedy, Sartre's *Les Mouches* is the story of Orestes and the problem of man's freedom. These are only four examples, taken from many, of plays on themes from classical antiquity, but all of them have been revived often in France and have become international successes as well.

The frankly religious theme, Biblical and Christian, has held a high place in the new French theater. Barrault's production for the Comédie-Française of Claudel's *Le Soulier de satin* has been recently revived. This work of gigantic proportions and difficulties is vastly different from Obey's skillful play on the subject of Noah. More accessible in tone and subject, *Noë* continues to be played in France and abroad. Even Anouilh attempted a religious subject in his play on Joan of Arc, *L'Alouette*. Montherlant's *Port-Royal,* on Jansenism and obedience to Rome, and the Bernanos adaptation, *Dialogues des Carmélites,* now re-adapted into an opera by Francis Poulenc, are among the contemporary successes that seem surest to survive.

A third category of subject matter or theme, preoccupation with metaphysical problems, involves to some extent the first two, the classical and the religious. But there is a certain number of important plays representing a rigorously philosophical bias (far more prominent in the plays than psychological study) and unrelated in any direct way to mythology and Christianity. Some of these plays are the most striking that have been written during the past twenty years, in terms of structure, brevity, intensity, and pessimism: *Huis Clos* of Sartre, *Les Bonnes* of Genet, *Les Chaises* of Ionesco, *En attendant Godot* of Beckett. Such plays reflect aspects of modern philosophy and art: existentialism, surrealism, and the work of Kafka and Pirandello and Joyce. In them, the drama of ideas seems to dominate the drama of characters. But they clearly manifest what is equally apparent in the plays on classical and religious themes—namely the conviction that the art of the theater is fundamentally and eternally an experiment with truth.

The plays in all three categories cannot possibly be looked upon as entertainment in the usual sense of diversion and escape and relaxation. They are studies, in the form of drama, of the conditions of life. Each one presents an ordeal, and each one that is successful in performance will present at the same time, in accordance with the age-old meaning of theater, a transcendence over this ordeal, a purificatory experience for the spectator. These plays best represent the theater's contribution to the central movement of modern literature. "It is an extraordinary victory of the French theater," writes Oreste Pucciani, "never to confuse the related though alien worlds of art and entertainment." Anxiety, which the existentialists have defined as inherent in existence itself, pervades and forms the action in these particular plays.

During the four years of the Occupation (1940-4), the French theater was prosperous, although there were only three or four exceptional productions: Claudel's *Le Soulier de satin,* Anouilh's *Antigone,* and *La Reine morte* of Montherlant. During the few years following the Occupation, there were many signs of transition and change. The work of the Cartel directors was practically over. Pitoëff had died at the beginning of the war. Jouvet, on his return to Paris after a long tour in South America, restricted his repertory to revivals and added only one new play, *Les Bonnes* of Genet. Baty gave up the theater and turned to marionettes. Dullin, a few years before his death, occupied the vast Théâtre Sarah-Bernhardt, quite unsuitable to his kind of production.

To some extent, the fate of the French theater fell into the hands of three pupils of Dullin: Barrault, founder of the company at the Marigny; Vilar, who became director of the Théâtre National Populaire; and André Barsacq, who took over Dullin's theater, L'Atelier. Barrault was the real successor to the Cartel, the director whose productions are most reminiscent of its style. He was trained principally by Dullin, but profited from the example and the friendship and the help of Copeau, Artaud, and the mime Decroux.

Since the war, no single playwright in France has occupied the exceptional place held by Giraudoux during the thirties. The only possible successor is Jean Anouilh, who has written twenty-one full-length plays during a span of twenty-six years. He has had three successes in London and New York: *Antigone, The Lark,* and *Waltz of the Torea-*

dors. A recent play, *Pauvre Bitos,* is a political manifesto that flatters some of the lower tastes of his audience. He is still a very controversial figure, and always faithful to a familiar antithesis in all his plays: the men and women who compromise with the world, and the pure in heart who are ultimately defeated. The second play of Samuel Beckett, *Fin de partie,* did not have the success of *Godot,* whereas Adamov's 1957 play, *Paolo Paoli,* may well be his best to date. The number of revivals of Ionesco plays seems to strengthen his position among contemporary playwrights. Sartre's pro-Soviet farce *Nekrassov* adds very little to his achievements as playwright.

During the course of each of the recent seasons, at least one of the drama critics takes time in his weekly columns, or in the collected reviews in a book, to point out the durability, the perennial quality of this art. It is unlike every other art, in that it lives or dies depending upon the support of a community. The theater is a social fact, a spectacle mounted with the hope of attracting and holding a public that has to be renewed every evening. The thought of man, as expressed in a literary text, and the physical appearance of man on the stage, form the substance of what is called theater, provided there is a paying audience in front of the stage, assembled in order to watch and hear the unfolding of some dramatic action. Theoretical writing on the theater is abundant in France, and in some instances it is of high quality. There are contributions from actor-directors (Jouvet, Barrault), from philosophers (Henri Gouhier), from theater administrators (Pierre-Aimé Touchard), from playwrights (Gabriel Marcel, Montherlant), from theater critics (Robert Kemp, Pierre Brisson). Each writer, in his own particular approach to the theater, has tried to explain the fundamental mystery of the art: the experience of communion, rather than mere communication, which has to take place between the man acting a given character on the stage and the spectator who follows the action and listens to the speeches. The theater in recent Paris seasons is based upon the experience of "participation," which is not totally unlike the participation at the distant origins of the theater when the priest performed a sacrifice before the people and when a dancer imitated the movements of an animal before an audience whose very livelihood depended on the action depicted.

If the question whether France has produced an outstanding playwright during the past twenty years is debatable, there is no doubt concerning the astonishing variety of plays performed and the high excellence of production. Just during the past few seasons the Paris theaters have offered such contrasts as Michel Vinaver's *Les Coréens,* a play on the Korean War by a young writer; Claudel's *Partage de midi,* a play on passion and God by the greatest French poet-dramatist; Marcel Aymé's *La Tête des autres,* which is a bitter attack on the French judicial system; Sartre's *Le Diable et le Bon Dieu,* in which it is argued that God does not exist; a translation of Tennessee Williams's *Cat on a Hot Tin Roof;* and an adaptation by Albert Camus of Faulkner's *Requiem for a Nun.* In the performance of each of these widely divergent plays, staged before what was, in a general sense, the same public, the same end was achieved, an end that is difficult to define in anything save semimystical terms. In each case, as the spectators became aware of the theme of the play, of the problems it posed and their solutions, another kind of experience was taking place, unique to the theater and affiliated to the religious experience of worship. A multiple and very mysterious bond was growing between spectators and actors, an awareness of communion which transcended the interpretation and the understanding of the play's text.

The commonplace word used to designate this experience is "pleasure" or the verb "to please." Aristotle, Molière, and Jouvet, in three different epochs of theater history, have claimed that the goal of a performance is to please the public, to afford pleasure. It is a pleasure that will not be generated unless it is shared, unless it is felt simultaneously to some degree by all the spectators. The significance of this experience, its origins, the universality of its expression and need and catharsis, are best explained (although it must be remembered that all explanations of such a complex subject are dimmed by the impossibility of ever discovering authentic facts) in a myth that existed before the time of Aristotle. Dionysus, the son of Semele and Zeus, who was raised by Silenus and the nymphs, became the god of ecstasy and death, of the most violent experiences that man knows. He is associated both with the experience of intoxication and that of persecution and martyrdom. He could take the form of the bull and hence represent fecundity and mad fury, but he also appeared as the god crucified. In the many legends of his activity, Dionysus always showed to man some extreme form of love or hate, of anguish or cruelty. He was the god of excess whose acts surpassed and transcended the ordinary action and experiences of human existence.

Dionysus is in truth the spirit of the theater. In whatever form he takes—we should say today, in whatever part he plays—he reveals to man, both to the actor playing him and to the spectator watching him, something more about man. Whenever the theater is looked upon as an art form that does good to the world or does harm to it, whenever it is described as a moral force of edification or as an evil force of temptation or exhibitionism, we can be sure that something is wrong, that the myth of Dionysus is being misconstrued. In itself the theater is neither something good nor something evil. It is the reflection of a very fundamental psychological fact in man: the need that man has always felt of testing and hence knowing the extremes of his powers and his weaknesses. This ability, visible in the story of Dionysus, to move from one extreme to the other, from the fullness of man's power or potentiality or transcendence to the opposite extreme of man's defeat or ignominy or death, may be the indication of man's principal attribute of divinity. Everyman is Dionysus to some extent. But every man cannot perform the acts that the theater can depict. The theater has been man's compensation for the life he cannot live, from the time of the earliest Dionysian dances through the tragedies performed in Athens, London, and Paris.

This compensatory experience can of course be found in other art forms, in the novel, in the dance, in the cinema, but the theater has always claimed, and justifiably, that a true purgation of the emotions can be realized only during the performance of a great play. The presence of living actors, engaged in the enactment of a serious dramatic action, is required to effect this supreme experience in the theater, whether seen in its modern form as psychoanalytical cure or as a broader reintegration within the social group, within the community. In this connection, it has often been argued that tragedy in its most exemplary and in its purest form is created during the most stable periods of history, when society is directed by a strong and even tyrannical government, when the laws governing men are rigid, when the moral, economic, and religious strictures are numerous. The age of Racine, for example, under Louis XIV, when social and political demands were so heavy that the performance of tragedy in the theater represented for the spectator acts dreamed of by him but which he could not imagine carrying out in his ordinary life. Their performance reminded him of the freedom that he jealously guarded within him but which he was unable to exercise in the exterior unfolding of his life.

This is almost a political theory of tragedy, and it is often referred to in our day when the changing unstable governments of the modern states would seem to form a strong obstacle to the development and flourishing of pure tragedy. If the plays of the modern French theater do not fulfill the laws of classical tragedy or classical comedy, the most successful among them do create and sustain an atmosphere of tragedy and an atmosphere of comedy. Some of the most permanent traits of tragedy and comedy are visible in the best of the recent plays. The fundamental divergence between the two genres of tragedy and comedy still exists in forms that only superficially give the impression of mingling or confusing the genres. In such plays as *Partage de midi, La Reine morte, Les Mouches,* and countless others, including even such experimental plays as *La Cantatrice chauve* of Ionesco and *Fin de partie* of Beckett, a tension is created by the drama; a Dionysian tension, in the sense that the spectator can easily feel his own fate merged with the fate of the character he is watching. The experience of death, for example, as it appears more and more imminent to the protagonists in these plays just referred to, may appear to the spectator related to his own death. This is one of the fundamental laws of tragedy, that the spectator is drawn into the catastrophe which is prepared and enacted on the stage. The atmosphere of tragedy makes possible this participation. The spectator will think, at least momentarily, that his own death is taking place. The atmosphere of comedy, on the contrary, will never permit the spectator to see himself in the dramatic action. It will be clearly someone else's death, for example, for which he feels no sympathy. In tragedy the spectator is subjected to the action of the play. In comedy he is separated from it; he is unable to identify himself with the actors and the characters. He is able to remain aloof and detached from comedy because he is able at every moment to rationalize about it. Comedy hence is more intellectual than tragedy. In tragedy the spectator's own feelings and passions play an important role.

This necessary liaison between public and actors varies in the form it takes from country to country, and from class to class, as it has varied in historical periods. Comedy —and farce in particular—seems more restricted than tragedy to a given historical time and to the given social class for which it was written. And yet Racine seemingly wrote his tragedies for a small, restricted public. And Giraudoux, in our day, claimed that the only class attentive to serious theater is the cultivated bourgeoisie. The French critics, especially those in the humanist tradition, have often stressed the belief that a knowledge of the past and a literary culture are necessary for an understanding and an enjoyment of serious plays. Two tragedies of Sophocles, for example, have been so fully incorporated into French civilization that they appear even today to the French as two modes or two levels of man's fate. *Oedipus,* on the one hand, is a kind of monstrous nightmare, and *Antigone,* as the second example, testifies to a pure form of heroism, to an almost awesome human greatness.

The exploits of these heroes did not interest Sophocles as much as their suffering. He believed that human nature had to be crushed and extinguished before it could rise and reach the status of heroism. The only action, therefore, that counts is inner and psychological. This particular focus has dominated French tragedy. It is avowedly so, and all-important, in the classical tragedies of Corneille and Racine. And on the whole, it continues as a workable formula in the French theater of the twentieth century. On many points the Greek view of human fate joins with the Christian. For Sophocles man's fate was more implacable, more absolute, than for a Christian writer, but Greek wisdom claimed that suffering comes from our nature and is measured out in relation to our faults. The choruses of Sophocles preach a submission to destiny. When man is subjected to the worst catastrophes, when he is a victim of the harshest blow of destiny, man is able to call it the tyranny of the gods, the tyranny of fate, and hence expresses a sublime experience of freedom. The freedom that the Greek hero practices in confronting disaster—this is the story both of Oedipus and Antigone—places him side by side with the Christian hero. Certain aspects of Greek tragedy would seem to make it a prefiguration of the drama of Calvary. In such plays as *Huis Clos* of Sartre and *Sud* of Julien Green, the unevenness of the fight, in the Greek sense, is very apparent. The forces opposing man far surpass his own powers, and they assure his spectacular failure.

What is the theater in its essence, in its dominant reality? What is a theatrical performance? It is a world of forms moving about on the stage. During the course of this mobility, an action is performed, a willed action is exteriorized. This action is of two kinds. When it is directed against some outside obstacle, it tends to be a physical or melodramatic action. When it is directed against an inner obstacle in the nature of man, it tends to be a spiritual or psychological action. But no matter what kind of action we are following on the stage, we are watching an even more basic condition for theatrical performance, the phenomenon of what Nietzsche called the mystery of metamorphosis. Before our eyes, a group of living men and women have been metamorphosed into characters who are totally different from themselves. This is why the dramatist has been called a demiurge, a god. He demands, for the presentation of his art, that actors exist on the stage in characterizations and actions that are not their own.

In two instances, in the modern French theater, this phenomenon has been examined and commented on by the playwright himself. Louis Jouvet in his book of theater memories (*Témoignages sur le théâtre*) has reminded us of these two scenes, one by Claudel and one by Giraudoux, in which the art of the theater is defined. In *L'Echange* of Claudel, an actress tries to explain what the theater is to a young girl who has never seen a play or been inside a theater. She says first that there is a stage and a place for the audience. Everything is closed in, and people come there in the evening and sit in rows, one behind the other, and look.

Il y a la scène et la salle
Tout étant clos, les gens viennent là, le soir et ils sont assis par rangées, les uns derrière les autres, regardant.

Then the young girl who is being instructed asks what they are looking at, since everything is closed in. The actress replies: they look at the curtain on the stage and what is behind when it goes up, and something happens as if it were true.

Ils regardent le rideau de la scène
Et ce qu'il y a derrière quand il est levé
Et il arrive quelque chose sur la scène comme si c'était vrai.

Jouvet sees in these five words, *comme si c'était vrai* ("as if it were true"), the entire enigma of the theater. From this brief formula enveloping the performance of the actors, the attention of the audience, and the work of the playwright, we learn that the illusion on the stage is a kind of reality, that the fiction we see acted is a part of our existence.

The young girl tries to understand this formula and says that if it isn't true, it must be like dreams we have when we are asleep. The actress then describes the "house" from her viewpoint. She has the impression of seeing bodies that are dressed and covering the walls like flies up to the ceiling. And she sees hundreds of white faces. And then she offers an explanation of why these people are there: Man is bored and he is ignorant from the day of his birth. And not knowing anything about how it begins or ends, that is why he goes to the theater.

L'homme s'ennuie, et l'ignorance lui est attachée depuis sa naissance.
Et ne sachant de rien comment cela commence ou finit, c'est pour cela qu'il va au théâtre.

There have been many theological, psychological, and moralistic theories on man's passion for the theater. In this seemingly very simple formula of Claudel, many famous affirmations concerning the theater are restated. We go to the theater in order to be rid of some deep-seated worry or anxiety, to overcome a feeling of emptiness, to feel joined with those people who sit in rows and watch. We go to the theater with the hope of finding a reason for existence, a belief that will lessen our uncertainty and our anguish.

The passage I am quoting is not quite over. The actress continues to say that in the theater the man in the audience looks at himself. He cries and laughs and doesn't want to leave.

Et il se regarde lui-même,
Et il pleure et il rit, et il n'a point envie de s'en aller.

The actress then lists a few types of people she imagines in the audience and her speech ends with the words: "And they watch and listen as if they were asleep."

Et ils regardent et écoutent comme s'ils dormaient.

This final statement seems to mean that the spectator, in his immobility and attentiveness, has lost an awareness of his own life in his identification with the life on the stage. And this seems almost to contradict Claudel's principal theory in this passage that we go to the theater to learn something about ourselves and about the world.

For the Frenchman this religious explanation of the theater is strongly reminiscent of Pascal. Jouvet alludes to this. By means of diversion—Pascal is thinking of the theater as well as of games and gambling—man seeks to forget his wretchedness and ignorance. Pascal even finds in this effort of man to see beyond himself, to transcend his normal state of ineffectualness and despair, a nobility and a greatness. It is even a form of heroism by which man seeks to recapture a lost happiness.

Jouvet, as a professional actor and director, says that these metaphysical explanations of the theater may well justify it. But he needs one further explanation, which he finds in a short play by his favorite playwright, Jean Giraudoux. In a speech in *L'Impromptu de Paris*, the writer attempts to tell us why people come to the theater and what they do there. He describes the moment when the house lights are dimmed and in the dark the people are tense and concentrated. It is in order to forget themselves and to give themselves. (*Si tout ce public, les lumières baissées, est maintenant tendu et recueilli dans l'ombre, c'est pour se perdre, pour se donner, s'abandonner.*) Jouvet claims that this description applies equally well to the actors—those already on the stage when the curtain goes up, and those in the wings waiting for their cue. They also are in a state of willingness to forget themselves and to give themselves.

That was the first half of the speech. Giraudoux adds, in the second half, that the spectator allows himself, by means of the play, to participate in a universal emotion. (*Il se laisse remettre en jeu dans l'émotion universelle.*) Jouvet tells us that this statement seems to him the most satisfying, the one by which the three people implicated in this experience—author, actor, and spectator—recover a sense of their real vocation. When one feels it, sitting in the dark of the theater and facing the lighted stage, a smile begins to form, or tears form in the eyes, or the heart is suddenly wrenched with anxiety. In a word, love overcomes one. (*Il se sent soudain le sourire à un centimètre de ses lèvres, les larmes de ses yeux, l'angoisse de son coeur. . . . Bref, il aime.*) Giraudoux refines on this last sentence of the speech when he says that the spectator does not love egotistically or narrowly. It is love filling his heart with generosity and tenderness and heroism. The experience of watching a play, and hence of participating in its action, is able so to magnify his capacity for love and so to purify his sentiments of love, that he moves beyond the pettiness and limitation of his own character.

This claim for the theater, phrased and rephrased by Jouvet, and for which he finds corroboration in the two scenes of Claudel and Giraudoux, is not in any literal sense a theory or a system. When Giraudoux said that the theater is an act of love, a need of communication and communion (*le théâtre est un acte d'amour . . . tout n'est que besoin de communication et de communion*) Jouvet felt that finally he had understood the art to which he had devoted much of his life. Throughout our lives we live a variety of feelings or sentiments. Life often seems constant oscillation between happiness and unhappiness, between anxiety and serenity, between despair and fulfillment. The variety of these sentiments, and our own ability to pass from one to the other and to know so many contrasting and conflicting experiences, is perhaps best explained by man's fundamental instinct for the dramatic. The very phrase "the instinct for the dramatic" best summarizes the entire gamut of our states of feeling. The theater, which Giraudoux calls "an act of love," is built on the instinct for the dramatic. If we quickly recognize ourselves and our feelings in what transpires on the stage, we do not remain, in the instances of great theater, merely amused or diverted. The theater is able to clarify and magnify this dramatic instinct and thus illuminate at least to some degree human destiny. It is difficult to account in any other way for the persistence of the theater through the centuries. The theater was born from a ceremony. Today, in the French plays of a Claudel and a Montherlant, and in the major plays of each country—those of Eliot, Lorca, Pirandello, Brecht—the art of the theater continues to consecrate the sentiment of destiny.

2. Theaters, Directors, and Actors

The French themselves are often very critical of the Comédie-Française, and they quickly concede that it has more prestige abroad than at home. Pierre-Aimé Touchard was director between 1947 and 1959. (See p. 35.) He suffered from criticism, which is the fate of every director, but he was responsible for at least some signs of revival of prestige in recent years. He was not able to pacify the partisan quarrels within the company. These are almost continuous and seem to the outsider strident and ferocious.

The Comédie-Française is the oldest theater in France, and one of the oldest in the world today. It was created in 1680 by Louis XIV for the production of Molière's plays. In a certain sense, it was originally Molière's company when it began playing in Paris, in 1659, after its long twelve-year tour in the provinces. It is referred to in France as Molière's theater, la maison de *Molière*. A few souvenirs of the master are still piously preserved: his watch, his signature on a document, the armchair in which he played *Le Malade imaginaire* a few hours before his death in 1673, and the famous register in which Charles de La Grange—a member of Molière's company—

entered the box-office receipts and the lists of the casts for the various plays.

The Comédie-Française has therefore been playing almost uninterruptedly for three hundred years. In 1799 it moved to the Salle Richelieu, near the gardens of the Palais-Royal. In 1946 a second theater was added, the Salle Luxembourg, on the Left Bank. Combined, the two houses seat nightly 2,600 people. The technical staff numbers four hundred. There are eighty actors, divided into two categories. The smaller, more permanent category is made up of thirty actors called *sociétaires* who are elected for a period of twenty years. Fifty *pensionnaires*, who are usually the younger actors and actresses, are engaged by the season. The *sociétaires* are the voting members of the company. The *pensionnaires*, who have no part in the government of the theater, form the group out of which the *sociétaires* are chosen. The annual state subsidy is four hundred million francs, or approximately one million dollars.

By its very nature the Comédie-Française is a kind of museum of French dramatic art. It is the opposite of a laboratory or an experimental theater. It is distrustful of vogues and fashions. It will therefore always appear behind the times. And even when it does add new plays to the repertory, the choices are not always satisfactory or sound. In recent years, only one outstanding play seems to have been added: *Port-Royal* of Montherlant. Its function, far from being that of discovering the new significant plays, is rather that of protecting the past, of constantly reviving and enlivening it. Traditionally and inexorably, the Comédie-Française is condemned to exist in cohabitation with greatness, with a hallowed time-tested past. The privilege of its actors is that of playing a number of different roles, through a number of years, and thus achieving a smoothness and harmony of ensemble which is almost impossible to achieve in the usual kind of theatrical company.

The play changes each evening, and the majority of the plays in the repertory echo the noblest human sentiments. The dramatic style sought for in its productions by the Comédie-Française, and almost always achieved, is hence the style of nobility, of classical finish. In attempting, for example, to make *Le Misanthrope* comprehensible to a contemporary audience, it will, more than newer companies, call upon traditional effects and interpretations, and even traditional gestures and intonations. Before a new production of a classical play is begun, the director and the actors have fully in mind a standard of measurement. We can be sure that the action will be clear, precise, and taut. We can be sure that it will combine in a harmonious way traits of a florid rhetorical tradition with the stylistic traits of a very simple, straightforward naturalistic present. Foreigners easily forget that the French language is very strict. The classical line of French poetry, the Alexandrine, has to be read in a certain way to be audible and comprehensible. It hardens into a fixed form much more quickly than, for example, iambic pentameter in English. And that is one highly important reason why the French actor has to add to the mere reading of his line a fairly complex system of inflection and gesture. It is far more difficult in French than in English to fuse temperament and speech.

Tragedy in its literary form is a more developed aggrandizement of life than comedy is. It demands for its projection in the theater a more deliberate stylization. The tempo must be slow and solemn. The emphases on key words and on significant moments must be carefully planned and meticulously modulated. At this time, in the Comédie-Française, the performances of tragedy, of Racine in particular, are less satisfactory than those of comedy. By virtue of their very simplicity the tragedies of Racine are more difficult to project, and perhaps especially today when traditional histrionics seem outmoded. During recent summers, the open-air festivals in such centers as Avignon,

Orange, and Angers have helped in restoring the atmosphere of tragedy and the need of accentuating gesture and diction. At the Comédie-Française, comedy is surer fare, and Molière remains steadfastly at the head in popularity. The recent production of *Les Fourberies de Scapin,* directed and played by Robert Hirsch, is an example of the extraordinary adaptability of a Molière text to the modern temperament and the modern taste for the theater.

In 1900, after a fire had destroyed the Salle Richelieu, a history of the theater in terms of impressive statistics was made public. In 220 years, 3,000 plays by 1,500 authors had been produced. Racine had played 6,270 times. Molière broke all records with 20,290 performances.

On April 8, 1959, André Malraux (as Minister of State for Cultural Affairs) announced a program to revitalize the French national theaters. The plan was put into practice in the fall of that year. This reform is essentially one of structure and repertory distribution, and reflects dissatisfaction with the recent history of the Comédie-Française. Under the new plan, Claude Bréart de Boisanger has been appointed director of the Comédie-Française, which has been deprived of one of its two theaters, the Salle Luxembourg. This hall, now the Théâtre de France, has been entrusted to Jean-Louis Barrault and his company, who opened in October 1959 with a production of Claudel's *Tête d'or* (never before produced in Paris), followed by productions of Anouilh's *Le Petit Molière* and Ionesco's *Le Rhinocéros.*

The new director of the Comédie-Française planned productions of Giraudoux's *Electre,* two plays of Anouilh, and new mountings of Racine's *Phèdre* and *Iphigénie.*

Malraux's reform also created two subsidized experimental theaters. One was to have been directed by Albert Camus and the other (Théâtre Récamier) by Jean Vilar, director of the Théâtre National Populaire.

At the time this book went to press, it was too early to

make any judgment on the operation of any of these changes; it is safe to guess, however, that the French theater will be affected profoundly by them.

The life of the French theater during the past three generations has been sustained largely through the labor and creative imagination of a series of directors. Each director's name designates a style and a particular theory of theatrical production. The combined activities of all of them represent a long-sustained and triumphant effort to rejuvenate the theater in Paris, or rather to found the modern French theater. Parisian theatergoers are more aware of the names of the leading directors and of their art than they are aware of the names and physical traits of the actors. This is a firm tradition in the French theater of the twentieth century, apparent especially in the younger members of the theater public, who demonstrate their enthusiasm or lack of enthusiasm for this or that director. They look upon the director as the real creator of the production. The technical term for his function is *metteur-en-scène,* but the French also use in the cases of the leading *metteurs-en-scène* the laudatory title of *animateur*. This is reserved for the greatest, those who have been able to infuse life into a literary text, and to use all the various accessories of the stage for the creation of the play: lighting, sets, properties. An *animateur,* such as a Copeau or a Jouvet, is the director of the theater as well as the creator of a dramatic style of acting and of a certain kind of theatrical production. He is the director of the play itself and is usually one of the actors. He is the unifier of all that is seen and heard on the stage, all that unfolds for the pleasure of the spectators.

André Antoine (1858-1943), who now has a theater named after him, was the first of the distinguished line of directors. His Théâtre Libre, founded in 1887, continued for only nine seasons, but this was long enough to establish his revolution and make out of it the standard type of realistic production which is the basis of the modern French theater. Antoine performed in France the theatrical renovation that Wagner carried out in Germany. He demolished the conventions that had dominated the French stage more or less since the time of Louis XIV: the declaiming of the Alexandrine line, stylized artificial acting, and the ornate, spectacular productions that the Sun King had once favored in the festivities of Versailles.

Antoine dominated the French stage for approximately twenty-five years. He instituted greater naturalness in speech and acting, and an extreme realism in his care for details and use of real objects on the stage. He was imitated in Berlin, in London, and especially in Russia, where Constantin Stanislavsky (1863-1938) founded the Moscow Art Theater in 1897. Only one director in Paris opposed, with any degree of success, the theories of Antoine. Lugné-Poë (1869-1940), in his Théâtre de l'Oeuvre, represented an antidote to Antoine's realism, in his effort to introduce symbolist theories, and to create on his stage a theater of dreams and poetry and intellectuality. He wanted to found, in opposition to the "slice of life" theory of Antoine, a theater of ideas. He introduced to Paris such different playwrights as D'Annunzio, Ibsen, Strindberg, Hofmannstahl, Shaw, Claudel. Stanislavsky fused the best elements of Antoine and Lugné-Poë. Copeau, likewise, profited from the two extremes of realist and symbolist theater. Both of these men inherited especially from the example of Antoine a conviction that the art they were engaged in was a religion and not a mere profession, that the actor was a priest and that acting was comparable to a sacerdotal vocation. In the performances of Chekhov, for example, the directorship of Stanislavsky revealed a spiritualized realism in acting in which the expression of pure human sentiment was emphasized over any systematic technique.

The activities, the theories, and the ideals of Jacques Copeau (1897-1949) form the most significant single contribution to the modern French theater. He was first a literary man who, with Gide and Jean Schlumberger, in 1908 founded *La Nouvelle Revue Française*, and remained the editor until 1913. This was the year in which he opened his own theater, Le Vieux-Colombier, with the help of his literary friends from the magazine. Léon-Paul Fargue was secretary, Roger Martin du Gard managed the coat room, Georges Duhamel was prompter. Jules Romains, Gide, and Ghéon lent Copeau moral support. The theater soon closed down because of the war, and after the war it continued until 1924. But for a quarter of a century after 1913, as successor to Antoine, Jacques Copeau dominated the French theater. Antoine himself said that the future of the French theater lay in the enterprise of Le Vieux-Colombier (*c'est sur cette maison que l'étoile se lèvera*). Particular homage was paid to Copeau's work by the Italian actress Eleanora Duse, by Stanislavsky, by Gordon Craig in England, by Appia in Switzerland, by Fuchs in Germany. The moral success of Le Vieux-Colombier far outdistanced its brief material success.

Copeau's austerity and the rigorous methods he used in training his actors accounted somewhat for his failure to keep alive Le Vieux-Colombier. The text of each play was submitted to a close literary study and analysis before rehearsals began. He encouraged and directed discussions of art and literature related to the text of the play, and insisted upon his actors performing physical exercises. The success of his first season, 1913, was due to the novelty of a theater on the Left Bank which did not use footlights and which manifested a veneration for the arts of the theater and a seriousness that contrasted with the lighter and more licentious tendencies of the *"théâtre du boulevard,"* and with the outmoded traditions of the Comédie-Française. Copeau was the first to use projectors (spotlight) for lighting. He had found a young technician and enthusiast whose name was Louis Jouvet. He had spotted a gifted young actor—who had played the part of Smerdiakov in his own adaptation of *Karamazov* in 1910 (Théâtre des Arts)—whose name was Charles Dullin. And he had discovered a young actress of charm and ability, an excellent Célimène, whose name was Valentine Tessier.

After the war, and despite Copeau's growing fame abroad, it became increasingly difficult to continue. Le Vieux-Colombier closed in May 1924. Those Parisians who wanted to be amused at the theater had dubbed Copeau's theater *"les Folies Calvin."* In 1925 Copeau retired to a small village in Burgundy, Pernand-Vergelesses, where he began training a small group of actors. They became known as Les Copiaux, and organized themselves into a small traveling company, La Compagnie des Quinze, which played in Paris, London, and New York. Material difficulties always upset the artistic successes of this group. It created André Obey's *Noë*, with the admirable Pierre Fresnay in the leading role. In the Burgundy center, Léon Chancerel was one of Copeau's most fervent disciples. He, more than any other single person, helped to propagate the ideas of the master. Many of the "little theater" groups in French universities and scout centers were founded by Chancerel. His Comédiens Routiers were the most active of the many groups he organized.

Copeau has unjustly been called a doctrinaire. He was primarily a discoverer, an experimentalist who learned how to reveal, in the movements and voices of the young men and women he trained, an extraordinary beauty of dramatic poetry. He constantly wrote down his thoughts and lectured widely on the one subject of his meditations.

At one time Copeau, who was a religious man, became interested in the work of Henri Ghéon and the possibility of a new religious theater in France. Although he grew wary of the pontifical and platitudinous tendencies of the texts he examined, the religious aspect of the theater, in a general sense, is very much at the center of Copeau's entire conception. He believed that the spirit of celebration should animate the drama. The public should gather in theater as it does on the annually recurring feast days of the liturgical calendar. At such gatherings men and women are able to think the same thing and believe the same thing. The experience of appeasement and serenity which should come to an audience witnessing a significant dramatic text will cause, according to Copeau, the disappearance of human hostilities and differences.

Copeau advocated a bare stage. He believed that the costume designers and the stage designers had gradually been assuming an overpreponderant place in the modern theater. The bare, improvised stage was enough to support farce and light comedy. A few stairs placed at the back of this stage would suffice for the enactment of tragedy (*qu'on nous laisse un tréteau nu!*). Copeau's ascetic tendencies, visible in the bareness of his stage— because of which he was alternately called "Calvinist" and "Jansenist"—was also expressed in the rigorous training to which he submitted his actors. Their temperaments were disciplined by group work, and their minds were cultivated and humanized by study. Copeau was not a play director in the ordinary sense. In fact, he feared and denounced the egoism and the pretense of the new type of *metteur-en-scène*. It is not the task, he claimed, of the *metteur-en-scène* to find novel ideas for his production, but to understand and embody the ideas of the playwright. To be able to read a great text is a gift comparable to the poet's gift of creating a text. A production is a connivance, a concerted understanding between the director and the playwright. The goal of a production should be a unity of conception. Copeau believed that the direction of the play, the *mise-en-scène,* is actually inscribed in the playwright's text itself.

Jacques Copeau was so tormented by the aesthetic and the ethical problems of his art that he was unable to continue for long as a theater director. The short-lived experiment of his Vieux-Colombier did not impede the propagation of his ideas. His strong personality was felt in Paris even during his twenty-year absence from the capital. The fervor of his apostleship in the French theater is unequaled in the twentieth century. He combined the roles of apostle and prophet. At the beginning of his career, when he was a literary critic, he denounced the dramaturgy and the plays of Rostand, Brieux, and Bernstein at the very moment of their greatest successes. Later, the financial failure of Le Vieux-Colombier was largely due to Copeau's unwillingness to flatter bad public taste and to compromise with the ideals of his art. He believed in an intellectual and professional order. He believed even that the theater would be able to bring about a new spiritualization in modern man. Gide's homage to his friend, in his *Journals*, stresses the fact that Copeau's particular contribution is best understood from a moral viewpoint. During the later part of his life, Copeau's public readings of Péguy and Molière and others of his favorite authors became famous in the capitals of Europe. These recitals revealed the actor's histrionic powers as well as his high idealism.

Copeau's work was continued especially by the four directors of the Cartel, who were approximately of the same age and who revealed similar traits of devotion and labor and imagination.

Charles Dullin (1885-1949), born in Savoie, was the last of nineteen children. After years of extreme poverty, he attracted attention by reciting poems of Villon and Corbière at the famous Montmartre café au Lapin Agile. Because of his success in the role of Smerdiakov in Copeau's *Karamazov*, he was engaged in the company of Le Vieux-Colombier, where he had his first intensive training as actor. He founded his own theater, L'Atelier, in 1921. The following year he took over a small theater in Montmartre, on the Place Dancourt, to which he gave the name L'Atelier, and where he presided until 1938. Of all the avant-garde theaters, Dullin's Atelier most closely resembled Copeau's Vieux-Colombier.

Dullin himself was primarily an actor. Among his most celebrated roles were Harpagon in Molière's *L'Avare*, Volpone in Ben Jonson's play, and the leading parts in Calderón's *Life Is a Dream* and Shakespeare's *Richard III* (in André Obey's adaptation). The productions he directed on the small circular stage of the Atelier were all characterized by Dullin's emphasis on the mysterious, poetic, and fantastic quality of the literary text. The costumes were designed by Copeau's daughter, Mme Marie-Hélène Dasté, who wisely collaborated with Dullin's general conception. Dullin was one of the first directors to use music as an integral part of his production, collaborating with such composers as Georges Auric and Darius Milhaud. His stylized settings were symbolic; they represented an opposition to the exact realism of much of modern stage design.

In every sense Charles Dullin was an *animateur*. He paid attention to all details of a production in order to create a harmonized synthesis. To each text he treated, he brought a profound understanding. He was perhaps the least theoretical or dogmatic of the four members of the Cartel. His basic belief was the unreality of the theater. By maintaining this sense of unreality in his productions, he believed he was best serving the essence of the texts. Like Copeau, he possessed remarkable powers of diction which remained with him up to his death. He fought doggedly and shrewdly for all he believed in. He was the discoverer and trainer of actors: Jean-Louis Barrault, for example, was a pupil of Dullin. And he was responsible for the first production of such playwrights as Salacrou, Achard, Anouilh, and Jean-Paul Sartre.

Georges Pitoëff (1886-1939) presented to the Paris public an exceptional number of plays betwen 1919 and 1939. He used several theaters during those twenty years: La Comédie des Champs-Elysées, Le Théâtre des Mathur-

ins, and especially Le Théâtre des Arts. Pitoëff was born
in Kiev. Despite his long career as a French actor, he
never lost his rather heavy Russian accent. He was as
selfless and as devoted to the theater as Copeau and
Dullin. In his art of actor and director he owned more to
Stanislavsky than did the other members of the Cartel. His
particular interpretation of the director's role was reminiscent of Stanislavsky's. He used to say that the *metteur-en-
scène* is an actor who is above the others and who becomes
the interpreter of the entire play. "Above all," he used to
advise, "enter into close communion with the work itself."

His repertory showed a marked predilection for foreign
playwrights. Chekhov especially (*Uncle Vanya, The Sea-
gull,* in which he played Trigorin, *The Three Sisters*);
George Bernard Shaw (*Androcles and the Lion, Candida,
Saint Joan,* in which he played the Dauphin, *Caesar and
Cleopatra,* in which he played Caesar); Ibsen (*Ghosts,* in
which he played Oswald, *Brand, The Doll's House*). From
the Shakespeare plays, he chose *Measure for Measure,
Romeo and Juliet,* and especially *Hamlet,* in which he
played the lead. Pitoëff created Cocteau's first important
play, *Orphée,* in 1926; and Gide's *Oedipe,* in 1932. He
put on the first plays of Jean Anouilh: *Le Voyageur sans
bagage,* in 1937, and *La Sauvage,* in 1938.

The long career of Pitoëff as creator of roles and interpreter of plays was marked by intermittent failures and
hardships. But he was indefatigable in his apostleship.
The example of the man was as noble as his multiple en-
terprises. His work was followed especially by the students
in Paris, who were sensitive to his *Hamlet,* for example, to
the originality and the boldness of his conceptions.

Pitoëff's wife, Ludmilla, was his principal actress. She
survived him by twelve years. They had seven children,
some of whom took up work in the theater. Ludmilla
Pitoëff spoke purer French than did her husband. She
was small of stature, girlish in appearance, with an un-
forgettable voice. Those who witnessed her part in *Uncle*

Vanya still speak of the pure intonation of her final words: *Nous nous reposerons . . . nous nous reposerons.* The accuracy with which some of her great scenes are still remembered are proof of the spell she cast over the youthful audiences in the twenties and thirties: Ophelia's mad scene in *Hamlet,* Medea's prayer to Jason in Seneca's *Medea,* the death scene in *La Dame aux camélias* of Dumas *fils,* the death scene of Joan in Shaw's *Saint Joan* and in *Le Procès de Jeanne d'Arc* (a dramatization based on the authentic text of the saint's trial). Both the Pitoëffs demonstrated a veneration for the theater and a selflessness in all phases of their career. He was the real creator of the production, and she always subordinated her voice and gestures to the idea of the whole.

Only one director of the famous Cartel was not an actor: Gaston Baty (1885-1952). Of the four, Baty's theory and art led him furthest from the theory and art of Copeau. Throughout his career he was obsessively fearful of the literary aspects of the theater. He feared the domination of the text of the play over the production, and emphasized in his skill as director the groupings of the characters, the plastic quality of their gestures and poses, the placing of objects on the stage, and the lighting effects. Baty never forgot his early love for the marionette theater. He subscribed to Gordon Craig's theory that the actor is the super-marionette whose wires are held by the director.

In 1921 Baty organized a company of actors, Les Compagnons de la Chimère, whose first performances, especially of *Martine* by Jean-Jacques Bernard, constituted a manifesto of his principal ideas. *Martine* was an ideal text with which to demonstrate his reform. It was an effort to reduce the importance of the text, of what Baty called in an essay, *"Sire, le mot."* Yet, he acknowledged in this important essay that "the text is the primal element of the production." But the text is not able to express everything. Baty claims that there extends a zone of silence beyond the text, an atmosphere and a climate that it is the function of the director to express. The director, in the highest sense of his calling, is the poet's collaborator. He reveals the most secret thought of the poet.

By 1930 Baty occupied his own theater, Le Théâtre Montparnasse. Two of his greatest successes were his own adaptations, one of *Crime and Punishment*, which ran for one whole season, 1933-4, and the other of *Madame Bovary*, in the 1936-7 season. Baty returned often to the plays of Alfred de Musset and devised for them new productions and, in some instances, new adaptations. *Les Caprices de Marianne*, which he put on in the 1935-6 season, was a revelation of subtlety and delicacy. In the subsequent choices of *Le Chandelier* and *Lorenzaccio*, the extremes of his method and stylization became more apparent. He took liberties with the text by adding scenes of miming and choral singing at the end. Often in his desire to explain a text he added embellishments that were unnecessary. He denounced, as Copeau had before him, the purely realistic theater, and sought to create an unreal world on the stage, one that would separate the public from its daily existence. The moral asceticism of Copeau found in the art of Gaston Baty its antidote where to the bare power of the word were added the supplementary powers of acting, miming, forms, colors, lights, voices, noises, silences.

If Baty is remembered as the opponent of the "word" in the theater, Louis Jouvet (1887-1951) stands as its principal defender, as the director who created essentially a verbal theater in which the text is given first place. No other actor-director considered with greater penetration and subtlety and frankness the problems and the mysteries of the theater. Immediately after his death a book of his writings, *Témoignages sur le théâtre*, was published, a personal record of his convictions and doubts, of successes and failures in his career. It is a kind of notebook of ruminations carried on by an actor who had always refused dogmas concerning the theater and beliefs in any one school of acting or directing.

Jouvet was trained by Copeau at Le Vieux-Colombier, where he was stagehand, mechanic, painter, *régisseur,* and actor. In the opening performance, he played Doctor Macroton—a tall cadaverous stammerer—in Molière's *Amour médecin.* He was somewhat typed by his first roles: a lanky clownish figure, deadpan, and with a voice of jerky articulation. He often resembled a Daumier portrait. One of Jouvet's earliest and most successful roles was that of Dr. Knock in the play of Jules Romains. He revived the play periodically throughout his career and played the part so often that the public came to associate it with Jouvet and to see characterizations of Knock in all of his other roles. Molière's buffoon doctor whom he played in 1913 had already some of the elements of the twentieth-century Dr. Knock. In reality, Jouvet was a versatile actor who played convincingly such diverse roles as Macroton, Philinte (*Le Misanthrope*), Mercure (*Amphitryon 38*), Knock, the old shepherd in *La Machine infernale,* Arnolphe (*L'Ecole des femmes*), Hector (*La Guerre de Troie n'aura pas lieu.*)

As a director, Jouvet faithfully served the cause of the playwrights. The outstanding trait of his art was the study he made of each play, the honesty with which he treated the text, and the close collaboration he established and respected with the various playwrights he served: Jules Romains, Bernard Zimmer, Stève Passeur, Marcel Achard, and especially Jean Giraudoux.

From 1928, when *Siegfried* was first performed, to Giraudoux's death in 1944, Jouvet was the perfect collaborator. The brilliant direction of Jouvet was responsible for the public's following of the subtle, complex, ornate thought of Giraudoux. The magic spell he created in each instance came from the text, which first he assimilated himself and then taught to his actors, who in turn collaborated with him: Valentine Tessier, Lucienne Bogaert,

Madeleine Ozeray, Pierre Renoir, among others. At the beginning of the 1934-5 season Jouvet took possession of his own theater, the Athénée, and opened with *Amphitryon 38*, which he had been playing at the Comédie des Champs-Elysées. By that time his company was well trained, and dedicated, as Jouvet was, to a literary theater. Giraudoux was the favorite author. In 1935 *La Guerre de Troie* was produced, with Jouvet playing Hector. The sumptuous beauty of the scenery and the production came from another collaboration, that between Jouvet and Christian Bérard.

After Giraudoux, Jouvet loved Molière. For the Athénée, he revived *L'Ecole des femmes* in a striking production that subsequently was taken on tour abroad. Jouvet played Arnolphe, a part admirably suited to his diction and acting. (When he was twenty, Jouvet had tried out for the Conservatoire with the fourth scene of the second act, and had been turned down by the jury. During the last years of his life, he served as teacher at the Conservatoire.) At the end of his life he played *Dom Juan* and *Tartuffe,* and gave to both roles unconventional interpretations.

Jouvet was an actor and never claimed to be anything else. He said that he lived in a perpetual and constantly renewed admiration for the text that he spoke. It became in a way his text, and he cultivated the illusion of thinking and speaking *his* text. Jouvet defined the function of the director as that of rediscovering the author's state of mind. It was an essentially spiritual exercise for him. Stage machinery and apparatus are means for copying the real in order to make it spiritual, he said. The theater was invented by men in order to explain the mystery of their lives. Even the childlike aspects of play-acting and histrionic imagination have something sacred about them. The legends associated with the origins of theater— Orpheus, Dionysus, Eleusis—are mysteries often involving descents into the lower world, either regions within oneself or outside of oneself. Jouvet has pointed out in his

Témoignages how the elements—wind, light, clouds, and sky—when they are represented on the stage, do not resemble the same elements in nature. The stage is another world, which does not possess the perils of the real world. The theater reminds us of the terrors of reality, but we are not terrified by them.

Jouvet is particularly brilliant in his analysis of the attraction of the theater, of the spell that it can cast over men. He believes that it is felt in the profoundest part of a man's sensibility, which is never satisfied with the events of daily existence and which yearns for the intensities of life when questions will be answered and worries forgotten and secret appetites indulged. This sense of the dramatic which is gratified in the theater is stronger and more complete than love, easier and more immediate than religion.

The apprenticeship of Jean-Louis Barrault (1910-   ) was spent in Dullin's company. Indefatigable, clear-minded, articulate, Barrault became during the years before the war a famous actor both on the screen and on the stage. During the years of the German occupation he was called to the Comédie-Française as a guest-director to supervise a series of productions. Barrault's *Cid, Hamlet,* and *Phèdre* became subjects of controversy in Paris. They bore the mark of a fresh, vigorous imagination. The edition of *Phèdre* prepared by Barrault contains detailed notes on the acting of the play, on the stage set and lighting, on the literary and even choreographic interpretation of the lines.

Barrault's most ambitious undertaking for the Comédie-Française was his production of Claudel's *Le Soulier de satin,* in which he played the role of Rodrigue. The long printed text had to be drastically reduced. Even after a large amount of cutting, the performance lasted over four hours. The opening took place on November 27, 1943. A remarkable cast had been assembled by Barrault—Clarirond, Yonnel, Brunot, Dux, Chevrier, Madeleine Renaud,

Marie Bell—and sixty performances in all were given. The major themes of this difficult play, separation, heroism, sacrifice, coincided with much of the anguish of the French at that moment. It was an example, among many, during the Occupation, when the theater sustained the courage and the faith of the people.

After the war, in 1946, Jean-Louis Barrault, with his wife, Madeleine Renaud, founded their own company at the Théâtre Marigny, on the Champs-Elysées. The new company seemed at first a rival of the Comédie-Française. Several of the actors had been trained at the Comédie-Française and had already had distinguished careers there: Madeleine Renaud, Jean Desailly, André Brunot, Jacques Dacqmine. Barrault took several of his younger actors from the Conservatoire, the official acting school that normally sends its best students to the Comédie-Française.

Barrault chose to open his theater with his very successful production of *Hamlet*, in the Gide translation. As a younger actor he had once played at the Comédie-Française a dramatization of Laforgue's *Hamlet* (from *Les Moralités légendaires*) and he still maintained in his Shakespeare role something of the earlier-conceived cerebral, intense, fast-moving Hamlet. This opening Shakespeare production was a personal success for Barrault. The second play performed, Marivaux's high comedy *Les Fausses Confidences*, was a personal success for Madeleine Renaud, who had been playing the part for three years at the Comédie-Française. This play, chosen from the best of the French tradition, with new sets and a new *mise-en-scène*, was faultlessly interpreted. In the very precise gracefulness of Madeleine Renaud, in the clarity of her voice and her poise, not a detail of subtlety was lost, not a moment of heaviness was permitted. Barrault himself played the valet Dubois. For this semingly French character, Barrault incorporated Italian traits of the Commedia dell'Arte Trivelin. He glided about the stage, ironically lucid, half clown, half spirit of love in revolt.

The following year Barrault revived Molière's very complex comedy, *Amphitryon*. A remarkable set was designed by Christian Bérard, in accord with the Italian stage of the eighteenth century. The white and gray motifs on the stage were an admirable background for the deft, musical Alexandrines of Molière. Desailly's Amphitryon had grace and strength, Madeleine Renaud's Alcmène had a satisfying degree of feminine coquettishness, and Barrault's Mercure had the expected agility.

Barrault as the dancing mime was even more prominent in his production of Molière's *Les Fourberies de Scapin*. He displayed a dazzling virtuosity in his choreographic use of Bérard's set, although the text itself was somewhat sacrificed to dance and stylized pantomime. Pierre Bertin, in the role of Géronte, won high praise for his performance, more restricted to the tradition of acting.

Jean-Louis Barrault was acclaimed for his performance in the film *Les Enfants du paradis*. The pantomine of Baptiste, which he played in a loose white Pierrot's costume, was a personal triumph for the actor. He incorporated traits of the commedia dell'arte and the technique of Etienne Decroux. His sharp face, with its high cheekbones, and his supple muscular body lent themselves to the clown's part in *Les Enfants du paradis*, which carried over somewhat into his Molière characterizations of Mercure and Scapin, and even into his Hamlet.

Barrault was perhaps the dominating personality in the French theater during the forties and the early years of the fifties. Energetic and imaginative, he is almost fanatical in his devotion to the theater. Almost every one of his major productions has been both castigated and praised: *The Trial* of Kafka, in Gide's adaptation; *L'Etat de siège* of Camus, one of his most distinct failures; *Les Nuits de la colère* of Salacrou, in which Barrault played the Resistance leader; *Malatesta* of Montherlant; and perhaps especially *Partage de midi* of Claudel.

Barrault's devotion to Claudel is comparable to Jouvet's

devotion to Giraudoux. Barrault's Marigny was more lavish than Jouvet's Athénée, and the repertory more varied. Molière and Shakespeare were in constant production with the contemporary plays of Anouilh, Camus, Claudel, Montherlant, Cocteau. Barrault has said that for him the theater is an act of love. He has put on plays in order to establish a communion with people like himself, in order to share. Barrault has always attracted a faithful fashionable audience to his productions. This audience has grown accustomed to his mimed robot kind of acting. Recently—and this is the fate of every director and every style of acting—the critics have been harsh on Barrault and have claimed that he is out of touch with life, out of touch with the changes that are taking place in the theater. As director of the new Théâtre de France he has new opportunity for achievement.

For several years, during the summer, Jean Vilar (1910-   ) directed an out-of-doors theater in Avignon, where the façade of the Palace of the Popes provided the background. In seven years he produced seventeen plays, including Shakspeare's *Richard II* and Molière's *Dom Juan,* which were considered two of his most successful. In 1951 Vilar was appointed director of the Théâtre National Populaire, a government-subsidized theater inaugurated in 1920 in order to bring productions of major plays to large audiences.

His initial production, in November 1951, at Suresnes, near Paris, was Corneille's *Le Cid,* with Gérard Philipe in the leading role. The lyric, dynamic acting of Philipe, and the production as a whole, made *Le Cid* into a love story, heightened by heroic adventure. Each scene was followed with unabated interest and enthusiasm. When Gérard Philipe, in the part of Rodrigue, rose up in the fourth act to deliver his famous battle speech, a spotlight showed him in black and gold armor, with a red cloak and a blue scarf. He resembled a heroic figure in Rude's bas-relief on the Arc de Triomphe.

Vilar has narrated his experience as director in a book, *De la Tradition théâtrale* (1955). He is the only director in France today who has succeeded in creating and holding a vast popular audience. He looks upon the director as the catalyzer of many elements, and especially as the one who reveals the meaning of the play in the bodily movement and the soul of the actor. His productions are stripped of all elements that might weigh down or deform the initial purity of the text. He considers the activity of the theater popular in its essence, and civic in its fundamental duty—and not because the state is Maecenas in his theater.

The type of production which characterizes Le Théâtre National Populaire differs widely from that of the Comédie-Française. The bareness and austerity of Vilar's production are reminiscent of the style of Dullin and Pitoëff, who had reduced the staging of their plays to a few props and sets. There is almost a rivalry between the two styles of production the more traditional Italianate stage (*scène à l'italienne*) with its full set and carefully delineated frame and attractive accessories, and its opposite, the bare stage (*le tréteau nu*) that uses a cyclorama rather than buildings and spotlights to indicate changes of scene. Vilar claims that the austerity of his production comes from his desire to give greater value to the text. He has abolished the habit of tipping the ushers, and considerably reduced the price of tickets. The audience he attracts at the Palais de Chaillot seems to be the familiar theatergoing public. The repertory of plays is not extensive and already there is some complaint that the productions resemble one another too closely. Vilar himself has played in *Dom Juan* and *Richard II*. Some of the foreign plays introduced by Vilar have been among the principal artistic successes in the last decade: *La Mère Courage* of Brecht, *La Mort de Danton* of Büchner, and *Le Prince de Hombourg* of Kleist.

After the war, in 1946, a limited number of state-directed companies were founded in the provinces, among them the Centre Dramatique de l'Est, the Comédie de Saint-Etienne, and the Grenier de Toulouse. There are other theater groups in the west and in Provence. Both state and local governments share in the financing of these companies. There are no university theaters in France, no professorships of dramatic art. Les Théophiliens of the Sorbonne were organized largely through the efforts of Professor Gustave Cohen and his students, to perform medieval plays. In 1957 the first official season of the Théâtre des Nations, at the Sarah-Bernhardt, extended from March to July, with ninety-seven performances in nine foreign languages. There were productions by such directors as Piscator, Vittorio Gassmann, Laurence Olivier, Jean-Louis Barrault. The creation of this international theater was largely the work of A. M. Julien, who was formerly an actor (trained by Copeau). In the past the French theater has always profited from contact with foreign plays: Corneille drew on the Spanish theater, Racine on Euripides, and Molière on Italian playwrights. In the twentieth century, the plays of Chekhov and Brecht in particular have had a salutary and invigorating effect on the Paris theaters.

Ever since the early seasons of Copeau's company at the Vieux-Colombier, before and after the First World War, the actor has been looked upon in France as a man trained to interpret a script, as an instrument in the service of a literary text. La Comédie des Champs-Elysées, L'Atelier in Montmartre, and Le Théâtre Montparnasse are among the leading examples of Paris theaters patterned after Copeau's Vieux-Colombier, which have made valiant efforts to endow Paris with theatrical productions of the highest quality. They have emphasized—perhaps more than any other one aspect of the theater—the training of actors, the building up of a troupe whose success is based on teamwork rather than solo performance.

For more than a century, perhaps two centuries, French acting has been admired throughout the world. Henry

James, in his theater notes of 1872, wrote that "one leaves the theatre an ardent Gallomaniac." Max Beerbohm has called France a nation of born mimes. Among many, during the past decade, who have acted in a consistently brilliant manner, one could name the actors Pierre Renoir, Pierre Bertin, Jean Marais, Gérard Philipe, Jean Vilar, Robert Hirsch, Michel Bouquet, Daniel Ivernel, Philippe Noiret; and the actresses Madeleine Renaud, Maria Casarès, Edwige Feuillère, Renée Faure, Tania Balachova, Suzanne Flon.

The actor in France has known many extremes of favor and disfavor. In the seventeenth century he was, because of his profession, excommunicated from the Church. In the twentieth century, success in the movies can make him a star and an idol of millions. The Jansenist Nicole, in Pascal's and Racine's century, condemned the actor as one who incites passion and lust in the audience. But Diderot in the eighteenth century exalted him as a moralist and a layman preacher. In the twentieth century, Antonin Artaud defined the ideal actor as being an instrument carefully fashioned and tempered, on whom the author can play as he wishes. The art of acting has grown into a highly organized training and profession. It reached the status of a moral system under such masters as Antoine, Copeau, Stanislavsky, Craig, Appia, and Jouvet. For all of the major figures in the modern theater, the actor is primarily an artisan and not a star. Diderot's famous treatise on the paradox of the actor, *Le Paradoxe sur le comédien,* poses the central problem of whether the actor should be moved or not moved in the performance of his art. Should his art be controlled by his intelligence or by his sensibility? The modern schools of acting are usually defined by the side they take for or against Diderot, who stressed the actor's intelligence. On the whole, the French directors, and notably Stanislavsky outside of France, have stressed the need for the actor to give himself over to his part. But Copeau reminds us that the actor cannot give himself before possessing himself. Stanislavsky restates this in his celebrated method of acting when he says that an actor is successful only when he has complete mastery over his own feelings.

There are two words for "actor" in French: *acteur* and *comédien*. In the seventeenth and eighteenth centuries a more rigid distinction between the terms was kept than exists today. *Acteur* was used to designate a man acting in a play, and *comédien* was a more general term applying to the profession of acting. Jouvet has claimed a slight distinction in the twentieth century. He said that *acteur* refers to a more specialized actor, to one who plays only certain roles. A *comédien* plays many diversified roles. In the profession, the word *comédien* seems to be preferred. He is the actor who has learned how to make himself habitable and accessible and free. Jouvet has called him the man "empty," who is ready to give himself to an existence not his own.

The public often associates a part in a play with an actor if he plays it a long time. This happened to Jouvet in his role of Knock. He created the role in 1923, and then during the next twenty-five years revived the play during fourteen seasons. In giving us these statistics in his book, Jouvet was trying to make an important point concerning the actor in general. If the Paris public grew to look upon Jouvet as Knock—and this was a fact—with Jouvet himself the character Knock had absolutely no bond or connection or relationship. In reality he was not at all Knock. The theater is an art of interpretation. Each of us in the audience, and each actor, is going to understand the play in accordance with his own intelligence and sensibility and temperament. But this variant of comprehension is, in the last analysis, more dependent on the art of the actor when he carries out the conception of the director, than on any other single force in the performance. Tartuffe may be, depending on the skill of the actor playing him, a false priest, a hypocrite, a lecher, a criminal, or a buffoon. The true actor will always know that he can never incarnate a role, that he can never be Tartuffe or Hamlet or Orestes. Such roles are inaccessible although they have been performed thousands of times.

The period of the past sixty years, between Antoine's Théâtre Libre and Vilar's Théâtre National Populaire, has been characterized by a dictatorship in the theater of the *metteur-en-scène*. This has not been true only of France. Jacques Rouché's book *L'Art théâtral moderne* (1910) calls attention to the reign of Georg Fuchs in Vienna, of Gordon Craig in England, and of Adolphe Appia in Switzerland. When Jacques Copeau, in the summer of 1913, opened Le Vieux-Colombier, midway between the Brasserie Lipp on the Boulevard Saint-Germain and the Church of Saint-Sulpice, he initiated a unique climate of opinion, a center around which an entire generation began thinking about the theater. To the public that attended his productions he revealed new interpretations of Molière, the Elizabethan enchantment of *Twelfth Night*, and new French plays such as *Le Paquebot Tenacity* of Vildrac, *L'Echange* of Claudel, *Saül* of Gide.

Copeau and the four subsequent directors who continued his work in a very special way, Dullin, Pitoëff, Baty, and Jouvet, put an end to the domination of the great actor, of the *vedette*. The tyranny of a Mounet-Sully and a Sarah Bernhardt seems, on the whole, to belong to the past. For Copeau, an actor is an instrument in the service of a text. He is only one part in a very complex process that will culminate in the production. All of these directors faced innumerable difficulties and setbacks in their struggles to endow Paris with a series of theaters that would represent a new tradition.

II. APPROACHES TO TRAGEDY

1. Giraudoux (1882-1944)

Ever since his first book—a collection of stories and sketches called *Provinciales*—appeared in 1909, Jean Giraudoux has been explained, by almost every critic who has referred to him, by the term "preciosity." He has been called a *précieux* with the same monotonous regularity that Gide has been called a "sincere" writer and Cocteau a "tightrope walker." The word is applicable, without much doubt, and yet literary styles are not easily classifiable. The very role of criticism is to question and at times to invalidate such generalities and such tenacious traps. If preciosity means the practice of studied and calculated effects, of swiftness in synthesizing and accumulating unusual images, Giraudoux would seem to illustrate this style. How does he characterize Americans, for example? "They come to France," Giraudoux writes, "to study the architecture of happiness in the hearts of French women, and go racing back to Minneapolis to plant it in the hearts of gigantic girls usually called Watson." (*Les Américains viennent en France pour étudier l'architecture du bonheur dans le coeur des femmes françaises et puis s'en vont au galop à Minneapolis pour l'implanter dans les coeurs de gigantesques jeunes filles généralement nommées Watson.*)

When used to describe Giraudoux's style, the word "preciosity" seems to mean an easy indulgence in brio, artifice, gracefulness, and a predilection for literary heroes. The climate of his novels and plays is temperate. It helps to diminish whatever tragic tension is created. The amiability of Giraudoux's world often masks a relentless tragic force at work. Giraudoux himself has defined preciosity as being a malady that causes him "to treat objects as if they were human, humans as if they were gods and virgins, and gods as if they were cats or weasels." It is a malady, he claims, "which provokes not study in libraries, but personal relationships with the seasons and small animals, an excessive pantheism, and politeness toward the creation." (*La préciosité, mal qui consiste à traiter les objets comme des humains, les humains comme s'ils étaient dieux et vierges, les dieux comme des chats ou des belettes, mal qui provoque, non pas la vie dans les bibliothèques, mais les relations personnelles avec les saisons, les petits animaux, un excessif panthéisme et de la politesse envers la création.*)

Giraudoux's art was achieved from an assimilation of traits that have been persistent throughout French literature. The preciosity of his images is constantly offset by conciseness and a bareness of expression. His themes of grandeur are counteracted by a tone of simplicity which the French might call *gentillesse*. He considers all the gravest of human problems, the conflicts between the life of the city and the laws of justice, between love and the cruel passing of time, between the purity of man's idealism and the necessity to be committed to an idea or a party or a nation.

Tragedy, no matter what literary form it takes in our day, is for Giraudoux the persistence of the most ancient and the most solemn of all traditions: human sacrifice. These two words designate the dual character of tragedy which is always present in some form: religious belief and the shedding of blood. To witness a tragedy in the theater is to diminish in the heart of the spectator whatever murderous intention he may have had. Giraudoux perpetuates a celebrated precept of Aristotle when he claims that tragedy by its symbolic re-enactment satisfies collectively the need of the public to commit a crime. The hero who dies on the stage thereby interprets the passion and the destiny of each spectator. The art of the dramatic poet is the image of man's most terrifying and most perfected destiny.

Classical tragedy, in its grandeur and bareness, seems to be the product of the great ages of civilization—Athens of the fifth century B.C., Elizabethan England, France under Louis XIV. Giraudoux never believed that his age measured up to such periods of history, and hence tragedies written in it could not aspire to the formal solemnity of a Sophocles or a Racine. Each age produces the tragedies it deserves, and Giraudoux's are adaptations to the style and the limitations of the twentieth century. They perpetuate the friendly dialogue with the creation which Giraudoux referred to in his definition of preciosity. Like Racine, one of Giraudoux's principal admirations, he chose for his heroes and heroines celebrated figures of mythology and the Bible, figures like Judith, Electra, Helen, who slumber in books when they are not fulfilling their destinies in works the poets have devised to keep them alive. Giraudoux called one of his plays *Amphitryon 38* to indicate the large number of versions of the same story which antedated his own. He has a predilection for those heroes who have lived through all the seasons and all the centuries in their special limbus out of which only the poet has the right to call them.

In the plays of Giraudoux these characters seem to be fully aware of what they represent and of what they mean to the world. They are cognizant of the fact that the playwright is not creating them, but is creating their speech. Whatever crimes they have to commit, whatever catastrophe awaits them in accord with their known fate, the tragedy is permitted to unfold on the stage thanks to the language of the playwright. Poetry, in the final analysis, is the only tamer of tragedy, the only force that will permit the spectator to stand tragedy.

For fifteen years, and particularly between 1930 and 1940, the texts of Giraudoux and their productions by Jouvet enchanted Paris. It was an unusually close association between a playwright and a specialist of the theater, in which Jouvet's scenic imagination matched Giraudoux's verbal virtuosity. Each man admired the other for his special gift. For Jouvet, Giraudoux had discovered the magic of dramatic speech. For Giraudoux, Jouvet was the great actor in France. In two important texts Giraudoux has discussed his understanding of the theater. First, in a speech given before the graduates of the Lycée de Châteauroux (his own lycée) in 1931, in which he claimed that the theater is able to create a secular religion since it is today for most nations the one form of moral and aesthetic education. Giraudoux discusses in his play *L'Impromptu de Paris* the historical and social mission of the theater. "Everything would go badly, but there is always the theater," he says. (*Tout irait mal, mais il y a le théâtre. . . .*)

The art of the theater is prophecy or divination, as Giraudoux calls it. It reveals to men the most surprising and the most simple truths, which they never fully realize, such as the inevitability of life, the inevitability of death, the meaning of happiness and catastrophe, the fact that life is both reality and dream. The language of the theater is liturgical both in its solemnity and its exuberance. He always pleaded for the primacy of the text in theatrical productions, and this was faithfully followed by Louis Jouvet. The purity and the importance of Giraudoux's text were such that Jouvet said that he had to teach his actors how to speak the text rather than act it. Both men always defended the literary theater at the expense of the more spectacular kind of production in which the text was sacrificed to the *mise-en-scène*.

When Giraudoux draws out from his reading the characters of his plays—Amphitryon, Hector, Judith—he treats them familiarly as friends despite their prestige and their great age. When Racine calls upon these characters (Hermione, Phèdre), he presents them dominated by a fatal passion. The totality of such passion is absent from the works of Giraudoux. His characters are chosen to illustrate contemporary problems: Siegfried, for example, studies the often repeated conflict between Germany and France; Hector poses the problems of the veteran soldier who is willing to accept dishonor if war can be avoided. Racine could impose his tragedies of phychological analysis and turmoil because the highly civilized public of Paris and Versailles was able to comprehend and appreciate. Racine's age was one that lived for eternity. But Giraudoux's world lived from day to day. As a playwright he could not profit from an age of great strength and a public of connoisseurs.

This "journalist of the theater," as he called himself, had to adapt his talents to the receptivity and the intelligence of his public. They accepted more easily the tragic dilemmas when presented with the irony and the literary wit of Giraudoux. He particularly inspired the youthful element of his public with his gentle irony, which seemed to free him from all respect for tradition and all traditional respect. The young people of his public realized that beneath the wit and the facility and the lightness of touch, Giraudoux believed fervently in the cause of literature. He believed that literature was the last recourse of mankind today. In other ages, under Louis XIV, for example, literature was an ornament, and perhaps the most dazzling of the ornaments of the age. But today it serves the far greater purpose of being the confidant and the resource of the greatest minds.

When the opening of *La Guerre de Troie n'aura pas lieu* (*Tiger at the Gates*) was announced for November 1935, the mystifying title was looked upon by the Parisians as a trait of the *"normalien"* (Giraudoux had studied at the Ecole Normale Supérieure) because everyone knew that the Trojan War had taken place. His art and his conception of tragedy are fully exemplified in this play, which is a combination of wit and seriousness, of the spectacular and the threat of war. The Trojan soldiers return from a victorious war. They are determined to preserve peace. Andromache, wife of Hector, the leading Trojan soldier, declares to her sister Cassandra that the Trojan War will not take place, that Ulysses will be politely welcomed and that Helen will be given back to him. Cassandra, who is a prophetess of calamity, contradicts her sister by maintaining that the Greek ambassador will be insulted, Helen will not be given back, and the War of Troy will take place.

The first act develops the particular danger for Troy, its recent victory. The citizens are affirmative. The world belongs to them. Hector does all he can. He closes the war gates and convinces Paris to give up Helen. He even convinces Helen that she no longer loves Paris. In the second act the poet Démokos stirs the people with his war songs and seizes upon the insulting words of a drunken Greek to call for war. Hector kills him but before he dies he shouts that a Greek killed him. The war gates open. The War of Troy will take place.

Hector answers and defeats one after the other all the human reasons for declaring war. But he is on the losing side because war, in Giraudoux's conception, is a fatality not controllable by man. The profoundest reason for war comes from man's love of war, albeit a shameful and hidden love. What is war? It is risk, adventure, a liking for danger. It is that force able to separate man from the comfortable forms of happiness into which he sinks so easily. By contrast he takes delight in the convulsion of

war which he sees on the battlefield or which he reads
about in his daily newspaper. In Giraudoux's world, woman
does not feel the same need for brutality. She has learned
to offset the monotony of comfortable living by simple
means. Andromache and Hecuba are horrified by the
virile instincts that war arouses.

But even if man himself overcame his warlike instincts,
Giraudoux would answer that destiny itself demands war.
The dramaturgy of *La Guerre de Troie* shows how destiny,
which wants the war, uses Hector himself as a pawn to
bring it about. Giraudoux's conclusion is bleak and despairing. War is hateful, but it is eternal because it comes
from the nature of man. And even if men reach some
temporary agreement, destiny, for whom it is a favorite
distraction, will release it.

Behind the legend of the Trojan War, Giraudoux seemed
to be referring, in 1935, to the coming of the Second World
War. This was the obvious interpretation of a line in
Act II, Scene 13: "Everyone knows it—we are going to
fight." (*L'univers le sait, nous allons nous battre. . . .*)
Despite such theories on war, Giraudoux's fundamental
philosophy is not pessimism. It is not the vision of man
placed in a world unsuited to him, in which his existence
will appear absurd. Giraudoux's view is far less intrin-
sically tragic. If there is a lack of harmony between man
and the world, the fault is man's. When man tries to bring
about some kind of reconciliation between himself and
the world, tragedy ensues, or what is called tragedy. We
must learn to see the world from the viewpoint of universal
harmony and not from the viewpoint of individual man.
In *Intermezzo* (*The Enchanted*), Isabelle explains to the
Inspector that catastrophes are necessary, and she tries to
teach the children in her care not to believe in the in-
justices of the world and nature. She refers to the *en-
semblier*, the spirit of the universe, who regulates everything, including wars and catastrophes. An individual life
is not so important as the countless bonds and relationships

that join an individual with the cosmos. We are not autonomous persons, but rather we are beings dependent on everything else in the cosmos.

The tragic heroes and heroines chosen by Giraudoux are precisely those who see themselves cut off from other men, who willfully separate themselves from mankind, who are determined not to accept the order of the world and even the order of humanity. Electra is one of those Giraudoux heroines who stubbornly wills to remind humanity of its tragic destiny.

This principle of Giraudoux is evident even in his social satire, *La Folle de Chaillot* (*The Madwoman of Chaillot*), first performed in December 1945, soon after the playwright's death. The Madwoman leads a crusade against the financiers. She represents the impoverished hard-working people of Paris. The world is evenly divided between the good and the wicked. It is an oversimplified Manichaean kind of world. But it reveals Giraudoux's social philosophy, his horror of usurpers and of the vulgarity they spread in their act of usurpation. There are passages that obviously relate to the contemporary social-political problems of France. The corrupt world of finance gathers at the Café Francis, on the Place de l'Alma. They form a kind of *mafia*, organized to exploit the masses. But the prevailing spirit in France, exemplified in Pierre and the Madwoman, is able to offset the spirit of greed. Giraudoux's belief in the greatness of France, in the virtues of generosity, tenderness, and hope which he finds in the hearts of the people, is implicit in *L'Impromptu de Paris* (first performed in December 1937). This is the play in which he describes the irritability and the distrust of the French concerning their government, and grants to the theater the power of awakening in them the opposite traits of sensibility and lofty vocation. When the corrupt bourgeois reads his newspaper at night, he says to himself: "All would be well if France did not exist." (*Tout n'irait pas trop mal, mais il y a cette sacrée France. . . .*)

Giraudoux in no one place in his writing defines his philosophy and hence never states his belief about the nature of tragedy. Yet a kind of philosophical wisdom emerges from his plays, a sense of balance which is to be found in the merging of individual happiness with the individual's responsibility toward mankind. What can be called fate inherent in man's character and which inevitably brings about tragedy, are pride, cruelty, stupidity, or stubbornness. But these are traits that may be overcome, and that are overcome in such characters as Hector, Alcmène, and Ondine. The lesson of moderation which Giraudoux avowedly respected in the writings of Montaigne and La Fontaine is somewhat his own. In watching a tragedy in the theater, Giraudoux would say that the audience is learning what it has always known. A tragedy —and Aristotle was the first theorist to stress this point— is an action that brings no surprise. We have always known that the Trojan War did take place. We remember we knew this when at the very end of Giraudoux's play, the war is announced, although the entire action of Hector was a convincing effort to avert war.

Even in his fairy-story play, *Ondine,* where the German romanticism of an old legend is refurbished with Giraudoux's Gallic wit and irony, a claim is made for the basic dignity and beauty of man's fate. Ondine, a water creature, falls in love with a man, and marries him on condition that if he ever deceives her, he will die. He does fall in love with a real woman. She pretends in vain that she deceived him, and he dies. Ondine represents a superhuman absolute passion. She cannot understand how love can come to an end between a man and woman. For Giraudoux a fairy such as Ondine is comparable to a saint or a hero who moves beyond the human condition and dies because of this. In order to study such a complex sentiment as love, Giraudoux needed a supernatural creature like Ondine. It is she who takes all the initiative. Hans, the man she loves, is an ordinary mortal and he lets himself be loved in a passive way. He is a knight and rises to one moment of nobility when he asks for the hand of Ondine in marriage.

Ondine seems to symbolize nature itself. At least she bears an extraordinary relationship to nature: *Il y a de grandes forces autour d'Ondine.* . . . In contrast to Ondine, Hans, like most men, has moved away from an exuberant contact with nature. His real potentialities have been lessened by the false powers of his pride and his pretensions. Ondine's adopted father, Auguste, a simple fisherman, speaks of all that nature tolerates on the part of man, and intimates that when man goes against nature, the result is catastrophe. But Hans, blinded like most men, does not understand the words of the fisherman and the secret powers in Ondine. Giraudoux's allegory is not hard to follow. Ondine's love for Hans is nature's benevolence toward man. A few of the characters, Auguste the fisherman and the poet at court, for example, understand the depth and the purity of Ondine's love, but the majority, and especially Bertha, are hostile to her. These two antagonistic divisions of society are comparable to the good and the wicked in *La Folle de Chaillot.* The character of Ondine is an extreme mythological figure, chosen by Giraudoux to show the reality and the absoluteness of love when it exists in total harmony with nature. But man is free in Giraudoux's world. He makes his own destiny. The life of Hans is destroyed because of his scorn of love.

The judge in *Ondine,* when commenting on love, expresses a thought applicable to all the instances when Giraudoux treats love in his plays. "When one begins to love in life, it is not in order to simplify it." (*Si l'on se met à aimer dans la vie, ce n'est pas pour l'alléger.* . . .) Hans is suffocated by the total passion that Ondine offers him. It seems to Hans, as it would seem to most men, an impossible kind of love to continue on earth. Ondine is one of several women in the plays of Giraudoux who represent total love and who, because of this, make life around them unbearable. Judith, after a night of love with Holofernes, kills him and then wants to kill herself in order to preserve the memory of her love and not allow it to be contaminated by an uncertain future. Electra's love for Orestes is comparable in its intensity. Lia (in *Sodome et Gomorrhe*) calls herself woman and love. She is intransigent in her love for her husband Jean.

Sodome et Gomorrhe, produced in October 1943, was written during the Occupation. It is Giraudoux's last play and his most pessimistic. Its theme is a favorite with Giraudoux, the problem of love in marriage, the relationship between husband and wife. In his usual manner, Giraudoux takes many liberties with his source, which in this case is the celebrated chapter in Genesis on the destruction of the two cities of the plain. The prelude of the play, spoken by the Archangel, announces its subject —the hidden reason for the coming disaster. In the Bible narrative, one just man would be enough to save the city of Sodom, but in the Giraudoux play, more is necessary. The Archangel says that heaven, to save Sodom, wants to find one man and wife united by love and representative of an undivided creation. (*Le ciel, pour sauver Sodome, veut un homme et une femme unis par l'amour, deux êtres égaux et complémentaires, représentants d'une Création indivise.*) This latter point refers to another liberty Giraudoux has taken with Genesis. At the beginning, for Giraudoux, was the couple. God did not create man and then woman, and one from the other. He created two twin bodies that were first joined by the flesh and then separated on the day when God created tenderness.

Throughout his plays Giraudoux emphasizes the importance of the couple over the individual: Ondine and Hans, Andromache and Hector, Alcmene and Amphitryon, and in his last play, Lia and Jean. The somberness of this final work is the picture of what love has become for Lia and Jean after five years of marriage. Lia has grown hateful and Jean discouraged. Life for both of them is a

prison. All the daily habits of living together, rather than
uniting this couple, have alienated one from the other.
Everything has turned into a source of bitterness. A curse
is on them, a malediction comparable to the one hanging
over the city itself. The Angel's proclamation is un-
equivocal: "Behold the human couple: a man who is
husband to the wives of other men, a woman who is wife
to the men of other couples." (*Voici le couple humain: un
homme qui est l'époux de toutes les femmes d'autrui, une
femme qui est l'épouse de tous les hommes des autres
couples. . . .*) And yet, Giraudoux, in his strong reminiscence of Plato's androgyne theory, claims that only the
couple is pleasing to God, that man and woman joined
in conjugal love are the foundation of human happiness
and dignity. *Sodome et Gomorrhe* confronts male with
female, and then demonstrates how love, in its effort to
join them, fails. Jean and Lia seem to be an ideal couple.
Heaven listens to them, and what is heard is the absence
of happiness, a monotonous diatribe of total incompatibility.

In analyzing the reasons for this failure of love, especially in the case of Lia, an explanation similar to that
given for the failure of Hans (in *Ondine*) is offered by the
playwright, in the words of the Angel. This statement
would seem to be the one hope in the play. Lia has lost
contact with nature, with the beauty and harmony of the
exterior world. She has confused life itself with her own
life. Four times during the course of the play, which correspond to four peripeteia, means of saving the city of
Sodom are offered. By testing the love of Jean and Lia, by
an exchange between two couples, by the example of
Samson and Delilah, and finally by the proposed sacrifice
of Lia's pride. Each possibility fails. At the end, in a
terrifying scene, the men are together on one side of the
stage and claim that they at last have peace of mind:
Nous sommes tranquilles. . . . And the women, together
on the other side, claim they have found happiness: *Nous*

sommes heureuses. . . . The city is doomed to destruction.

In the earlier play, *Amphitryon 38*, first produced in 1929, the love between Alcmene and Amphitryon is preserved, despite the trick of Jupiter. Everyone in the central action is duped, with the exception of Mercury, who is not involved. But Alcmene's love is triumphant and the play represents a far more hopeful interpretation of conjugal love. Alcmene is solicited by Jupiter himself, but in order to succeed, he has to take on the appearance of the husband he intends to cuckold. In fact, Alcmene forces him to confess that he is her husband! According to mythology, this union engendered Hercules, but Alcmene on the following morning refused to believe that anything unusual took place. A double involuntary adultery is the central action of the play and transpires almost in the spirit of burlesque. But the elegance and refinement of Giraudoux's language elevate the imbroglio. The role of divinity in *Amphitryon 38* is just the opposite of what it is in *Sodome et Gomorrhe*. And yet Giraudoux goes to great pains to point out that the love between Alcmene and Amphitryon is purely human.

This play is a celebration of conjugal love. Alcmene says she will not open her doors to a lover even if her husband wants to play the role of lover. The lover, she claims, is always closer to love than to the beloved. The brilliance and subtlety of Giraudoux are inexhaustible in his praise of marriage. French plays have so often exalted the "lover," that *Amphitryon 38* appears as a paradox in which Giraudoux exalts the virtue of fidelity and ridicules the lover.

Amphitryon 38 was Giradoux's second play, and the first he wrote specifically for Louis Jouvet. It was performed on November 8, 1929, at the Comédie des Champs-Elysées, with Jouvet in the role of Mercury, Pierre Renoir as Jupiter, Valentine Tessier as Alcmene, and Lucienne Bogaert as Leda. It was a marked success. Valentine Tessier, especially, gained a personal triumph in what is perhaps the most erotic role ever written for an actress.

In the same theater, in February 1957, nearly thirty years later, *Amphitryon 38* was revived with Philippe Nicaud as Mercury and Jean-Pierre Aumont as Jupiter. A comparison of the two productions does not favor the second. The text is more difficult to listen to today than it was in 1929 when it played 236 performances in Paris. The virtuosity seems now more gratuitous despite the subtle things Giraudoux says about love and war. The manner of reciting Giraudoux is all-important. Jouvet knew how to articulate and have articulated the abundant, fluid prose of the playwright. He knew how to break up the seemingly uninterrupted flow of speech and convert it into a dialogue between himself and Pierre Renoir, for example. Giraudoux was always something of a magician and a trickster. To perform him adequately today, so that the old charm will again work, a very skillful and subtle dramatic art has to be marshaled. Preciosity, when badly recited, will sound insipid. The very refinement of Giraudoux's style will inevitably appear, in certain periods of history, a weakness, a lack of vitality.

The poetic fervor with which Giraudoux wrote his plays and his critical writing on Racine, La Fontaine, Laclos, and Nerval point to the exceptionally high esteem he felt for the art of literature. Until very recently his preciosity and brilliant wit obscured other claims to greatness. In his efforts to understand human problems, to find solutions for ancient controversies of a political and sociological nature, Giraudoux has taken on the proportions of a thinker. His underlying serenity of mind and his determination to consider an individual life in terms of its relationship with everything in the world justify to some extent the term "Apollonian" which has been applied to his world-view or his philosophy. The critic R. M. Albérès, in his book *La Révolte des ecrivains d'aujourd'hui* (1949), was the first to develop this critical notion in a sympathetic and laudatory essay. This view has been further developed by M. L. Bidal in his recent *Giraudoux tel qu'en lui-même* (1956), in which he studies the courage and boldness with which Giraudoux moved away from a narrowness of outlook on human affairs in order to propose his belief in a more generous order of humanity. Man's happiness will be found in acknowledging his own role and function in the world and in fulfilling this function, which is only one minute part of a vast system. Whatever can be derived from Giraudoux's plays seems to be in opposition to the contemporary acknowledgement of a basic absurdity in human existence.

2. Cocteau (1892-   )

The seriousness of Cocteau's plays is so carefully disguised that they form today the least understood part of his writings, the part that is often neglected or even vigorously discarded with the swiftly reached opinion, "outmoded." The recent assessments of Cocteau, inspired by his investiture in 1955 as a member of the Académie Française, grant him, without much discussion, a place in the history of the novel (*Les Enfants terribles*), and a place in the history of the cinema (*Orphée*). Still more unquestioned is his position as essayist and critic, as commentator on art and artists, on aesthetic and moral issues, on himself in his abundant warm friendships with writers and painters.

It is difficult (and perhaps unjust) to isolate one form of Cocteau's creative activity. The poet, the critic, the essayist, and even the cinematographer are all present in the dramatist. And yet the plays, in their first performances, in their revivals, in their published texts where they are today studied in many nations of the world, offer the surest basis for an objective critical evaluation. If these plays survive, thanks to their dramatic construction and to the understanding of tragedy which they demonstrate,

Jean Cocteau will survive as a French writer. His innovations and the risks that he has always taken in all the varied forms of his work are more grave in his writings for the stage. The rules of playwriting are rigorous, the highly developed and almost unpredictable critical sense of the French audience still more so. Despite this state of affairs, which characterizes the world of the theater in Paris, Cocteau has produced play after play, with success and with failure, throughout a quarter of a century.

Despite defeats, Cocteau has never been defeated. He possesses a resiliency that survives every attack. His eternal youthfulness permits him to renew himself periodically and renovate the varied forms of the theater in which he has chosen to write. Because he is fervently himself in whatever form he selects, he can permit himself all the genres: a Greek play (*Antigone*), a story of Greek mythology, *Orphée*), a contemporary psychological tragedy (*Les Parents terribles*), a romantic drama (*L'Aigle à deux têtes*), a French medieval myth (*Les Chevaliers de la Table Ronde*), a Renaissance melodrama (*Bacchus*), a surrealist fantasy (*Les Mariés de la Tour Eiffel*), a tragic monologue (*La Voix humaine*).

The theater is a deeply rooted, persistent need in Cocteau's nature. It is the most repetitive, the most often recurring form, in which he must express himself and release the phantoms that people his mind and imagination. He calls the theater an early malady, first contracted when his father and mother left the house in order to attend a play. The effects of this malady became really serious when he himself first began attending the theater and was caught by the splendor of the red and gold decorating the inside: *Depuis l'enfance et les départs de ma mère et de mon père pour le théâtre, j'ai contracté le mal rouge et or.* (*La Difficulté d'être.*)

When Jean Cocteau first began writing for the theater, at the end of the First World War, the important dramatists were Brieux, Curel, Porto-Riche, Bataille, and a few others who today are totally neglected and without posterity. Claudel had been writing for twenty years, but his plays were still unknown. Giraudoux was not to produce his first play until ten years later. Dada was in 1917, the year of Cocteau's *Parade*, the new artistic movement, but it was negative and even nihilistic. Les Ballets Russes were in fashion. They dominated the theater in Paris by their lavishness, their spectacular beauty, by their perfection of a synthesis of all the arts.

Cocteau's first three works for the stage came from his intimate knowledge of the Ballets Russes and from his desire to simplify that art and restore it to its more primitive form of pure theater. *Parade* (1917) was a pantomime divested of the lavishness and richness of the ballets, more affiliated perhaps with what the French call *le music-hall*, and even with the circus, the fair, the out-of-door theater. The action was half pantomime, half dance. Erik Satie composed the music, and Picasso painted the set. The realistic gestures of the various characters— the little American girl, the Chinese magician, acrobats, managers, and even a horse (who was to continue his destiny later in *Orphée*)—were all transposed into a style reminiscent of the classical ballet. A gesture in this first choreography of Cocteau was not a simple transcription of reality. It was a gesture that signified something else. It was that which effected a transformation, a metamorphosis. It was, in a word—and this is its fundamental significance in the evolution of Cocteau's dramaturgy—a magical gesture capable of changing the real, a gesture calculated to reach far back into the mysterious religious origins of the theater where a gesture was hieratic, serious, propitiatory.

In Cocteau's next two experiments, *Le Boeuf sur le toit* (1920) and *Les Mariés de la Tour Eiffel* (1921), he continued with this basic concept of theater and evolved, especially with *Les Mariés,* in the direction of a literary theater. From the example of Les Ballets Russes, he inherited the need of collaboration with many artists, of achieving a synthesis of the arts with each theatrical experiment. *Le Boeuf sur le toit* was mimed by the Fratellini brothers. The set was the work of Raoul Dufy and the music was composed by Darius Milhaud. Speech was used in *Les Mariés de la Tour Eiffel*. Cocteau's preface to this third work for the stage has often been looked upon as a manifesto for the revival of the poetic theater in France. Strictly speaking, there has been no revival of a poetic theater in France. Cocteau alludes in his preface to a special kind of "poetic" language for the stage—not poetry in a technical sense—which would reveal the hidden meaning of objects. Each of the major experimentalists has tried to create a poetic language along these lines—Cocteau, Giraudoux, Pichette, Schehadé, Beckett, Ionesco—by means of which the world would appear new and virginal. This is in fact part of the surrealist movement in modern art. The theater, by rehabilitating the commonplace word and the commonplace situation, by "poetizing" them, has sought to give a new meaning to daily life, to see it form in new perspective.

These first three plays of Cocteau, if one can call them that, met with little success and with an almost universal lack of comprehension. They helped to create, at the very beginning of his career, the false notion that he was a jokester and a dilettante. It was difficult for a long time to understand the meaning of the "poetry" that Cocteau claimed lay at the foundation of his dramatic conceptions.

Undaunted, he turned to a study of Shakespeare and to Greek tragedy, in order to learn his craft, in order to practice with the construction of a real play. He adapted *Romeo and Juliet* in 1918, but did not produce it until 1924. This adaptation has no value today—Cocteau himself has acknowledged this—but in devising its *mise-en-scène* and its choreography, the young author confirmed for himself his passion for the theater and spent some of his boundless energy in caring for and in supervising every aspect of the production. Two plays of Sophocles, *Antigone* and *Oedipus,* were far more suitable to the particular kind of adaptation or "operation," as he called it, which Cocteau wished to make. What he had tried to find under the richness of language and complexity of action in *Romeo and Juliet,* "the bone" of the play, its dramatic necessity, he found more easily in the Greek tragedies. Cocteau has described these adaptations as abridgments, as photographs taken from an airplane which reveal only the most essential parts of the subject. The results are swiftly moving, intense dramatic sketches, exercises in acting and in a basic kind of dramaturgy. *Antigone* in particular is still today a useful text. It was first performed in the Atelier, in 1922, with Dullin's company and a set by Picasso. *Oedipe-Roi,* although written in 1925, was not performed until 1937, in the Théâtre Antoine.

Greek mythology is the basis of Cocteau's first original full-length play: *Orphée* in 1925, performed in 1926 by the Pitoëffs in the Théâtre des Arts. The tragedy, as the prologue tells us, is played very high up in the air. Its action is as purely magical as could be devised. Like a poem, in the Cocteau sense, it has cut itself off from all material and realistic strategies, and, like some trapeze formation, it is enacted in a sphere other than the usual one. And yet, as in a tightrope stunt, we recognize familiar beings and occurrences: a man, a woman, a horse, a window-repairer. But the danger exists throughout the tragedy that the players may fall, and our excitement is enhanced by knowing that there is no one to catch them.

Orpheus and Eurydice are engaged in a domestic quarrel. On the one hand, Orpheus is under the spell of a horse, an unusual horse that has given him such a strange message that he is going to immortalize it in poetry. And Eurydice is under the spell of a wicked woman in town, Aglaonice, who seems to be bewitching all the women. When Orpheus recites to his wife the mysterious phrase

of the horse, *Madame Eurydice reviendra des enfers*
("Eurydice will come back from hell"), the whole action
is thrown into the future, or higher into the air than
ever. The sense of the supernatural grows stronger and we
are willingly convinced that the actions we watch are
being dictated by the gods. The context seems to be both
supernatural and comically natural. Orpheus as well as the
spectators feel the need of a bomb or a scandal to clear
the air. The quarrel culminates when Orpheus darkly suggests that Eurydice breaks a pane of glass each day in
order to have the window-repairer come up. He himself
breaks the window this day and leaves his wife with
Heurtebise. We begin to see the multiple services and
uses of this man. He has brought from Aglaonice some
poison, in the form of a piece of sugar, for the horse, and
a self-addressed envelope in which Eurydice is to return a
compromising letter. Just before the poison is administered
to the horse, Orpheus returns unexpectedly for his birth
certificate. Heurtebise jumps on a chair and pretends to
be busy at the broken window. When Orpheus absent-
mindedly removes the chair, the man remains quite
placidly suspended in the air, and in a few minutes the
chair is put back under him. But Eurydice has seen all.
It was not enough to have a speaking horse in the house,
now she has a friend who is able to float in the air. We
begin to realize that the large panes of glass which Heurtebise carries strapped on his back are perhaps wings.
Orpheus has gone out again, but Eurydice, for whom all
mystery is an enemy, has lost confidence in her friend.
She licks the envelope from Aglaonice, only to collapse
a few minutes later. She has been poisoned by Aglaonice,
who with her wicked women is gradually taking on in the
play the characteristics of the Bacchantes. Heurtebise puts
Eurydice in her room and goes out to find Orpheus.

The action of the play has been slowly accelerating ever
since the beginning, but we become especially aware of
its increased tempo in the next central scene, when Death,

as a beautiful woman in evening dress, with her two aids dressed as surgeons, Raphael and Azrael, come in to perform the death of Eurydice. Death first gives the sugar to the horse, who disappears, and then enacts the ceremonial, half surgical, half mythical, on the absent body of Eurydice. It is over and they have gone, when Orpheus and Heurtebise return. When Orpheus in his grief swears that he will take his wife away from Death, Heurtebise says that there is a way, since Death forgot to take with her her rubber gloves, which are still on the table. The way to Death is through the mirror, and Orpheus, wearing the rubber gloves, enters the mirror, and disappears for a second of our time when the mailman delivers a letter to Heurtebise. Orpheus comes back through the mirror leading Eurydice. Only one detail has to be remembered: Orpheus must never look at his wife or she will disappear. But the myth is inexorable, for this is exactly what happens during the course of the renewed domestic quarrel. Orpheus, along with Heurtebise, now reads the letter that had come when he was in the realm of the dead. It is anonymous and announces that Aglaonice and her women, infuriated by discovering that the first letters of Orpheus' celebrated sentence spell a vile word, are marching on his house and want his death. The play ends rapidly with the murder of Orpheus by the Bacchantes and with the disappearance of his body. Only his head remains and finds its place on a pedestal. The last scene is in heaven, where Heurtebise is undisguisedly the guardian angel and is taking lunch with his two wards, Orpheus and Eurydice, who have finally brought peace to their domestic situation.

Such an action permits Cocteau to treat lightly and subtly very profound preoccupations and problems and causes of human anxiety. As children often do, Cocteau willfully tries to puzzle and perturb by the fantastic secrecy of his writing. A sentence in Breton's surrealist manifesto might apply to *Orphée:* "What is admirable in the fantastic is that it ends by becoming real."

Orphée is a meditation on death wherein Cocteau miraculously rescues death from disappearing in a void. In the play, death escapes death or the fate of nothingness. Cocteau can usually be found wandering between life and the void. This is the meaning of Cocteau's angelism, or the lesson of equilibrium he is always teaching. His favorite setting is the circus tightrope, with heaven above and death below. He is the Parisian artist, the upstart who was trained by severe muses, but who has rid himself of all pedagogic traces. His simplicity is very deceptive. *Orphée* should be played with the swiftness and direct- ness and ease of a trick in prestidigitation. But it is a play of condensed richness, a surrealist enactment of the most tender and the most profound myth of mankind: the descent of a living man into the realm of Death and his return from there. Men cannot accept truth directly. Cocteau says in one of his aphorisms that truth is too naked: it has to be at least partially clothed in order to attract or excite men. (*La vérité est trop nue; elle n'excite pas les hommes. . . .*) It is almost in these terms that the surrealists attacked realism.

Orphée succeeds in making of the myth of death, or the fantasy of death, something extraordinarily real. At the beginning of the play Orpheus is attracted toward death by the horse, whose messages come from the realm of the dead, and then he is attracted toward it, more insistently still, by the death of Eurydice. Cocteau conceives of death as a magical substitution for life, as a passage through a mirror. The limits that separate life and death lose in his play all hardness and precision. The swiftness of the action and the mathematical neatness with which everything is evolved are in themselves sufficient to create the illusion of the supernatural. Orpheus and Eurydice fulfill their destiny on time, as Cocteau, who has very little sense of the mystical, places his bet on the magic of the myth: conundrums, mirrors, poison.

Orphée was the first work of Cocteau to reach a fairly wide public. Reinhardt produced the play in Berlin, and Rilke had begun a translation of the text into German just before he died. In the season of 1926-7 the play represented beyond any doubt an example of avant-garde writing, but the seriousness of its theme and its intentions made it into much more than a purely experimental play. It marked a definite break with what the French call *théâtre de boulevard*, or the then currently popular melodrama and realistic play. It was seen to be an effort of a contemporary to attach the theater to its origins, to renovate one of the oldest myths of mankind, and to preserve in the new treatment of the myth the secrecy, the mysteriousness, and the suggestiveness that are the constant ingredients of myth.

In a general sense, *Orphée* plays a part in the resurrection of tragedy today, and in a specific sense it continued and deepened Cocteau's interpretation of the poet. Here the poet would seem to be a combination of the two characters Orpheus and Angel Heurtebise. Cocteau never forgets that Orphism is religion based upon the magical power of language, even if he forces the myth to take on the strange atmosphere of a supernatural police court. The power of metamorphosis and the rite of exorcism, so integrated with the original forms of tragedy, are in *Orphée* applied to commonplace objects and words. The action of the play is both familiar and esoteric. Orpheus is both poet and hierophant, both husband and priest.

La Machine infernale (*The Infernal Machine*), like *Orphée*, has become a permanent classic in the avant-garde theater. Cocteau's treatment of the Oedipus theme is very much his own. He focuses on the machinations and the ingeniousness of the gods, of Olympus, in destroying man. He moves closer in this play to the Greek prototypes of tragedy than to the seventeenth-century Corneille and Racine. Against the machine of the gods, in its perpetration of woe and death, there is no defense. Each of the earlier plays had been an effort to discover a vocabulary, a situation, and a style that would not contradict the fundamental illusion that the theater must always provide. The stage is always the scene for something that is not. Dramatic art is illusion and travesty. Very few contemporary playwrights, except Pirandello, Lorca, and Cocteau, have emphasized this doctrine. But the plays of these three writers are largely concerned with this very problem of illusion and reality.

In *La Machine infernale* Cocteau reached his full power as illusionist, and he has been able to call upon it at will in the subsequent major plays: *Les Chevaliers de la Table Ronde* (1937), *Les Parents terribles* (1938), *Bacchus* (1951). Oedipus himself is the prototype and the most famous searcher for truth behind the lie and the illusion. The central problem for the hero is how he can know his destiny. Orpheus turns to Death, who appears in the form of a beautiful woman. Oedipus turns to the Sphinx and to Tiresias. Galahad turns to the monster inhabiting him. Michel, in *Les Parents terribles*, turns to his mother. Hans, in *Bacchus*, turns to Cardinal Zampi. This search and this eternal questioning have never been better illustrated than in the myth of Oedipus, which Cocteau refurbished with his own uncanny sense of situation, enigma, timing, and characterization.

La Machine infernale was produced by Jouvet in 1934. The original settings, designed by Christian Bérard, were used in the revival of 1954. The first act, specifically inspired by *Hamlet*, transpires on the ramparts of Thebes, where some soldiers are anxiously awaiting the nightly return of the ghost of the assassinated king. The soothsayer Tiresias, who knows the punishment the gods (the infernal machine) reserves for those who try to see into the supernatural, is unable to keep the Queen, Jocasta, from trying to see the ghost and discovering the means of appeasing him. But the ghost, who wants to warn the people of Thebes about impending disaster, cannot make himself heard.

The second act is set in the countryside, where young Oedipus, who has just killed his father, meets the Sphinx. She is a young girl who is tired of killing and who tries to escape from the power of the god Anubis by falling in love with Oedipus. She gives away the riddle's secret and is therefore conquered by Oedipus. The action of the first two acts takes place at the same time. Act I treats the victims. Act II treats the gods.

The third act is the marriage night of Oedipus and Jocasta. Neither knows who the other is, but they almost reach the truth throughout a perpetually maintained ambiguity. But the will of the gods keeps them blind. The Bérard set for this act shows the bed of incest almost in the form of a funeral pyre or sacrificial altar. Bérard had understood Cocteau's atmosphere of phosphorescence and the symbolism of the infernal machine, which counts out the time granted to man to enjoy his illusions, and which, when the time is over, explodes and destroys. Cocteau has always been obsessed by this belief in supernatural surveillance and intervention.

Seventeen years separate the third and fourth acts. In this final act, Cocteau adheres closely to the Sophoclean model. Oedipus learns of his crimes: that he is the murderer of his father and the husband of his mother. He puts out his eyes, Jocasta hangs herself, the daughter Antigone will go with her father into exile.

The fall 1954 revival of *La Machine infernale*, at the Théâtre des Bouffes-Parisiens, was a production supervised by Cocteau himself. There were no catcalls, no rowdy manifestations in the house. It took only twenty years to prove that the play was not a farce or a trick. Even the long monologue of the Sphinx, which was questioned by those who approved of the play in 1934, was well received in 1954. The great scene of the Sphinx, Anubis, and

Oedipus seemed to be the most remarkable in this new production. The pure inventions of Cocteau remain the strongest elements of *La Machine:* his conception of the Sphinx, weary of killing and in love with Oedipus, the marriage night of Jocasta and Oedipus, the reappearance of Jocasta in the last act where, invisible to all, she leads Oedipus to his destiny.

In *Les Parents terribles (Intimate Relations)* Cocteau turned to tragedy in modern dress, to a form of tragedy in our own age. The work is deprived, therefore, of the poetry of myth, and the tragedy takes place within the hearts of the characters. Twice productions of *Les Parents terribles* created a scandal in Paris. It was first forbidden as being "incestuous," and in 1941, during the Occupation, the theater was closed by the Germans. The revival, in 1945, however, met with unusual success. At that time even the most hostile critics of Cocteau approved of it. The film, made by Cocteau in 1948, used the same actors and the same text. The situation of the play might have turned it into melodrama. The father and son in love with the same woman was a familiar plot for plays of the *boulevard* tradition in Paris, but Cocteau's treatment is so rigorously bare and honest that the tone and atmosphere, the suffering and the dilemma of the characters, relate the work to a strict form of tragedy.

The theme of the play is the frustration and the impossibility of love. The key words that resound from beginning to end in the text are "order" and "disorder," and they are easily seen to be parallel terms for "reality" and "illusion" in the other plays. Cocteau never moves away from his central preoccupation. He renews the same problem but creates a new work. The play is about three parents: two sisters, Yvonne and Léo, and Yvonne's husband, Georges, who is loved by Léo. The son Michel precipitates the crisis of "disorder" by not coming home one night. The girl he has fallen in love with, Madeleine, turns out to be the mistress of his father. The parents try to break their son's engagement: the mother, through jealous love for her son, and the father, through jealous love for his mistress. The aunt, Léo, dominates the family by her wealth and her authority. She is a kind of Tiresias in this bourgeois family, but much more involved in the lives around her than the blind soothsayer in the royal family of Thebes.

Cocteau's most recent play, *Bacchus,* produced in December 1951 by Jean-Louis Barrault at the Marigny, created a minor scandal in the form of an attack by François Mauriac. Cocteau has discussed this open letter in his *Journal d'un inconnu.* The accusations of Mauriac, which were largely of a personal nature, did not affect the success of the play. In reality, he seems to have launched his attack against the legendary Cocteau. Rather than basing his attack on the text of the play, which he knew very imperfectly, he revived the traits and misdemeanors of a celebrated figure which have only a partial basis in fact.

The action of *Bacchus* takes place in sixteenth-century Germany. It was written when Sartre was writing his play on the same historical period, *Le Diable et le Bon Dieu.* Beyond this same background, the two plays have nothing in common. *Bacchus* is perhaps Cocteau's longest and most argumentative play. Two philosophies are opposed in it: the anarchistic, in the young hero Hans, and ecclesiastical authority, in Cardinal Zampi, who has been sent from Rome to investigate the rise of heresy in Germany. Hans represents the free man in the face of what he believes to be tyranny in a political and ecclesiastical sense, and Cardinal Zampi, who is sympathetic to the ardor and honesty of Hans, preaches a return to order and a method of calculation and adjustment. The two theories and the two points of view representing revolution and order are exposed especially during the long second act. At the end of the play, Hans becomes the political martyr. He is slain by the populace he tried to help.

Literary art, in all of its forms, is always a risk, but the theater is the greatest risk of all. This sense of precariousness has always been felt and understood by Cocteau. In fact, he encourages this risk and works under its domination. From his earliest *Parade* and *Mariés de la Tour Eiffel*, through his adaptations of Sophocles (where he learned his scales and the form of tragedy), to the major dramatic works *Orphée, La Machine infernale, Les Parents terribles,* and *Bacchus,* he presented experimentation on the stage, with the tireless enthusiasm of a dramatist enamored of the theater and of the idea of a spectacle. Because of his irresistible sense of vocation, Cocteau has always felt that each new play is a new beginning and a new risk. The witchcraft and the spell of the theater are worth this perpetual risk.

The Muses, about whom Cocteau speaks with some degree of familiarity, have appeared in his work in some of their most extreme roles, as the destructive Bacchantes in the myth of Orpheus, or as the Sisters of tenderness and love, as in the poem *"Plain-Chant."* The poet's relationships with the varying and contradictory temperaments of the Muses form his power and originality and provide him with the necessary experiences by which he may approach his status of demigod. Cocteau has not hesitated to make for poets the noblest and most exalted claims. The immortality of the poet is a very special and very real accomplishment for him. The poet's close association with death is not a terrifying experience but a necessary initiation to his immortality. In the earliest works and in the latest, death has been for Cocteau not a unique experience but a daily experience that is his means of knowing truth, his means of coming into contact with truth, his means of understanding the ordinary objects in his life and the daily occurrences that befall him. Death is the total vision for Cocteau, the aggrandizement and the triumph over constriction.

Metaphorically he explains that the relationship between life and death is that between the two sides of the same coin. The first two acts of *La Machine infernale,* which take place at the same time, he calls the two faces of the same picture or the same medallion, *l'endroit et l'envers*. The poet in his greatest moments of illumination knows what transpires on both sides. There is the stage in the theater for one presentation, but there are also the wings for another, where the characters take off their masks, where the Beast turns into the Prince. In the play *Orphée*, Orpheus and Heurtebise move back and forth between life and death; and in the film *Orphée*, the communications between the two worlds are more constantly established. This moving back and forth between life and death affects, at least to some degree, the features of the angel and of man. One appears more human and one more angelic, but this is the result of the poet's practice.

Angelism, as Cocteau seems to understand it, is a system of contradictions, because it is essentially an explosion of the divine in the human. The supernatural is found to be everywhere, in the most commonplace and ordinary objects. This discovery is not unrelated to Cocteau's fundamental aesthetic. As an artist his goal is perfection found in simplicity. On every occasion when he has defined his integrity, he has stated his distrust of the artificially beautiful and ornamental. Such doctrine seemed an innovation when Cocteau first defined it. But it is always difficult to assess the innovator. During the forty years of Cocteau's career, he has moved from innovator and experimentalist to a classic figure, to the stature of a stylist who represents his age because now his age copies him. Only during the process of his development did he seem to be defiant and shocking.

3. Montherlant (1896-   )

In 1954, when *Port-Royal* was first performed at the Comédie-Française, Henry de Montherlant announced that he would write no more plays. *Port-Royal* was his eighth play, if one does not count the early, never-performed *L'Exil* and the fragment of a play, *Pasiphaé*. His first, *La Reine morte*, was written and performed at the Comédie-Française in the Occupation year 1942. The eight plays in twelve years, which received extensive critical attention and some degree of popularity, were followed by a formal farewell to the theater, recalling Racine's farewell in 1677, after the cabal against *Phèdre*, his ninth tragedy. After his famous retreat, Racine did return with his two Biblical plays for Mme. de Maintenon's Ecole de Saint-Cyr; Montherlant, as early as 1956, produced with the utmost care the seemingly definitive edition of his *Théâtre*, in the Pléiade Series. The volume is a model of editorship, with the text of each play carefully surrounded by bibliographical notes, prefaces, casts, and, as conclusion, with Montherlant's journal of comments on playwriting.

The announced departure from the theater and the Pléiade edition of the plays—the kind usually accorded a completed literary work—have already, to some degree, separated the man Montherlant from his work as play-wright. Much of the criticism of the plays had been a vain effort to relate their themes and meanings to what was known or believed to have been known concerning the personality and temperament of the writer. The work now appears more detached from the playwright, and totally distinct in its style and preoccupations from other works in the French contemporary theater.

Montherlant was born in Paris in 1896, in a family whose ancestors had been devoted to the ideals of mon-archy and the Catholic Church. Both Brittany and Spain are in his background. The word "feudal" has often been used in describing the temperament of Montherlant, who appears still today aloof from social and political problems, engrossed in the editing of his work, in his reputation as moralist and playwright. He is an isolated figure in French literature who in his seeming stoical indifference recalls the figure of Vigny in the "ivory tower" of his family château in Charente. The themes of his novels are intense and tragic: his school experiences (particularly in the Catholic school Sainte-Croix de Neuilly), sports, taurom-achy, colonial life. Montherlant always preferred his travels in Spain, Italy, and North Africa to the intellectual and worldly life of Paris. His vocation as writer came early and has never been doubted. It is the justification of his life. His books and his plays have considered uninter-ruptedly a heroic kind of life, a life of action and exalta-tion where a human existence is tested, where knowledge is derived from living, where an atmosphere of greatness and nobility prevails.

In October 1941 Jean-Louis Vaudoyer was director of the Comédie-Française. He gave to Montherlant three volumes of sixteenth-century Spanish plays, with the re-quest that he translate one. Montherlant read all fourteen plays in the volumes, but decided against the labor of translation or adaptation. One of the plays, however, sug-gested to him the idea of an original play; this became

La Reine morte. In May 1942 Montherlant retired to the town of Grasse on the Mediterranean, to devote himself to the writing of the play that had been slowly germinating in his mind. He set himself five weeks for this work and accomplished it a bit earlier.

La Reine morte is a play on the conflict between love and politics, between the demands of the heart and the demands of the state. The aging King of Portugal, Ferrante, plans the marriage of his son, Don Pedro, and the very young Infanta of Navarre, who is in the palace on the King's invitation. The love of Inès de Castro for Don Pedro is the obstacle to the state marriage. Ferrante learns of this love at the beginning of the play. Then he learns of the secret marriage between Inès and Pedro. And finally, at the end, learns that Inès is pregnant. His anger falls on Inès, whom he orders killed. Ferrante throughout the play denies love, denies its power and reality as persistently as Inès proclaims it. A very subtle friendship grows up between Ferrante and Inès as he questions her about her love and reveals to her the aridity of his own soul. At the end of the play, his irritability and senile illogicality, far more than any reason of state, cause him to turn on Inès and demand her death.

It is impossible to refer to all the interweaving themes and characters and observations that make of *La Reine morte* an exceptionally rich text. Despite the baroque richness, the abundance of moralistic and aphoristic speech, there is an underlying asceticism, as is evident in the carefully constructed scenes and in the deliberate focus on a few characters and a few problems. Inès and Ferrante are powerfully drawn characters. The Infanta and Pedro, despite their far briefer appearances on the stage, are also vigorously and dramatically projected. We can believe that Pedro, after the conclusion of the play, will begin to grow in power and evil, but we see him during the play at a moment in his life of great tenderness for Inès and deep despair over the political machinations of his father.

His is the most reduced role, overshadowed by the complexity of his father and the passionate loyalty of his wife. The Infanta's pride is strident. She is restless and destructive. In the subtle scene of the second act between her and Inès, more serious aspects of her character are revealed than her Navarrese pride. Her scorn for men is in reality her hatred for their sex, and her invitation to Inès to accompany her back to Navarre comes not so much from a desire to save her from execution, which the King's advisers are demanding, but as the sign of a nascent love. A similar passionate secret is concealed in the speech and action of Coelho, the King's prime minister. At the beginning of the second act Coelho argues with Ferrante for the death of Inès. Behind the reasons of state which he articulates, are his hatred of woman and an executioner's sadism.

The victim of all the major scenes—Ferrante's, the Infanta's, Coelho's—is Inès de Castro, whose strength and passion are pure. The nobility of her instincts is heightened by the love she feels for her husband and for the child in her womb. She has no secrets and no guile. And yet the action of the drama turns as much around her as around the dominant character of the King. Ferrante combines majesty with a bitter disgust for mankind. He knows his kingly duties, and his power too, but he is growing old and this condition, this daily approach to death, ends by dominating all his thinking and directing his actions. He is disgusted with the political evil of the men around him. He has all the make-up of a philosopher-king. But his loathing for the evil instincts of men has won out. This is revealed in the powerful scene between him and Inès. As Inès thinks of the hope of life, of the future she bears in her body, Ferrante longs for a way to destroy the future. In ordering his henchmen to slay Inès, he is destroying the future and hence all elements of hope, which seems imbecilic to him. The exterior speech of Ferrante is admirable and dignified, and one is always aware of the deep inner suffering and disillusion that it is expressing. In his age he has maintained the youthfulness of pessimism, the active almost adolescent power of denunciation and bitterness. An extreme of cynicism is reached in such a formula as: *Je crois que j'aime en elle le mal que je lui fais.* . . . The masks and the exercises of cynicism that he has employed throughout a long life have become his very character and produced a humanity of contradictions unparalleled in the contemporary French theater.

La Reine morte was the first play of the years that Montherlant devoted to the theater, between 1942 and 1954, and which served him as *un motif d'ébrouement* ("a new kind of neighing"). He speaks of this in his dedicatory letter to Jean-Louis Vaudoyer. Whereas the usual play is built around the coherence of character, *La Reine morte* is built around the incoherence of Ferrante, a kind of philosopher experiencing the horror of his own philosophy. He turns against his son because of his love for his son as a child and because he cannot love a mediocre character. As he dies, he pulls the page Dino del Moro against him because Dino reminds him of his son Pedro as a boy. He kills Inès in order to end an impossible situation, but also through sadism and because of a hatred for life itself, which he knows is ending for him. Such complexities as these justify the excessive language of Montherlant's creatures, a language that is as close to their nature as their passion is.

Fils de personne, written in Grasse in 1943, would be classified by the French as a *drame bourgeois*. In an exterior sense, at least, it appears in strong contrast with the baroque historical *La Reine morte*. Montherlant has stated that he wanted to write a play of inner psychological action, of total simplicity in plot and language. He has compared it to an athlete's body stripped and massaged, divested of all nonessential matter. It has a skeletal quality, also visible in the play that is its continuation, *Demain il fera jour* (written in 1948).

The action of *Fils de personne* takes place in Cannes during the winter of 1940-1. Georges Carrion, a lawyer, is living with his former mistress, Marie Sandoval, and their son Gillou, whom he has not recognized legally. The boy is fourteen. Just before the beginning of the war, when Gillou was twelve, Carrion had met the boy and his mother by chance in the Métro in Paris, and had become interested in playing the role of father. The action of the play centers around the struggle between the father's fine intelligence and the son's mediocrity, or his adolescent fascination for bad music, bad films, and ungrammatical speech. Gillou is a normal nongifted boy, affectionate, heedless, terrified at not pleasing his father, incapable of realizing the high standard of "quality" which Carrion insists upon. The father and son unquestionably love one another, but in the painful dialogues between them, there is no point of contact, no accord. Each is tragic in his own plight: the boy unable to please his father in speech or reaction, and the father unable to inculcate in the boy the interests and tastes that he esteems. The mother tries to justify the boy and reconcile the father to him, but she usually makes matters worse.

The end of the play is precipitous and revelatory. Marie has been asking to live in Le Havre. Georges tries to keep Gillou with him in Cannes, but at first the boy prefers to accompany his mother. At the end, he betrays his mother in telling Georges she is returning to a lover in Le Havre, and this causes Georges to turn against the boy. The final rapid scene is sacrificial in nature. Gillou is sacrificed by Georges Carrion to the ideal "quality" of human nature he believes in.

Fils de personne is not a morality play in the sense that Corneille's tragedies are. It is the exposition of a psychological case history. The French classical theater was in the seventeenth century unaffectedly allied with the cause of morality. Today the theater on the whole refuses to serve such a cause. The moral issues are all present in the three characters: in Gillou, the bastard son; in Georges Carrion, the father who neglected his son for twelve years, who refused to acknowledge him in the eyes of society and who finally repudiated him; and in the mistress Marie, who has brought up her son and who at the end of the play returns to a newer lover. Carrion is as difficult and as demanding with himself as Corneille's Horace is, but he has not the lofty motive for his cruelty which the Corneillian hero exemplifies. Carrion acknowledges the fact that he sacrifices his son to a principle (*je l'immole à un principe*), but this principle is hardly comparable to the cruel decision of the older Horace and the younger Horace in the seventeenth-century tragedy. Carrion realizes that the motives of his act would be abhorrent to the majority of Frenchmen today. Montherlant is proud of this, proud of the passion with which he has invested such a word as *qualité*, proud of his attitude of scorn and aloofness. Carrion attacks not only his son and his son's mother, but the majority of his compatriots in 1941.

The theme of paternal love, with which *Fils de personne* is concerned, has received little attention in literature, despite its universality in daily life. Montherlant's treatment is radically different from Shakespeare's *Lear* and Balzac's *Père Goriot*. The suffering of the high-minded father as he listens to the triteness of Gillou's speech and waits for some extraordinary expression of a depth of character which does not exist is fairly reminiscent of Alceste tortured by the eternal coquettishness of Célimène rather than of any literary example of a father-son relationship. The quarrel scene in *Phèdre* between Thésée and Hippolyte is, for example, on a far higher level. The disappointment of a father in his son is a daily familiar tragedy. Montherlant is successful in portraying this tragic sentiment, but with it he portrays all the concomitant awkwardness of the situation, of its silent suffering, of its unarticulateness, of its shame. At one moment in the play, at the end of the third act, the father opens his heart to his son, and speaks with genuine pathos and feeling. But Gillou is unable to concentrate for long and turns the pages of a magazine. All hope ends here.

Montherlant carefully made Gillou the bastard son of Carrion and not the legitimate son. Thus he places his tragedy in a purer domain above social laws and obligations. Carrion is attached to Gillou by a very pure love, and he remains free in his capacity to dissolve this love for Gillou by a greater passion still, which is nothing less than the passion of morality. The tragedy is just as total, just as irremediable for Gillou as it is for his father. Gillou remains totally alone in his mediocrity.

Malatesta was not performed until the end of 1950, but it was written in Grasse in 1943-4. It preceded, therefore, in the order of composition, *Le Maître de Santiago*, with which it has often been compared. Malatesta and Alvaro (in *Le Maître de Santiago*) have traits in common —nobility, aloofness, cruelty, violence. Such traits exist also, in Ferrante (of *La Reine morte*) and Carrion (of *Fils de personne*). Portugal, France, and Spain have all produced for Montherlant a dominant character, ambiguous in his nobility and cruelty, in his Christian and pagan traits, in his seductiveness and fearfulness.

The Italian Renaissance, with its alternating sensibility and violence, is incarnated in Malatesta. Enraged in his belief that Paul II wants to take Rimini from him, Malatesta dreams of poisoning the Pope. But in the presence of the Holy Father, Malatesta falls to his knees and weeps. He is kept in the Vatican, inactive and feared by everyone. When he falls ill his admirable wife, Isotta, has him released, but once back in Rimini, he is poisoned by his protégé Porcellio, the author of a treatise on poisons. Sigismond Malatesta is, for Montherlant, a study of vital energy, anger, impulsiveness. He has the incoherence of genius, passing quickly from hatred to love, from wrath against the Pope to total tearful submission, from confidence in Porcellio to death from Porcellio's poison.

The atmosphere of the Renaissance, impregnated with its memories of pagan antiquity, is the background for the most Jove-like character in the theater of Montherlant. The playwright has called his Alvaro (*Le Maître de Santiago*) saturnine (*un saturnien*) and Malatesta *un jovien*. The action of the play is Malatesta's self-destruction. Despite his fire and physical prowess and craftiness, he is a prisoner in the machinations of the Pope. The presentation of this character, and therefore the play itself, was attacked by the majority of the reviewers in 1950-1. The attacks were aimed not only against Malatesta as an incomprehensible character, but also against Jean-Louis Barrault as an unsuitable actor for the part, and more especially—with an obvious degree of personal enmity—against Henry de Montherlant, whom the critics insisted on confusing with Malatesta.

The accusations leveled against the historical Malatesta are all referred to in the text: the murder of his first wife, the murder of his second wife, the murder of a German woman and the rape of her corpse, the attempted sodomistic attack against his own son Robert. He was excommunicated and condemned to death by fire by Pope Pius II in 1462, and two years later, by the same Pope, was solemnly blessed, and in 1466, by Paul II, was decorated with the Golden Rose, the highest honor a pope could bestow. In fifteenth-century Italy there was nothing extraordinary in the character of this man, in his changeableness, violence, in his combined pagan-Christian tendencies. The openness and naturalness of his character are difficult for a certain kind of Frenchman to accept—the conforming and cerebral Frenchman. Stendhal has written at length about the impossibility for a Frenchman to understand certain traits of the Italian temperament. Montherlant gives to Paul II a larger degree of spirituality than history accords him, and to Malatesta a kind of spirituality in his love for his wife Isotta, in his belief in himself, and in the reality of his temporal deeds.

The end of the play—the poisoning of Malatesta—is not historical. Montherlant has acknowledged this point in his comments. (This playwright is the best exegete of his own plays.) But the historical matters are more unlikely, more difficult to accept, than the inventions in the play. Malatesta did actually go to Rome, with a concealed dagger, to kill the Pope. And in the presence of His Holiness, he fell to his knees and sobbed like a child. This is the dramatic and unpredictable scene of Montherlant's second act. Sigismond Malatesta is the incarnation of diversity and of perpetual mobility within this diversity. Each trait of his character is immediately followed by an opposite trait that seems to contradict the first: nobility of action and ignominious action; strength and weakness; masculinity and the unstable nerves of a woman; a humanistic culture and coarseness. He rarely exists between these extremes. He is either exalted or downcast. The atmosphere created by Montherlant in *La Reine morte* is recreated in Malatesta, where every scene unfolds in an extreme intensity of feeling. A sense of nobility presides over each scene, no matter how brief or insignificant. This is apparent, for example, both in the scene where the Pope surrounds himself with his courtiers in order to receive Malatesta, and in the following scene where he sends them off in order to remain alone with his dangerous visitor from Rimini. Malatesta moves from failure to failure, and yet the action of the play builds up to a sense of achievement, because his eyes are constantly fixed on posterity—on his *Life,* which he is dictating—and on the comparison of his exploits with those of other warriors who appear before him just before he dies. The play, in reality, is an expression given to his ideas and his dreams, and all the humiliations he undergoes fail to affect him as they might otherwise.

Written in 1945 and first performed in 1948 (Théâtre Hébertot), *Le Maître de Santiago* was warmly received and looked upon, from the beginning, as Montherlant's typical play. The action is simple and of a psychological nature. The style is continuously sober and elevated. The character of the protagonist (Alvaro) has been closely associated with Montherlant, and this time with perhaps greater justification than in the cases of Ferrante (*La Reine morte*) and Carrion (*Fils de personne*) and Malatesta.

The action takes place in Avila, in 1519. Whereas the King of Spain is the titular head of the Order of Santiago, Alvaro is the true head. The last faithful members of the Order meet in his house. Don Bernal, who comes to the meeting early, tells Alvaro's daughter Mariana that several of the knights are to be sent to "India," that is, the New World, and her father among them. This will permit Alvaro to acquire a much needed fortune and marry his daughter to Jacinte, son of Don Bernal. Alvaro refuses to participate in the expedition. He denounces America as the temptation of evil. Bernal resorts to a trick. He sends Count Soria to entreat Alvaro, in the name of the King, to take part in the expedition. Alvaro hesitates and at this moment the remarkable character of Mariana is revealed. She, to whom Alvaro had given little heed heretofore, reveals the stratagem. The King had not made the demand. Alvaro asks pardon of his daughter for his neglect and misunderstanding. She sacrifices the idea of marriage and turns toward the convent. Alvaro himself has denounced any desire for worldly and political glory and any desire for gain. The theme of sacrifice dominates the play and the denunciation of Spain's bad reasons for the conquest of her continent.

Although the character of Don Alvaro strongly resembles that of the typical Castilian nobleman, all the elements of the plot in *Le Maître de Santiago* are invented by the playwright. Montherlant does not pretend to present a basically Christian character in Alvaro. At best, he represents one aspect of the Christian ideal, the *nada* or the will to renounce all possession of the world and all claims to worldliness and glory. The final scene of the play accentuates

Alvaro's belief in the nothingness of man, in the infinite distance separating God and man. (*Dieu ne veut ni ne cherche: il est l'éternel calme. C'est en ne voulant rien que tu refléteras Dieu . . .* [*Alvaro to Mariana*].)

Montherlant has pointed out himself how often the theme of Abraham's sacrifice recurs in his plays. Alvaro sacrifices his daughter Mariana in the name of his religious and philosophical convictions. Ferrante sacrifices his son Pedro to the state (*La Reine morte*). Carrion sacrifices his son Gillou to his ideal of human dignity (*Fils de personne*).

God's love, as taught in the Gospels, is absent from *Le Maître de Santiago*. The leading motivation, for example, for Mariana's willing sacrifice, is in her love for her father and not for God. The lofty idealizations about mankind articulated by Alvaro do not derive from any theological conception, but from Alvaro's anthropocentric humanism. He has no love for man as man, or for man as the creature of God. He admires the ideal man in himself. There are many today who consider themselves Christians and whose psychological make-up matches Alvaro's. When Mariana speaks of wealth and says that she will welcome it as suffering and try to overcome it (*je l'accueillerai comme une épreuve, et je m'efforcerai de la surmonter*), there is usually an audible tittering in the audience. This is perhaps the one authentically Christian sentiment in the play, but today's public of Christians is unable to recognize it. Montherlant defines his Alvaro as belonging to the intransigent type of primitive Christian, easily judged today as monstrous or pathological or insane. To justify the portrait he gives of Alvaro, Montherlant draws, not upon Jansenist writers or Spanish theologians, but upon the Gospels themselves. To justify, for example, Alvaro's lack of feeling for his daughters, Montherlant elects a passage from Luke 14:26: "If any man comes to me without hating his father and mother and wife and children and brethren and sisters, yes, and his own life too, he can be no disciple of mine." For every trait of the protagonist's character, for every trait that appears shocking to today's morality, Montherlant calls upon Holy Scripture for his direction and his authority, and records his astonishment that Catholics in France have not recognized the aspects of their religion as they are presented in *Le Maître de Santiago.*

In the intractable hardness of Alvaro's character, critics hostile to Henry de Montherlant have tried to see the self-portrait of the playwright. This is as unjustified as to look upon Racine as equal in perversity to his own Nero. The contradictory interpretations of the play, especially those in terms of politics and psychoanalysis, clearly point out the stupidity and vanity of such theories. The public is sensitive to the violence of such a text, to the hostility Montherlant shows toward all forms of mediocrity, and it is thereby unsure of its reactions and even appalled by what it hears. The despair in such a character as Alvaro, and his world-weariness, are difficult to accept. But his cruelty is in accord with his character. The horror he feels for life derives from his conception of religion. He is of one piece, fully integrated, and basically simple in a psychological sense.

Demain il fera jour, written in 1948, was given thirty performances the following year. It is a sequel to *Fils de personne,* and its failure has been accounted for in many ways, including reference to the drabness of the actual writing. An entire book about the play was written by Michel de Saint-Pierre, *Montherlant, bourreau de soi-même,* which is a eulogy of the text and the playwright.

The action takes place in 1944, four years after the action of *Fils de personne.* Of the three characters, Gillou changes the least. He is still affectionate, good-hearted, and not very intelligent. He requests permission to join the Resistance as a young Frenchman who believes in it and is willing to take the supreme risk. Marie has changed somewhat. She is no longer a mistress. Love for her son dominates her life and ennobles it. George Carrion has lost much of the power and dignity he had in the earlier play. All love for his son is gone. At first he refuses Gillou permission to join the Resistance, but when he is threatened by enemies suspecting him to be a collaborator, he sacrifices his son to his own fear and sends him into the Resistance, where he is killed.

In his commentary on *Demain il fera jour,* a text he calls *Postface,* Montherlant argues that he is contradicting the Aristotelian rule that the public will not be interested in a character who is totally wicked. The play, in the degradation of the character of Georges, is a defiance of the public. Unwilling to acknowledge any possible weakness in his work, he ascribes its failure to the childishness of the public and to his innumerable detractors among both collaborators and noncollaborators. The father's love for his son, visible in *Fils de personne,* has changed into a state of indifference in the second play. But his character has undergone an even greater change. He believes in nothing. He has no conviction, in 1944, about the Resistance and about collaboration. He has become the tragic skeptic who will sacrifice his son to his own weakness and egoism.

First performed in 1950, and revived in 1957, *Celles qu'on prend dans ses bras* is the barest of Montherlant's plays, the closest in style and structure to the French classical tragedy. The wealthy antique dealer Ravier is fifty-eight years old and is discovering that he no longer has the power to attract every woman he desires. He has fallen in love with a very young girl, Christine, who at first refuses to become his mistress. Ravier has an elderly woman-friend, Mlle Andriot, who has been rejected by men all her life and who is secretly in love with Ravier. A single incident interrupts the situation and changes it. To save the honor of her father, who is to be apprehended by the law, Christine asks help of Ravier. He provides it and she in turn offers herself.

A mere analysis of the action can in nowise indicate the

grim sobriety and the power of this text. The language is exclusively common everyday speech, but its terseness and inexorable truthfulness give it unusual strength. The answers seem flashes of wit and cruelty as they fly back and forth. No one loves the right person. (One remembers the similar impossible situation in Racine's *Andromaque*.) When Christine capitulates out of gratitude, Ravier at first declines and then accepts her as the final curtain falls. He acknowledges that nothing is lower than the way in which he is taking her, but everything in this world is of impure origin. (*Rien n'est plus bas ni plus vulgaire que la façon dont je t'accepte, mais à peu près tout de qui naît est d'origine impure. . . .*) Throughout the text, in comparable aphoristic phrases and formulas, the sentiment of insolence and quasi-vulgarity opposes the experience of passion.

The final scene of the play is interrupted by a seemingly trivial incident. It is in reality an interruption adroitly placed in order to provide a powerful analogy with the imminent capitulation. One M. Le Vadey excitedly breaks into the room in order to purchase an armchair (*une bergère*) on which Christine has been sitting. He realizes it is not an authentic antique but wants it nevertheless. The scene is farcical, but the principal speech if the purchaser—*le meuble est faux, j'en aurai des ennuis. N'importe, je le prends, parce que j'en ai envie . . .* — is the complement of Ravier's action in taking Christine. Moreover, the episode points up the mystery of preference in love, of why Ravier prefers Christine rather than some other girl. This mystery of preference accounts for the grotesqueness of love and its tragedy, both of which are present in *Celles qu'on prend dans ses bras*. This ambiguity is felt and revealed because of the exceptional boldness and frankness of Ravier's speech. One again thinks instinctively of the immodesty of certain characters of Racine in their most poignant scenes of confession: Hermione, for example, and Phèdre.

In the notes appended in the Pléiade edition, Montherlant refers, as usual, to the many varying and contradictory criticisms the play has received. The problem of verisimilitude, of the likeliness of Christine's offering of herself out of gratitude, was raised by Montherlant himself in inquiries he made of many young women. Their answer was always affirmative: this act would be in keeping with her character. And it too symbolizes, as in the case of the *bergère*, a deeper principle, the willingness of a woman, or her obstinacy, in returning over and over again to that very man who she knows will do her the greatest harm. There is a more profound, more despairing note in *Celles qu'on prend* than in the other plays.

The title of the play *La Ville dont le prince est un enfant*, is taken from a verse in the book of Ecclesiastes, which condemns a country whose prince is a child. The work, first published in book form in 1951, has as its setting a boy's school in Paris, directed by a religious order. The time is today.

Montherlant classifies this play with two others—*Le Maître de Santiago* and *Port-Royal*—as his Catholic plays. He calls them his three *autos sacramentales*. *La Ville* he specifically calls a tragedy of sacrifice. It is at least a key, if not the principal key, to all the writings of Montherlant. It bears a relationship to his early play *L'Exil*, to the novel about his own experiences in a Catholic school, *La Relève du matin*, to *Malatesta*, and to *Port-Royal*.

The playwright was fully aware of the extreme delicacy of the subject and decided not to have the play performed in any professional way. The public interest in the work was from the beginning tremendous, and Catholic circles were deeply interested in it. An article by Daniel-Rops, published in *L'Aurore* upon the publication of the text, went very far in encouraging a sympathetic Catholic reaction to the dangerous theme of sentimental attachments that can develop between boys at school, and the role of spiritual directors. M. Touchard, director of the Comédie-Française, requested permission to present the play. Before reaching a decision, Montherlant wrote to Archbishop Feltin of Paris, to ask his advice. The answer praised the play but advised against any performance at the moment. A similar request for performance was made by Jean-Louis Barrault and Madeleine Renaud for their Théâtre Marigny, and a series of other theaters repeated this request. Montherlant has persisted thus far in denying permission. There have been private performances or readings and a recording of the text was made early in 1958.

La Ville dont le prince est un enfant centers about the conflict in the heart of Abbé de Pradts, which ends by weakening his love for God. He is a disciplinary administrator who has manifested an unusual indulgence for Sandrier, a pupil in the third class, aged fourteen. Without the protection of Abbé de Pradts, Sandrier would have been expelled on two occasions. A close friendship has grown up during the past few months between Sandrier and the star pupil Sevrais, aged sixteen. This friendship, discovered by the priest, is publicly condemned because of its strong sentimental nature. (Nowhere in the play is there reference to sexuality as such. Abbé de Pradts, in his role of confessor and disciplinarian, and the Superior of the Order in the final act of the play, are concerned with arresting the development of relationships between boys which are "platonic" but decidedly amorous.)

When Sevrais freely offers to break with Sandrier, Abbé de Pradts engages in a Machiavellian trick. He revokes his decision and permits the boys to see one another. When he finds them together, he falsely accuses Sevrais, whom he asks to have expelled. The Superior, who appears at the end of the play, severely castigates the priest for his love of Sandrier and analyzes the kind of love that has been growing in the priest's heart. The younger boy is expelled also and the Superior exacts the promise from the Abbé that he will never see his charge again.

Only one theme is studied in this play, but it is presented with so many different nuances that it seems to be several themes. The paternity of the priest, whom so many call "Father," can be a source of great personal suffering, as it is in the case of Abbé de Pradts, and the source of a grave spiritual peril. Even the relationship between Sevrais and Sandrier has something of the confessor and penitent in it. The final scene, movingly tragic and inexorable, between the Superior and the priest, is the climax of a series of similar relationships. To the pure in heart everything is pure. The reader or the spectator would have to be profoundly Catholic in conviction and knowledge in order to accept in all of its meticulously worked-out psychological and theological details a text such as *La Ville dont le prince est un enfant*.

The crisis of this drama is reached and resolved within the strict confines of the school. The friendship between the two boys is referred to in Montherlant's text by the phrase *amitié particulière*, which has for the general public in France an obscene or scandalous meaning that it does not have in *La Ville*. This is undoubtedly one of Montherlant's reasons for prohibiting a production. The text is Montherlant's purest in structure and most human in feeling and pathos. There is a total absence of eroticism. The sentiments and emotions in the characters are treated on the highest level. It is difficult to imagine any public deforming the intention of *La Ville*. Its rigorous style protects its situations and permits the playwright to say everything and to speak only the truth concerning these situations.

On many occasions, Henry de Montherlant has written that he has no pretension of proving anything in his plays. This principle applies exactly to *La Ville*. In the final dialogue between the Superior and Abbé de Pradts there is no debate on *les amitiés particulières*. The Abbé articulates the arguments of his heart and the Superior articulates the arguments of a pious, theologically sound school principal. The city referred to in the title of the play is a condemned city. The arguments of the Superior are the longer and the more convincing. The order of the establishment is threatened in the strong attachment of Abbé de Pradts. The order of chivalry is referred to and exalted for a moment in the brief episode of the joining of blood (the "eighth sacrament") in the scene between Sevrais and Sandrier. But the school itself in this case, *le collège,* has its order, superior to the order of friendship.

For his announced final play (which in reality was not ultimate), *Port-Royal*, Montherlant chose an austere subject from the history of Jansenism. An earlier version, on a different aspect of Port-Royal, was not incorporated in the second text. The subject is a day in August 1664 when the nuns of Port-Royal refuse to sign the Formulaire. Twelve of them, designated by one of the nuns as the most rebellious, have been dispatched to different convents. When the curtain goes up, it is quickly established that the struggle between Jansenism and the Catholic Church is practically over. The long theological debate over grace and predestination is not even referred to. It has been replaced by a moral and social conflict. The crisis of the entire religious community is projected especially in the inner struggle of two nuns. One of the youngest nuns, Soeur Françoise, discovers in herself an unusual combative strength, an unqualified sharing in Jansenist intransigency. The other nun, Soeur Angélique, a niece of "le Grand Arnauld," one of the spiritual directors of Port-Royal, undergoes a devastating experience of religious doubt. It is because of her that the play has been called a tragedy of fear. She is one of the strongest, one of the most highly endowed sisters of the community. Her suffering because of the imminent persecution is in reality her suffering over her religious doubts, which she feels are beginning to manifest themselves.

Montherlant's style—without ornamentation, of bare but powerful and varied formulas—is admirably suited to the characters and the dramatic situation of *Port-Royal.* The action is inner and psychological, and so devoid of exterior action that in his preface Montherlant invokes the name of Racine and the Greek tragic writers. One might argue with Montherlant over his justification for referring to *Bérénice,* so dominated by passionate love, and *Antigone,* which ends in a crescendo of horrors. He has persistently avoided any melodramatic effects in his theater.

In the two psychological developments of Port-Royal, in the characters of Soeur Françoise, resolutely turned toward what she considers the light, and Soeur Angélique, turning in spite of herself toward darkness, we follow two spiritual itineraries that are without complexity and mystery. There is no entr'acte, no time given the audience for relaxing their attention. The principal struggle is between the Archbishop of Paris, whose reasons for condemning the community of Port-Royal are strong and defendable, and the obstinacy of the frail-looking nuns who oppose the established order. The text of Montherlant does project from this struggle a grandeur of pathos, which in the dramatic sense has little to do with theology. The theological points of the Formulaire are not so important to the nuns as the fact that they have been asked to sign it. Their doggedness in the central scene with the Archbishop appears as a kind of blind rebellion. The fight is lost before it is waged and this fact provides the pathos. Theologically minded critics, such as Thierry Maulnier, have pointed out that the victimized nuns may appear before today's public as the real champions of freedom. Actually, in the historical sense, the persecutors of Port-Royal were the defenders of free will, and the persecuted defended a thesis that was practically that of predestination.

In the many public discussions and debates concerning the theology and the dramaturgy of *Port-Royal,* Montherlant has resolutely argued for the basic Christian belief in the fecundity of all suffering, for the maintenance of Christianity in the suffering of its martyrs. He has defended the intransigency of Soeur Angélique, in her treatment of others, as being historically accurate. One of the public debates brought together a Dominican, Père Carré; a Jesuit, Père Daniélou; the two philosophers Gabriel Marcel and Henri Gouhier; and Henry de Montherlant. Père Daniélou stressed the fact that in the play *Port-Royal*, the theology is of little consequence, and raised the point that the truth of the cause for which man suffers has its importance, and not solely the fact that man suffers. He believed that Montherlant reveals in *Port-Royal* a morbid kind of Christianity which belongs neither to Jansenism nor to Orthodox Christianity. He protested that the theme of despair in the play is Montherlant's own and not that of historical Jansenism.

Port-Royal is Montherlant's eighth play, and the one in which all action in its obvious meaning—exterior, melodramatic, visible—is reduced to its maximum simplicity. It exists—what there is of it—as a pretext for that inner psychological action which Montherlant has always claimed uniquely interests him. What in English-speaking countries would be called the plot of this play is a series of moments of the soul which the playwright has successfully projected with a maximum of truthfulness and intensity.

4. Anouilh (1910-   )

Jean Anouilh's play of 1956, *Pauvre Bitos ou le dîner de têtes*, called forth something that is very rare in Paris: a unanimous and vehement disapproval on the part of the dramatic critics. It is a play on hatred and moral turpitude, but so prevalent, so deeply ingrained in all the characters, that the effect of horror turns finally to one of boredom. The critics, in their denunciations of the play and their fears that such a text would confirm and strengthen anti-French feelings abroad, paid little heed to the dramatic structure of *Bitos*, which, as always in Anouilh, is skillful and ingenious. The first act gives the background of Bitos —his wretched childhood of poverty; the cruelty of his schoolmates, who beat him because he was poor and because he received the highest marks; his active role in the Resistance; the high position he reached in his native town after the war. He became the leading citizen, honest, incorruptible.

His old school enemies plan a revenge. They organize a dinner where the guests wear wigs and headdress to designate them as characters from the French Revolution. Bitos comes fully dressed as Robespierre (a serious error). The cruelty is now more subtle and more perverse. Bitos faints when he recognizes the Gendarme Merda—who broke Robespierre's jaw—incarnated by a victim of Bitos, condemned to twenty years imprisonment but now released. The false Merda shoots a blank cartridge at the false Robespierre. Bitos believes that he is dead. The second act constitutes his dream. He relives episodes in the life of Robespierre so arranged, in defiance of chronological truth, that Anouilh's thesis becomes clear: Robespierre was bloodthirsty and wicked, and he had grown into that kind of character because of his early poverty and because of the beatings he had received in childhood. The indictment against poverty is a strong theme in *Pauvre Bitos*.

There is a still stronger theme in this play which explains much of the hostility it has encountered in France, and yet which in its fundamental meaning is inherent in all the writings of Anouilh: an interpretation of the history of France as being a battle of bandits of the lowest kind, some poorer than others. Except in very few great works of satire—Juvenal, Dante, D'Aubigné—hatred is an ungainly muse. In Anouilh it turns quickly to disgust and filth, to a monotonous repetition of expletives.

In the third act of *Pauvre Bitos*, Bitos has recovered from his fainting spell. He is further humiliated by his torturers and forced by them to become a gangster capitalist. More blatantly than in his other plays, but not in contradiction with them, Jean Anouilh has in this work reduced every instinct of nobility and purity to its opposite of cowardice, villainy, vulgarity. The language is as coarse as the sentiments. The playwright's deep seated resentment against humanity is here fully expressed, fully exposed.

The same fundamental bitterness of tone characterizes all the plays of Anouilh, but in the earlier plays it seemed to come from a more noble, more philosophical kind of despair and torment. There have, however, always been traces of the popular novel and the melodrama in the Anouilh plays, but they were usually offset by an imperious spiritual suffering, by a new kind of *mal du siècle*. He has written uniquely for the theater. Giraudoux and Montherlant came to the theater from the novel, and Claudel from poetry. Anouilh is purely the playwright, and because of this exceptional characteristic, his career has been followed with close attention, with intermittent hopes that he is the representative French playwright today, that he best continues the tradition of Molière in being solely and purely a man of the theater.

Pauvre Bitos, playing in the 1956-7 season in Paris, at the time of the Algerian crisis, the Hungarian revolt, and the Suez Canal conflict, was caustically received by the French, largely perhaps because of the international drama and the problem of national prestige. It is the fate of the theater in every country to suffer and profit from the state of the nation. On the occasion of each new play of Anouilh, the skillfulness of its construction, of its dramaturgy, is commented on, and the general atmosphere of the play as well. The bitterness of his satire is not new. His view of the world and of human existence has not altered through the years. He has Antigone say: "I refuse Life." (*Je refuse la vie. . . .*) Between his heroes and the world, Anouilh reveals and studies with an implacable perseverance a deep incompatibility. His heroines—Antigone, Jeanne d'Arc—and his heroes, like Bitos, live in terms of an absolute that the world will not permit. Good and evil are clearly defined and tragically separated by Anouilh.

In a metaphysical sense, Anouilh is constantly rewriting the same comedy. Technically he introduces innovations. He takes every liberty possible in his arrangement and choreography of the play. He employs every device, from farce and vaudeville to tense, somber tragedy, but he demonstrates a fundamental unity in theme and philosophy. At the time of Henry Bernstein, the term "well-made play," *la pièce bien faite*, designated the ideal in playwriting. It meant a careful ordering of scenes, an organization of suspense, exposition, climax. This characterization applies

better to the realist theater of a Bernstein, for example,
than to the plays of Molière, Marivaux, or Anouilh, where
the construction is more musical and choreographic. In the
history of the French theater, perhaps only Racine has
felt totally at ease within the rigorous rules of a given
dramatic form.

The central figure, then, in an Anouilh play, is the one
who says "no," who contradicts life: Creon's niece in
Antigone, Thérèse in *La Sauvage,* Jeanne d'Arc in
L'Alouette, and Eurydice in *Eurydice (Legend of Lovers).*
These are all fundamentally the same heroine whose
purity of being and purity of purpose are contaminated by
a corrupting family relationship, by some social pressure,
or by the memory of family and social entanglements.
Even if the heroine is wholly innocent, she cannot live
because of what others say about her. Anouilh centers his
dramatic action on the cruel difference between what an
act is for his character and what it is for those around her,
who observe and judge her and who consistently refuse to
believe in her innocence. A human action is capable of
eliciting two diametrically opposite interpretations.
Anouilh's pessimism is revealed in his willingness to ascribe
to these two interpretations the same degree of reality. The
individual is fatally compromised by his world, by his
family and society and friends. In several of his plays, in
Pauvre Bitos, for example, and *L'Invitation au château
(Ring Round the Moon),* Anouilh accords an almost
mystical power to money. He seems to look upon money
as the determining factor in the evolution of human destiny. Poverty and wealth are equally potent fatalities. On
this score in particular, Marxist and Christian thinkers have
bitterly attacked the psychology of Anouilh.

Unlike Giraudoux, unlike Montherlant, Jean Anouilh has
published no theory concerning his plays, no dialectical
exposition that can be confronted with the texts themselves. Moreover, Anouilh has never been a public figure.
He has maintained the utmost secrecy about himself and

Short Biography

his life. He was born in 1910, in Bordeaux. His student years were spent in Paris, where he attended the Collège Chaptal. At the age of nineteen he was engaged by Jouvet as secretary to the Comédie des Champs-Elysées, where he remained a year and a half and then left for military service. He studied law and worked briefly in an advertising firm. His first play, *L'Hermine,* was produced in 1932. Since that time he has lived solely by writing for the theater, and, intermittently, for the movies.

By 1959, Anouilh had written and produced more than twenty plays. The constancy of theme in these plays gives his work, taken as a whole, the appearance and the forcefulness of an ideology. He is perpetually opposing two types of attitude, best illustrated in Antigone and Creon. Antigone's attitude is stalwart refusal of any kind of happiness which will be marred by compromise or impurity. Usually the play is dominated by a single protagonist, such as Antigone, whose purity of intention reveals the ugliness of the world. "All would have gone smoothly if it hadn't been for Antigone," one of the characters remarks. (*Sans la petite Antigone, vous auriez tous été bien tranquilles. . . .*)

Like Molière's Anouilh's plays usually concern a family. The reality that the play develops is the forced hypocrisy that such a group of characters represents. The leading action is almost always the stifling of the protagonist's purity. But to be pure, according to Anouilh, is to be without a past, and since this is impossible, even the purest, an Antigone, a Jeanne d'Arc, a Thérèse, are destined to failure.

The two most popular successes of Anouilh have been *Antigone* and *L'Alouette* (*The Lark*). Already *Antigone* has had more than one thousand performances in Paris alone, and some of the scenes are now regularly used as "try-outs" by aspiring young actresses. *L'Alouette,* a much more recent play, has had more than three hundred performances.

The story of Antigone is one of the three or four

classical tragic situations. The victim is not responsible for the tragedy that befalls her. It is upsetting to the moral judgment of the spectators. Anouilh's treatment of Antigone omits any intervention of the gods. There is a total absence of any religious interpretation of the protagonist's fate. This means that Anouilh's understanding of tragedy is as far removed from Sophocles' as it is from Claudel's. But Antigone's fate, in Anouilh's version, is known from the start. At the beginning of the dramatic action, she is fully aware of her fate and of the uselessness of opposing it. In this sense, Anouilh's understanding of tragedy appears in opposition to the Sartrean or existentialist understanding of tragedy, which is based upon a belief in the individual's freedom to choose.

The character of Antigone, as Anouilh presents her, is one of such innate pessimism and such difficult willfulness, that this in itself may be sufficient explanation for her fate. In the opening *agon* between her and Creon, everything seems settled in advance and she is able to taunt her uncle with these words: "I knew you would have me killed." (*J'étais certaine que vous me feriez mourir*. . . .) When Creon asks her point-blank for whom she performed the act of disobedience of trying to bury her brother's body: she answers, "For no one. For myself." (*Pour personne. Pour moi.*) With these caustic words, she sets herself off at some distance from the Sophoclean Antigone. The French heroine rejects hope (*le sale espoir*). This theme is repeated by the chorus, which defines tragedy as something restful and clean because it is stripped of all elements of hope. (*C'est propre, la tragédie, c'est reposant, parce qu'on sait qu'il n'y a plus d'espoir*. . . .)

In opposition to Antigone, Creon is the politician concerned with imposing and maintaining order. Anouilh's Creon has illusions about the stupidity of his edict, but it is good enough for the populace. At all costs he wants to avoid scandal and preserve peace in the state. He is without fear and he has at times impulses of affection and human warmth. The type of human being his nature cannot tolerate is the anarchist Antigone. In her search for truth she is as unbending as Creon is in his upholding of the law. The tragedy of Sophocles presents two strong individuals, but especially a conflict of a metaphysical nature between a practical system of order and the truth of an eternal law. The tragedy of Jean Anouilh also presents two strong individuals, but especially a pattern of temperamental conflict, a clash of a psychological nature between a man and a woman. Almost more than the struggle between order and truth, we follow in the Anouilh play the examples of Antigone's and Creon's terrifying solitude.

At one moment in the play, when Antigone defines the kind of being she is, she defines at the same time the leading trait of Anouilh's characters, and indeed an austere psychological trait visible in much of contemporary French literature. Antigone claims that she is one of those who ask questions up to the very end. (*Nous sommes de ceux qui posent les questions jusqu'au bout. . . .*) There is no facile human answer to the questions asked by the characters of Anouilh, and this would be fully applicable to the characters of Julien Green and Mauriac and Bernanos. These characters have in common the fact that they are placed in exceptional situations, in great tests of moral experience, where they are mercilessly revealed and exhibited. The moral struggle they carry on within themselves reveals the corruption of the world around them. Anouilh's *Antigone* underscored with as much vigor and precision as Camus's *L'Etranger* and Sartre's *Les Mouches* the new French consciousness in the early 1940's of the concepts of freedom and responsibility. These three works are perhaps the clearest expression of man's moral adventure unfolding in a world characterized as "absurd" in the light of war, deportations, and a foreign occupation.

The extreme liberty taken by Anouilh in the organization and writing of his plays is particularly visible in *La*

Valse des toréadors (*The Waltz of the Toreadors*) of 1952.
This play has elements of classical comedy, of vaudeville
(in the French sense), of opera with arias, of fantasy. But
Anouilh is perfectly capable also of writing the strictest
kind of comedy. In the composition of his plays, Anouilh
starts with the characters. He has said on many occasions
that the decisive event in his career as playwright was a
performance he attended of Pirandello's *Six Characters in
Search of an Author*. In this play, the six characters appear
on a stage where there is no set and no dramatic situation
to play. A theatrical fantasy is gradually generated by them
and organized around them. After only a few speeches, a
plot begins to form. The characters themselves create their
own setting and their own drama. The example of the
Pirandello play is never totally absent from the works of
Anouilh.

La Valse des toréadors is a continuation of a previous
play, *Ardèle ou la Marguerite,* where one of the characters,
at the end of the play, is left stranded in an elevator. Near
the end of the play, this character, the wife of General
de Saint-Pé, emerges for a moment for a violent scene of
accusations, but she is put back into her elevator before the
last curtain.

La Valse is the "blackest" of Anouilh's plays, his most
brilliant demonstration of unrelenting pessimism. General
de Saint-Pé had appeared in *Ardèle* essentially as a dis-
solute sensualist and woman-chaser. In *La Valse des toréadors* a finer side of his character is revealed. For seventeen
years, despite an unbearable existence with his wife—who
has been unfaithful, shrewish, screaming, and paralytic—
he has never abandoned her. And during the same period
of time he has loved a young woman and refused to make
her his mistress because he would have preferred to have
offered to marry her. Two major occurrences sustain the
play's action. He discovers that his wife has always been
unfaithful, and that the young girl with whom he danced
la valse des toréadors seventeen years ago has fallen in

love with his secretary, a young man named Gaston, who turns out, at the end of the play to be the general's own illegitimate son.

One scene in particular, in the fourth act, between the general and his wife, reaches a paroxysm of tragedy. The entire story of the marriage is rehearsed. The dialogue is violent and brutal and unerringly realistic. The terms of love and hate are indistinguishable. Each one has become an object of horror for himself through the other. The "tone" of the rest of the play is quite different, more light and whimsical. For this reason the quarrel scene seems more violent than perhaps it is, more shocking in its particular context.

The basic Anouilh theme of incommunicability is again established in *La Valse:* incommunicability between the heroes of this playwright and their world. Wherever a sense of the absolute exists in a human being, the power of communication diminishes. And at the same time, the power to compromise or adjust. Around his central character, Saint-Pé, Anouilh assembles a group that resembles stock characters or marionettes: a naïve young man, an old maid, a grumpy, aged servant-woman. The skillfully arranged entrances and exits of these characters reinforce the marionette-show effect. This is a basic kind of theater where the action moves so fast that the spectators are delighted and captivated. The comic effects are multiple and controlled by a master hand. The voice of the general's wife is heard during the first act. She appears in the second act, but collapses and is taken away. Her big scene of explanation is constantly being put off, but the public realizes her great importance in the play. In the third act she is really introduced, but in a semipleasant, semicomic way, at lunch, around the table, where the conversation intimates the basic theme, but avoids any frankness with it. The fourth act is the terrible center of the play, in the bedroom where the general's wife appears with all her masks, wig, ribbons, rouge, and the lace-covered bed—a kind of altar where each night the general is sacrificed. The bedroom scene is the fatal trap that has caught the protagonist. The triumphant aria sung by the wife is malicious and vile and unbearable. Seventeen years of hate and venom are rehearsed until the general strangles the mad woman. This is a Greek scene of tragedy dominated by a demonic Fury.

The lesson that the young secretary learns from all this woe is a kind of message. He finds happiness in his marriage with a woman much older than himself but who will never repeat the horrors of the general's wife. The fifth act is a poignant portrayal of the general's sad, empty existence, so personal and so deeply felt that one instinctively feels that it is the playwright himself speaking.

It happens often in Paris that a play will become a popular success and enjoy a long run, despite a hostile press or at least despite opposition from major dramatic critics. This was the case with *L'Alouette*, presented in 1953 at the Théâtre Montparnasse Gaston-Baty.

When the curtain goes up, Jeanne d'Arc is in the presence of her judges. The Englishman Warwick and Cauchon are in a hurry to conclude the affair. As the questions continue, the episodes of Jeanne's life become the play: her childhood, her departure from home, her visit to Baudricourt, the recognition of the King at Chinon, her departure for Orléans. Anouilh sidesteps the burning at the stake, and the end of the play is Jeanne's preparation for the coronation of her king at Reims.

Anouilh's Jeanne is vastly different from two other incarnations still present in the memory of many French: Shaw's Joan, played by the frail, sensitive Ludmilla Pitoëff, and, more recently, Péguy's Jeanne, played by Maria Casarès in front of the Church of Saint-Jean in Lyon. The very gifted actress Suzanne Flon played Anouilh's lark. Her performance was universally praised, but this was not sufficient to placate the critics in their disapproval of the text. Certain of Jeanne's characteristics seemed to come from other Anouilh heroines, from Thérèse of *La Sauvage*, from Eurydice, from Antigone. Perhaps especially from Antigone. There is the same grouping of traditional characters around the central character: the narrow-minded and coarse father of Jeanne; the rascally mother, who gives her daughter the advice of a procuress; the Queen; and Agnès Sorel, who is the King's mistress. The process of caricature, always visible to some extent in Anouilh's plays, is perhaps more swiftly, more dexterously applied in *L'Alouette* than in the others. The art at times even recalls that of the Parisian *chansonniers* in its popular medley of pathos, wit, and vulgarity.

It would be ludicrous to expect from Anouilh the attitude of a Claudel before the subject of Jeanne d'Arc. But there is a change in tone from the destructiveness and hatred so apparent in *Ardèle* and *La Valse des toréadors*. And yet the satiric impulse is never impeded in *L'Alouette*. Antigone's famous "no" to life becomes something else as Jeanne repeats it to the innumerable solicitations of doubt, of coarseness, of abdication. Her "no" is so insistent that it becomes "yes" to other values such as action and courage. Anouilh's Jeanne has a certain degree of maliciousness in her nature, married with good common sense. But her smile and her sense of familiarity never lose their mystery. It is perhaps this mysteriousness of her nature that allows her to triumph over the narrow-mindedness or lack of energy in those she argues with: Charles VII, Baudricourt, La Hire. Her commonplace speech and her tireless willfulness end by transforming those she needs to transform. She combines the tenderness of a young girl with the heavy wit of a peasant.

The subject of sanctity is perhaps the most delicate and the most complex that the theater attempts to treat, even when it is disguised, as it is in *L'Alouette*, by a sense of directness and wholeheartedness which explicate sanctity in purely human terms. The disguise is skillfully effective and the construction of the play in a series of short sketches sustains the disguise and never allows it to fall. Each character moves in turn into the full glare of the spotlight and recites his particular part that will demonstrate the extraordinary human qualities of Jeanne without insisting on any supernatural explanation. Deliberate juggling with chronology, often practiced by Anouilh, is here employed to offset any possible intrusion of theology. The ladies of the court discuss their headdress and the texture of their cloth as if Christian Dior were present. The High Inquisitor of the Church speaks somewhat in the style of a right-wing politician. The "set piece" reserved for each of the principal characters, and the rapid succession of these set pieces when a nonchronological effect is often comic, give to *L'Alouette* the tone of a "review." Although in all justice to Anouilh it must be said that the brilliance of the dialogue, the skillful handling of transitions and juxtapositions, place this work in the domain of drama.

The reception accorded to *L'Alouette* was somewhat comparable to that accorded *Cyrano de Bergerac* in 1898. At that time there was a sense of joy in coming upon a work purely Gallic, limpid, entertaining as well as moving, in the midst of a period dominated by Scandinavian realism. It was received with too much enthusiasm to last. All levels of the public were too satisfied at once. In time, the *panache* of *Cyrano* turned out to be a caricature of true greatness, of true courage. In time, the hearty treatment of the saint in *L'Alouette* will also turn out to be false. The laughter that the play elicits is too close to the laughter of mockery. Some of the most successful scenes are built on commonplaces. Jeanne's triumph over Baudricourt, for example, illustrates the fact that soldiers are stupid and that women are clever, and that women win out by telling men they are handsome and intelligent.

In the whole array of devices which *L'Alouette* exploits so dexterously, the most significant is Anouilh's refusal to end his play with the burning at the stake. It has just begun when it is interrupted with the assurance that

Jeanne's story is joyous, and suddenly we hear the cathedral organ and bells, and we see the banners and flags of the coronation at Reims. The burning scene would have been too harsh an ending for such a play. Anouilh sees to it that the public will leave his theater in a state of euphoria. All the moments of bad taste in his play (what I suppose the French would call *vulgarité*) have been adroitly camouflaged. Far more than one realizes, Jean Anouilh in *L'Alouette* is mocking the saint, the Church, French peasants, French royalty, mankind.

For twenty years now, Anouilh has been writing what he himself characterizes as *pièces noires* and *pièces roses* or *brillantes* or *grinçantes*. These are his personal terms for genres that more or less resemble tragedy and comedy. The dark-colored plays have perhaps been his greatest successes: *La Sauvage, Eurydice, Antigone, L'Alouette*. The heroine in each case dominates the work by her revolt, her clamor, her willful and at times sentimental opposition to the ways of the world. She is in each notable case a challenge to the actress incarnating her. She is a "vehicle" for the star, and this explains to some extent the contemporary success of the *pièces noires*. The light-colored plays are more complex. To this category belong *L'Invitation au château, Le Bal des voleurs, Ardèle ou la Marguerite, La Valse des toréadors*. These plays reflect some of the most serious psychological problems of our period. The extraordinary range of Anouilh's talent is visible here: his sense of the comic, his powers of observation. In the long run, his comedies may well represent the surer part of his art. His tragic heroines lack the final all-important component for tragedy, a total sincerity. And perhaps the best scenes in his tragedies are those that might easily belong with his *pièces roses*.

Anouilh's comic art has not yet, I think, been fully realized. One is aware of it too often at moments in his plays when he uses it as a device to effect some relaxation, some respite from the problem at hand at a point when the problem reaches a moment of tension and anguish. Anouilh's complexity comes from the conflict in himself between a fundamental pessimistic outlook and a theatrical presentation that is as basically comic as it was in Molière. If this conflict is ever resolved so that the dramaturgy of the idea, of the philosophic concept, will be totally focused on the comic, Anouilh may well become a major writer in the history of the French theater. He is certainly of his time, fully aware of the manias and the problems of his age. But in order that the public in France today may laugh with him, without shame, and for future publics in France and elsewhere to continue to laugh without shame, he will have to effect a more drastic aesthetic transposition than he has yet achieved.

The third term that Anouilh has used to designate the genre of his plays, *pièces brillantes,* announces in itself the necessary modification. Their "brilliancy" is precisely this mixture of thematic seriousness and lightness of touch, lightness of style. But mixture is not enough for the final achievement of the work. It will have to be a fusion—an art resembling the sureness of a Molière comedy, where we can laugh without being ashamed. In two of his richest comedies, *Colombe* and *La Répétition,* the theme is not new, but it is profound and provocative. It is a debate (somewhat discernible in all of Anouilh's plays, but lucidly presented in *Colombe* and *La Répétition*) between two philosophies: one that is determined to exploit human life and profit from it, and another that demands of human life more than it can ever give. On the one side is the character who believes that life has to be tricked and plotted against; and on the other is the character who is determined to ask from life, without subterfuge, without hypocrisy, the ultimate, the absolute. This ideological conflict is paralleled in the amazing contrast, within the texture and the style, between a virtuoso's technique and the gravity of a revolt against human fate.

If Anouilh ever finds the mysterious form or formula

(and only he can find it for himself), the dialogue between truth and falsehood that never comes to an end in his plays would at least find in each play a solution and a conclusion. During the course of the past twenty years, and during the composition of as many plays, Anouilh has constructed the world, not so much of a theater as of a mythology. An opposition between good and evil, as old as the world itself, is at the basis of this mythology. But the author, whose world it is, refuses to allow any triumph of either good or evil, of either love or hate. It would seem that Anouilh, in an almost masochistic fashion, is determined to prolong his own suffering from an unwillingness or an impossibility of concluding—of depicting the triumph of good or evil.

III. RELIGIOUS THEATER

1. Claudel (1868-1955)

It is quite possible that the term "drama," in its fullest sense, never applied to the French theater until Claudel began writing his plays. From the sixteenth to the nineteenth centuries tragedy and comedy were strict forms in France, adhering closely to the Aristotelian precepts and the classical models. Victor Hugo, in the nineteenth century, attempted to create *le drame* by fusing the comic and the tragic. The formula he worked out was weak. Claudel created a dramatic form that is unique in French and that bears some affiliation with the drama of Shakespeare and Lope de Vega. His drama is not a combination of the comic and the tragic. It is a work of one piece and one texture. It is simultaneously speech of the theater and poetry of language.

His characters speak with the voices of real men and women who feel that humanity forms one body in that each man is responsible at every moment of his existence for all other men. In each scene of his many plays we have the impression of following some aspect or other of one of the most difficult and mystical dogmas of all, that of the communion of saints. For Claudel the universe is total at every moment of every man's existence. Every story he undertakes to unravel he finds to be an anecdote or an element of the same drama of man which is continuously unfolding in the world. Claudel has spoken of the "passion of the universe" which he feels, and of the exaltation he derives from contemplating the millions of things that exist at the same time. (*Que j'aime ce million de choses qui existent ensemble!* . . .)

The first version of his first play, *Tête d'or,* was written in 1889. It is his only non-Christian play. (Not until Christmas 1890, four years after his conversion, did Claudel make his communion at Notre-Dame and his formal return to the Church.) Claudel always attached a great deal of importance to this play. Long after its composition he called it the "introduction to his work" and "the drama of the possession of the earth." In its theme, and even partially in its style, it is the closest of all of Claudel's works to Rimbaud. Rimbaud died in the hospital at Marseille in October 1891, two years after the first version of *Tête d'or.* In 1893 Claudel began his own career of travel, and composed in China in 1894 the second version of the play. It is the drama of an adventurer who attempts to elevate himself by the sole means of his own strength and intelligence. This early text shows the poet's effort to master it and translate an inspiration that is a spiritual tumult. It poses all the problems of man's fate, without, however, the problem of woman's love, which is to be central in the later plays.

At the beginning of the play, the hero, Simon Agnel, is burying the woman he has loved and whose body he has brought back to their native soil. He recognizes the younger man, Cébès, who had loved the same woman. This first part of the drama is a lament over the grave, spoken by the adolescent Cébès and by Simon. In the second part of the drama, Simon becomes *"Tête d'or,"* the conqueror. He conquers all of Europe as far as a Caucasian pass where he meets defeat and death. Behind the obvious impulse in *Tête d'or* to seize the earth is the problem of love, which is to develop in the subsequent plays into Claudel's principal theme. The tragedy in *Tête d'or* comes from the hero's belief that he can find in himself his equilibrium and his salvation. He had not listened to the deepest voice within himself at the moments of his harshest lessons: the death of his wife, the death of Cébès, and his own death. In *Vers d'exil,* written a year after the second version of *Tête d'or,* Claudel reveals in a single line of a poem a clue to his dramaturgy:

Quelqu'un qui soit en moi, plus moi-même que moi.
(Someone who is in me, more myself than I am)

This is Claudel's version of Rimbaud's celebrated *Je suis un autre.* The dialogue between man and God, the struggle between submission and resistance, is to inspire some of the loftiest and most dramatic passages in the theater of Claudel.

La Ville (The City), Claudel's second play, written in 1890 and considerably revised in 1897, is on the meaning of the city and the organization of men. Besme is head of the city, the owner of vast gardens and an engineer. His brother Lambert is a not too vigorous politician, who despite his age, wishes to marry a young girl, Lâla. Avare is the spirit of violence and destruction in the city. He recalls the character Simon in *Tête d'or.* In his revolutionary judgment, the city might be Sodom or Babylon. Coeuvre is the poet of the city. His scene with Besme, at the beginning of the play, is a dialogue between the two opposing but necessary temperaments of the poet: the isolated, excommunicated member of the group, and the leader who has discovered the vanity of all things. Lâla turns toward Coeuvre and their marriage marks the end of the first act. This is the moment when Lambert accepts the idea of his death, when his brother Besme gives himself over to total despair, and when the revolutionary Avare prepares the destruction of the city.

The one woman of the play, Lâla, dominates the second

act. She is now living with Avare, the spirit of the future, and has abandoned Coeuvre, the poet, who always for Claudel represents the present. When the city is in ruins— the setting of the third act—Avare leaves because his mission is over. Ivors, the son of Lâla and Coeuvre, is lieutenant and in charge of the new city. Coeuvre returns to it in his new role of bishop. His life continues to be a search, but he speaks with authority about the constitution of the city, about the need to organize it as if it were a single body with all its organs and members, from the prince to the lowliest contemplative. Lâla, one of the first of Claudel's heroines, already possesses the principal trait of the poet's women. She is unseizable, unknowable, but she is looked upon by man when he is unable to see God. Between *Tête d'or*—the study of man alone with his powers—and *La Ville* there is a marked progress in Claudel's religious understanding of the world. After the study of man in himself, in his power of conqueror (*"Tête d'or"*), Claudel chose for the object of his contemplation the arrangement of the city.

In all the many versions he has written of his best-known play, *L'Annonce faite à Marie* (*The Tidings Brought to Mary;* first called *La Jeune Fille Violaine*), Claudel stresses the mystical paradox of human relationships. This is particularly clear in the prologue, the scene between the young girl Violaine and Pierre de Craon, the builder of cathedrals. The bonds uniting these two are as mysterious and as strong as those uniting Prouhèze and Rodrigue of the later play *Le Soulier de satin.* Pierre loves Violaine, and she represents for him everything he is called upon to give up: woman, happiness, the world itself. His love scene is actually his scene of farewell to the world. This opening dialogue contains the whole meaning of the text and what lies beyond the text, because it analyzes the secret role that every Christian is called upon to play in the world— the role of pilgrim, the one who accepts the idea of separation. A kiss usually binds two lovers, but the kiss that

Pierre gives to Violaine at the end of their scene is the sign of their separation. He has guessed the real meaning of her vocation. She is the victim who combines heroism with humility. Her example is the morality of the play and of all of Claudel's plays. If it is true that the world has no value by comparison with life, then the ultimate value of life is in its capacity to give itself. Pierre as mason, architect, and builder of churches, and the other characters in the play discover their vocations in accord with the seasons and the earth. Violaine stands apart from them all, in that she represents the symbol of eternity within time, of spirit within matter. Her vocation in the play itself adds a further dimension to the characters around her. By her existence she reveals a meaning in those close to her: her father and mother, her sister, her fiancé, and Pierre de Craon.

Violaine is the type of mystic that represents for Claudel an analogue with the poet. Although the goals of mystic and poet are different, many of their activities and disciplines bear striking resemblances. For certain degrees of knowledge the poet has to reach a deep inner silence, a freedom of the spirit, a detachment. This necessary stage precedes the real function of the poet, who is by definition the maker of something. He is creator not in the sense that God is, who is able to create out of nothing. The poet is creator out of what the world provides. Claudel, coming after Baudelaire's important lesson on "correspondences," has stressed this need of a collaboration between the artist and the world. A poem begins when a relationship is perceived.

At its inception *L'Annonce faite à Marie* resembles a folk tale or a village story. Out of its familiar plot centering on two sisters, one good and one bad, Claudel achieved one of the loftiest examples of poetic drama in French literature. Mara (whose name in Hebrew means "bitter") is envious of her older sister Violaine. Like Cain and Abel, they come from the same origins and yet grow into two opposing temperaments. Mara's passion is for the material things of the earth: the farm of Combernon and the inheritance. The role of Pierre de Craon grows in importance with each new version of the play. He is the stranger, the "guest" who has no home of his own. The kiss that Violaine gives him at dawn will be sufficient to break off her marriage with Jacques Hury. Pierre is a leper, and Violaine in turn succumbs to the disease through her act of charity and love. Pierre in a sense is the image of the suffering king Amfortas, the sinner whose health is necessary to the health of all the inhabitants. He is a builder of churches in Claudel's own province, which is rich in masterpieces of the Gothic period: Reims, Soissons, Laon. The period of the play is the time of Jeanne d'Arc and of the Hundred Years' War, a period of great distress for France, when the concepts of nation and national pride were beginning to emerge.

The second act, dominated by the scene between Violaine and Jacques, has the character of a consecration. Violaine is the victim reserved for a holy purpose. *Ecce ancilla Domini.* She has prepared herself for the sacrifice and is even wearing the sacerdotal habit of the religious in the convent of Montsanvierge. She tries to explain to her fiancé why she cannot marry him. The race is to end with her. As the Virgin is the last of the tree of Jesse, so Violaine is the last of her family. Her relationship with Montsanvierge is as close as that uniting Mara with Combernon. The entire play is based upon an intimate relationship between nature and grace. Violaine's mystical vocation, which had been guessed and accepted by Pierre in the prologue, is not understood at first by Jacques.

The third act is the miracle. Violaine is a leper and ostracized. Mara's baby daughter has died and she approaches her sister as a last hope for resurrecting the child. The dialogue between the two sisters is as profound as that between Ismene and Antigone. Life returns to the baby at the moment of the first mass at Christmas. *Puer natus est nobis.* The miracle is accomplished in a liturgical way on the stage. The epilogue is the awakening of Jacques. He realizes at last the innocence of Violaine and the superfluous evil of Mara. He knows, with the example of Violaine's death before him, caused by his wife, that love is the gift of ourselves, the power to give of ourselves what we do not know. In purely human terms, the lesson is harsh, and it will pervade all the plays of Claudel. The sorrow of human love comes from its desire for complete possession. The soul cannot possess anything or anyone. Love has nothing to do with justice. These are the words spoken by Violaine in her renunciation scene of the second act.

The brilliant première of *Partage de midi* took place on December 16, 1948, in Paris, at the Théâtre Marigny, exactly forty-two years after the play was written. In 1906, one hundred and fifty copies of the play had been privately printed. But further publication had been withheld by Claudel until 1948, when he reissued the text and gave permission for its performance. Ten years previously, Jean-Louis Barrault had asked Claudel for the right to put on *Partage de midi.* The poet had refused, saying at the time: "You will play it after my death." During the Occupation, Barrault's production at the Comédie-Française of *Le Soulier de satin* was a triumph, and Claudel finally consented to a production of his older play, *Partage de midi,* perhaps because he felt himself so far removed from the younger man who had written it. He was present at the rehearsals and introduced many changes in the text, but in speaking with the actors about himself in connection with *Partage de midi,* he would say, "the author of the play." It is well-known that the play is the literary expression of an episode in Claudel's personal life.

Partage de midi occupies a peculiarly central position in the entire work of Claudel. The drama concerns only four characters. Their speeches are long, but sober and bare.

Each scene resembles a musical composition of few voices that produce a great variety of moods and tempi. The language controls and dominates all the movement, as if the actors had only to understand it and recite it in order to discover their action and their moods. The play remains at all times a majestic verbal quartet each motif of which is audible and in harmony with all other motifs. The principal theme is adultery and the secondary theme is the struggle in a man between a religious vocation and sexual love. Ysé, the heroine (admirably played at the première by Edwige Feuillère), pursues in the three men around her—her husband and two lovers—an assurance or a stability that no one can give her and that she will find only in death. She is the dominant character of the play and incarnates the principal idea, defined in Claudel's own terms, as "the spirit desiring against the flesh." (*L'esprit désire contre la chair*. . . .) At the beginning of the play, she is a coquette, both provocative and seductive. But soon she reveals herself also as something of the bourgeoise, created for marriage and children, bent upon assuring for herself a maternal and spiritual security. But fundamentally she is a biological cosmic force opposing relentlessly the power of the spirit and manifesting for Claudel the religious poet the mystery of a creature's imperfection. Her femaleness wants to reach and enfold everyone, and those whom she cannot join she will degrade.

Mesa, the leading male character (played by Barrault), is precisely the one whom Ysé desires the most and who is for her the most inaccessible. He incarnates not only the lover who comes to a woman for the first time, but also that secret force in a man which he is eternally unwilling to yield to human love. The religious idea of *Partage de midi* might well be the impossibility of perfect human love, coming from the fact that we are beings separated from one another. The particular anguish expressed so abundantly in the love scenes between Ysé and Mesa comes from the desire in physical possession of a spiritual union, of a joining with the absolute.

In his own comments on *Partage de midi,* Claudel has stressed the character of Mesa, who, at the beginning of the play, at the noon (*midi*) of his life, at the close of his youth, is returning to China after losing out on an effort to win a religious vocation. He is a bourgeois in the narrowest and meanest sense (Ysé calls him *un sacré petit bourgeois*), totally preoccupied with himself. On the ship he meets the woman who has been placed there to cause him to prefer someone else to himself, and, eventually and mysteriously, God to himself. But the play is more subtle than Claudel's interpretation of it, which would seem to turn God into a magician and men into beings resembling puppets. Ysé is one of the most complex characters in the French theater. Amalric, her first lover (played by Pierre Brasseur), sees her not as a coquette, but as a warrior, as a conqueror who wants to subjugate or tyrannize or give herself like some huge animal in pain. Amalric sees her as a stranger among them all, outside of her land and race, looking for some tremendous duties and obligations. She is more present than Mesa. She speaks and loves within her own solitude and composes her tragedy around a ghost. From the beginning of the play, Mesa appears as a character existing outside of any struggle. He has been conquered already and no longer seems to participate in his own life. Ysé wages a combat against someone who has ceased being a fighter.

The atmosphere of the first act, a remarkable depiction of an ocean desert, never disappears from the play. It gradually becomes the desert of Ysé's life. Claudel has provided for the stage version of his text a background explanation of the desert theme. When Ysé and her husband, De Ciz, appear in the first act, she states that they have been living in Harrar, where De Ciz in his trade as a gunrunner was an associate of a certain Rimbaud, a man who had paid no attention to her. Turning away from her husband, she contemplates each of the other two men. She discovers in Mesa the Christian, and is attracted by him because, after all, she is a woman searching for the absolute in love. In Amalric she discovers the type of man who knows what he wants, the colonial materialist accustomed to tyrannizing and controlling large numbers of natives. Together the characters form a quartet of criminals. The action of the play transpires between the moment of noon (*partage de midi*) when each character makes a decision separating himself from his previous life, and the moment of midnight (*partage de minuit*) when the tragedy occurs and death in the form of violence and sacrifice comes to join Ysé and Mesa.

Partage de midi demonstrates Claudel's growing power as dramatist and thinker. One sentence in the text describes the emerging of the soul from the body as if it were a sword half unsheathed. (*L'âme outrée, sortie de ton corps comme une épée, à demi dégaînée.*) The play is the drama of this apparition. In Claudel's own preface to the play, he calls it "the flesh desiring against the spirit, and the spirit desiring against the flesh." But it is at the same time the flesh desiring the spirit, and the spirit desiring the flesh. The drama of physical love in *Partage de midi* is the anguish of a possession that is far more than the possession of the body. One thinks instinctively of Phèdre, who in Racine's tragedy desires far more than the body of Hippolyte. She yearns for the purity of which he is the physical image. The drama in *Partage de midi* is more the woman's than the man's. Mesa's case is far more simple than Ysé's. His passion for Ysé is never total. At every moment through the action of the play he knows that he cannot belong to Ysé. He therefore represents for Ysé what is ultimately inaccessible in a human being. She discovers in Mesa—and this is her principal action in the play—that part of man which is never relinquished to human love. By comparison with Ysé, Mesa appears almost passive. She lives on many levels, and far more intensely than he does. Her great fault, infinitely more grievous than her adultery, is her will to debase what she cannot possess.

Partage de midi is more awesome than the other plays of Claudel. It is the barest and the closest to pure tragedy, despite the melodramatic ending. There is no supernatural intervention. It is rigorously a play on human freedom and responsibility. The subject of eternity is never absent from the complex psychological problems, but it is always enmeshed in the complications of immediate life. At every moment, the play risks appearing trivial in its familiar adventure of violence, sensuality, adultery, coquetry. But the action is dominated by the power of the sky. The force above these lives is either solar (*partage de midi*) or astral (*partage de minuit*), moving them toward a world that is the consummation of their world.

Claudel's greatest play, *Le Soulier de satin* (*The Satin Slipper*), is at once one of the most complicated plays ever written and one of the simplest. The three principal characters form one of the most familiar plots in the history of the theater: an aged husband, a young wife, and a lover. Behind the personal relationships of these three characters, Claudel has developed the historical drama of the Renaissance and the destiny of Spain. Even if dates and events are deliberately juggled with, one has the impression of watching the birth of a new era, of seeing a new world emerge from the medieval world of Saint Thomas. Rodrigue and Don Camille are types of conquerors and adventurers of that period. Their quest is as deeply spiritual as it is materialistic. An obvious bond joins them with more modern adventurers, such as Rimbaud and T. E. Lawrence, with travelers like Guillaume Apollinaire and Claudel himself.

In the Claudelian conception of drama, the relationship between man and woman and between man and God is an eternal relationship. If salvation is the goal of each human existence, love is the means for reaching this goal.

Lovers in Claudel's plays appear as potential mystics. In *Le Soulier de satin* and *Partage de midi* he presents a case of love so total that it would seem to exclude love of God, and yet Claudel believes so deeply in the identity of all love that he would say: human love, as it grows in intensity, will end by seeing what it really is.

In these two plays especially, Claudel has re-examined the problem of human passion. The questions about the fatality of passion, asked in such works as *Tristan, Phèdre, Manon,* are reiterated by Claudel: the meaning of passion, the reason for human love, the reason for its particular force, its destructiveness, the Christian attitude toward it, its spiritual meaning. Claudel's answers to these eternal questions, or at least his comments on them, form a significant aspect of his work which has not yet been fully realized or studied. These two dramas are violent in terms of the mystery surrounding the problem.

He calls woman, in *Partage de midi,* the promise that cannot be held. (*La femme est la promesse qui ne peut être tenue. . . .*) She is not limitless, and yet man's desire, his longing, is infinite. Her need for the infinite, which is at the basis of human love, is always being deceived by the limitations of love. It must be remembered that Claudel is not speaking of conjugal love in either play. He is quite literally and with unusual boldness studying the kind of passion analyzed previously in *Tristan, Phèdre,* and *Manon Lescaut.* Claudel's fundamental thought seems to be that a human being cannot be the end of the satisfaction of another human being. The beauty of such human love is all the greater if there is an absence of satisfaction. There are no human means for reaching this satisfaction. As soon as a man is separated from the one he loves, he yearns for death.

Claudel spent five years in composing *Le Soulier de satin,* between 1919 and 1924. He was living in Japan during most of this time. The earthquake in Tokyo occurred when he was there, and in fact he lost a part of the manuscript at the moment of the catastrophe. The première took place twenty years later during the German occupation of Paris, on November 27, 1943, at the Comédie-Française. For this production Claudel rewrote the play in a considerably shortened version. It was staged by Jean-Louis Barrault and the music was composed by Arthur Honegger.

The hero of the drama, Rodrigue, is a conqueror type, a *tête d'or,* and the situation he finds himself in is comparable to that of *Partage de midi.* Claudel places his drama in the sixteenth century because, contrary to the opinion of most historians, he finds it a triumphant period for Catholicism. He considers it a century of apostolic fervor, of conquest, of struggle against heresy, of discovery of Plato and Greece. The voyages of Vasco da Gama, Columbus, Magellan, parallel the founding of religious orders. Divine love was never more fervently expressed than in the experiences of Saint Teresa of Avila and Saint John of the Cross. The action of the play covers an entire century. There is mention of the Council of Trent (1545-63), and of the paintings of Rubens (1577-1640). Claudel freed himself from all the rules of unity. The universe itself is the site of the action.

The play opens with a mid-ocean scene where a dying Jesuit priest, tied to a sinking mast, is praying. Then follow scenes in Spain, Italy, Africa, America. The hemispheres carry on a dialogue with one another. In one scene, of great mystical importance, the earth itself takes on the size of a rosary bead. In the Third Day, scenes seven and eight, Don Camille places in the hand of Dona Prouhèze, who sleeps, a crystal rosary bead she had lost. In her dream, in which she speaks with her guardian angel, the bead becomes the globe and then a single point in a star-filled sky where a gigantic image of the Immaculate Conception appears to her. (*O Marie, Reine du Ciel, autour de qui s'enroule tout le chapelet des Cieux, ayez pitié de ces peuples qui attendent!*)

In the opening monologue, spoken by the dying priest, the subject of the play is clearly announced: the salvation of his brother Rodrigue's soul, which the priest prays for. The influence of this first character, who appears only in the monologue, is felt throughout the play. The action is built upon a constant intervention of Providence in the plans of man. As in *Partage de midi,* two men are rivals for the hand of Dona Prouhèze. (This name, Claudel confided to Louis Gillet, was discovered by him on a shoemaker's sign in the rue Cassette, in Paris.) The experience of love makes the lover into a plaything of the Almighty. Therein He has His greatest hold on a human creature, because love is the source of grace. It has also an obscure relationship with sin. Love is the sign by which we are chosen.

Dona Prouhèze's first marriage, to Don Pélage, a worthy judge and worshipful husband, had been the life of peace and inactivity for which she was not made. She is a woman of action who lives the most intensely in the presence of danger. At Mogador she feels attracted by the frivolous Don Camille. There also she falls deeply in love with Rodrigue, whom she nurses back to health. She knows that this love is absolute and for all time. On the point of leaving Spain she had prayed before the statue of the Virgin and placed in the hand of the figure one of her satin slippers. "When I rush toward evil, may I go limping." (*Je vous préviens que tout à l'heure je ne vous verrai plus et que je vais tout mettre en oeuvre contre vous. Mais quand j'essayerai de m'élancer vers le mal, que ce soit avec un pied boiteux!*) Such an episode as this would have furnished the subject matter of a miracle play in the fourteenth century. It is the beginning of the drama between Rodrigue and Prouhèze, which, with two or three secondary plots, fills the "four days" or the four long acts of *Le Soulier de satin,* for which Claudel uses an entire world of characters.

This is a play on the subject of love, but there is no love scene in the usual sense. The playwright separates his lovers, and keeps inventing ways to hold them apart. Only twice do they see one another, at the end of the Second Day and at the end of the Third. They are usually at opposite parts of the earth: Prouhèze, as governor of Mogador (in her husband's name), and Rodrigue, as viceroy of India. This story of love is a drama of absence, where each of the lovers accepts the fate of separation. Happiness in love is no subject matter for art. Nothing is more monotonous to watch than the cooing of love birds. Dante does not marry Beatrice. The wound in Prouhèze and in Rodrigue is precisely the place where God works. Prouhèze is far from being reconciled to her fate. Rodrigue is no pure young man. He is the founder of empires, and jealous of his rival, Don Camille. He wants Prouhèze in order to satisfy his physical desire and to vilify her.

In Rodrigue is something even more powerful and more relentless than his love for Prouhèze. This love, which is not satisfied, is a suffering in him, a wound, an opening in his body which has to be forced. Otherwise he would have suffocated. The angel tells Prouhèze that God created this love. Prouhèze had marveled that God was not jealous of her love for Rodrigue, and the angel explains carefully that even love in sin is able to serve God.

Dona Prouhèze:—L'homme entre les bras de la femme oublie Dieu.
L'Ange Gardien:—Est-ce l'oublier que d'être avec Lui? est-ce ailleurs qu'avec Lui d'être associé au mystère de sa création, Franchissant de nouveau pour un instant l'Eden par la porte de l'humiliation et de la mort?
Dona Prouhèze:—L'amour hors du sacrement n'est-il pas le péché?
L'Ange Gardien:—Même le péché! Le péché aussi sert.

This important scene between the angel and Prouhèze, which mingles theology, drama, poetry, and pathos, reveals the technique of salvation, which is the central issue at stake throughout the long work. Salvation is compared to the art of fishing. Prouhèze is not only a capture for the angel, she serves also as a bait for Rodrigue.

The Fourth Day is different in tone from the other three. It takes place on the sea, close to Spain, where the King of Spain holds court. High comedy and persiflage dominate the scenes. The Armada is referred to, although it is not to take place for twenty years. Only the King has an intuition about the disaster that the Armada will bring to his country. Rodrigue is old, impoverished, and infirm. He has lost a leg. (This may well be another reminiscence of Rimbaud, whose leg was amputated in a Marseille hospital.) In terms of the world, Rodrigue's disgrace is complete. He insults everyone. By comparison with his vigor and boldness and total freedom of expression, the court and the King appear as puppets, as humans deprived of their dignity. Rodrigue is with the daughter of Prouhèze, Marie de Sept Epées, a child she had with Don Camille and whom she had given over to the care of Rodrigue before her death. In the presence of the court, Rodrigue develops a plan of world government and distribution of wealth. This is received as treason. With Brother Léon, Rodrigue laments the death of Prouhèze. He looks at the sky and the stars, and knows that he cannot escape them and that it is impossible for him to die.

The conception of *Le Soulier de satin* is gigantic, and the beauty of some of the scenes is unparalleled in the French lyric theater. In his preface, Claudel states that the play is the conclusion to *Partage de midi*. He had dreamed of composing a total drama. Its realization is complex and lengthy. It will appeal to those readers and spectators who have affinity with the baroque style. Henri Peyre says that "it deserves, better than any other literary work of recent times, to be called baroque, if baroque means tension, a luxuriance of offshoots and an intricate blending of genres, nonchalant disregard of unities, acrobatic turbulence, lack of prosaic verisimilitude, and the whole world becoming a stage for a struggle toward divine love through human love," Another kind of art would have exercised greater rigor and prudence in choosing the elements. One can best say about Claudel that he has more to choose from than most playwrights. The enormousness of his means must be accepted before he can be read: the opulence of his language, his verbal incontinence, his characters recruited among saints, angels, and stars.

Between *Tête d'or* of 1890 and *Le Soulier de satin* of 1924, French poetry moved through a rich period of experimentation. It practiced with many kinds of license, abuse, and peril. From today's viewpoint Claudel's position is at the very head of the experiments with language which characterize symbolism and surrealism. In many ways *Le Soulier* seems consecrated to the tenth muse, Grace, but it is also composed in a new understanding of poetic freedom. No one word can define it: it is poetry, science, art, and theology combined.

Before its composition, during the years preceding the First World War, Claudel had reached a degree of glory —not celebrity—that was equivalent to the glory of two other figures of the same period, Bergson and Rodin. It was certainly "glory" to have his plays compared with those of Aeschylus and Shakespeare. Then, after the war, Claudel lost favor with the literary world. The younger writers could not forgive him for being an "official," a dignitary. The postwar ferment of artistic experimentation blinded them to the fact that Claudel had always been essentially an experimentalist. This was the moment, too, when the Catholic world began to realize that Claudel existed. The hostility against Wagner which this new generation felt was the same kind of hostility as that against Claudel. Apollinaire was the triumphant poet for the young, who formed a group around Picasso and launched the music of Satie and Les Six. Darius Milhaud alone remained faithful to Claudel.

Claudel returned to favor at the end of the 1930's. All of the facets of his writing were discovered and rediscovered at this time, and by young and old alike. The moment was propitious for the première of *Le Soulier de satin* in 1943, despite the tragedy of that year in France. The new readers found in Claudel an intellectual stimulation. He was not obscure in the cubist or surrealist manner. His verbal mannerisms simply contained a greater degree of intelligibility than ordinary language. The salutary effect his work now offered was the feeling of a full physical, sensual life, of violence and brutality. He had marvelously profited from the achievements of the symbolists, from thirty years of poetic acrobatics, in order to create his own eloquence, with its remarkable suppleness and abundance and weight. His repertory of lusty full-blooded characters: Tête d'or, Avare, Pierre de Craon, Amalric, Rodrigue, were men of combined flesh and spirit. Over and over again in these plays humanity was represented as one gigantic body for which each one of us is responsible every moment of our life. The universe is a network of crisscrossing influences and responsibilities. Claudel, far more than the other voyager-poets, Blaise Cendrars and Apollinaire, uses the entire world as his field of action.

Le Soulier de satin is comparable to a camera that sees everything: the historical drama of the Renaissance when the great schism split asunder the Church and a new civilization was founded; a drama of action and adventure where strong men created new empires or wandered over the face of the earth to find a place with nothing in it to remind them of their native land; a drama of human relationships existing despite long and distant separations; a drama of love, finally, where love is never passivity or rhetorical effusion. This last-named aspect of *Le Soulier de satin* is the longest to be remembered by the demanding power that this love demonstrates. Throughout his drama Claudel is saying that love of man for woman is love of an illusion, love of something that seems to exist. The romantics had preached that love is God and Claudel reverses the terms of this phrase in order to restate, through the example of Rodrigue and Prouhèze, the Scriptural message that God is love.

2. The Problem of a Religious Theater: Bernanos (1888-1948) and Mauriac (1885-   )

The Christian tradition has given masterpieces to French literature in almost every century. In the theater of the twentieth century this tradition has persisted, although there are very few successful plays in which the religious sentiment or the religious conflict dominates. The plays of Gabriel Marcel and Henri Ghéon have not projected conflicts of faith and religious destiny as dramatically as certain isolated plays by authors not as Catholic-minded as they are: *Sud* by Julien Green, for example, and *Port-Royal* by Montherlant. The plays of François Mauriac are not as successful as his novels, but he is concerned in the plays, as well as in the novels, with the case of the Christian pharisee. The final work of Georges Bernanos, *Dialogues des Carmélites*, seems to be an authentic masterpiece in the Christian tradition. Finally, the dramatic works of Paul Claudel would be sufficient claim for a French religious theater in the twentieth century. Since 1940 the name of Claudel has dominated the Paris theaters. His plays have made a veritable conquest. There have been three revivals of *L'Annonce faite à Marie*, a revival of

L'Otage at the Comédie-Française, and one of *L'Echange* with Ludmilla Pitoëff. Interspersed with these revivals there have been five premières: *Le Soulier de satin,* in 1943, at the Comédie-Française (revived in 1949); *Tobie et Sara,* at Avignon in 1947; *Le Père humilié,* in 1948, at the Champs-Elysées; *Partage de midi,* at the Marigny in 1948; *Le Pain dur,* in 1949, at the Atelier; and *Tête d'or,* in 1959, at the new Théâtre de France.

Certain prophetic writers of the nineteenth century announced an age of catastrophe. Rimbaud's phrase, *voici le temps des assassins,* seems applicable to much more than a poetic vision. The influence of Léon Bloy in particular is felt in every aspect of what has been called the spiritual revival (*le renouveau spirituel*) in French literature. This term is more applicable to the 1920's when the examples of Péguy and Psichari and the early writings of Jacques Maritain held the attention of a large public in France. During the thirties and forties the "religious revival," in the sense of a literary movement, gradually diminished. And yet, isolated works, novels and plays especially, written during those two decades attempted to explore the specifically Christian meaning of tragedy as it had been earlier analyzed in the work of such seminal writers as Kierkegaard, Berdyaev, and Péguy.

The picture of man proposed by these writers—and constituting the Christian interpretation of man in the plays of Mauriac, Bernanos, and Claudel—is that of one struggling against forces that defeat and divide and harass him. He has not found harmony in the cosmos of his theology. His vision of the world and of mankind in the world is the same as the existentialist vision. With very few exceptions, the Christian dramatist does not present edifying situations. Man is seen as oscillating between salvation and damnation. The existentialist absurdity of life is just as visible in the plays of Mauriac, Bernanos, and Graham Greene as is the concept of a destiny. After committing a crime, for example, a Christian character will feel more ill at ease, more incomplete in his life than before. A Christian life is not depicted in the new literature as a routine or pious observance of laws, but as a commitment of a man to a destiny whose accomplishments will be either positive or negative.

The Christian theater centers on the unfolding of a tragic fate vulnerable both to sin and divine love. Since there can never be certainty for man concerning his salvation, the problem of salvation is constant and tragic. Life is treated by the new Christian as a risk. He is unwilling to present it in the form of a contract in which guarantees or assurances are made. In this sense, Christianity is defined as the terrifying privilege of freedom given to man. After all, the most exalted instance of an existential life is the story of Christ, of God who exercised His freedom by taking the side of man against Himself. It has been pointed out that the Orestes of Sartre (*Les Mouches*) is a Christ-figure. There is of course a gigantic difference in that Orestes, before liberating his people and assuming responsibility for their guilt, committed a crime. A Christian will ultimately feel that his anxieties over the void, the absurdity of his life, his endless search for values, and his human suffering are proofs of the existence of God, incontrovertible guarantees that he is loved by God.

There is an absence in the contemporary theater of religious plays that are edifying and militant. Apologetics, when used in a play, inevitably formulates a thesis. And a thesis inevitably transforms a play into a demonstration. In the case of Claudel, who defines the law of the Christian universe as a principle of contradiction, we have a playwright who believes that the demands of the world and the demands of religion force man to live in a permanent state of mobilization. Certain plays of the French theater demand a Christian understanding, but this understanding could be followed by a non-Christian spectator during the performance. The dramatic action of Corneille's *Polyeucte* would be interpreted as fanaticism in a non-Christian context, and the religious conscience of Dona Prouhèze in Claudel's *Le Soulier de satin* seems monotonous unless it is accepted as a Catholic conscience. It is no more difficult for a modern audience to recognize and accept the conscience of Dona Prouhèze than it is for the same audience to recognize and accept that of Hamlet.

The last work of Georges Bernanos, written in 1948, was intended to be a film. *Dialogues de Carmélites* was inspired by a work of Gertrude von Le Fort, *Die Letzte am Schofott* (*The Last on the Scaffold*). It was adapted for the stage by Marcelle Tassencourt and Albert Béguin, and is, outside the dramas of Claudel, the most moving religious play of the century. The play is based upon a historical episode, the guillotining of sixteen Carmelite nuns on July 17, 1794. Gertrude von Le Fort had added a character, Blanche de la Force. Bernanos keeps this character because the principal psychological drama centers in her.

Unexpected noises and dangers, both small and large, have a terrifying effect upon Blanche de la Force. She is unable to overcome an instinctive deep-seated fear. Enough is revealed concerning her birth and childhood to explain this easily aroused state of panic, for which she has feelings of guilt and shame. The dialogues penetrate deeply into the character of Blanche, who was born in tragedy and remained terrified of tragedy all her life. On the day that she arrives at the convent, the prioress, who is dying, offers up her death so that this timid young girl will not weaken before the experience of death.

This moving scene of the first act announces and prepares the final scene of the play. When the persecutions of the revolutionaries begin, the nuns take the vow of martyrdom. Blanche de la Force, who has taken in religion the name Soeur Blanche de la Sainte Agonie, is terrified at the taking of the vow and escapes. She returns home at the moment when the "citizens" take over the convent. At the time of the vow, Mère Marie de l'Incarnation is the head of the community. She is eager for martyrdom and expresses some scorn for the sister who fled and who thereby brought some degree of dishonor on the convent. Soeur Blanche is not present at the court proceedings nor at the reading of the death sentence. Only when the nuns are mounting the steps of the scaffold and singing the *Veni Creator* does she appear, "the last at the scaffold." The sufferer from fear wills her martyrdom. This moment of grace, when Blanche is able to transcend supernaturally all her deep-seated instincts of fear, is reminiscent of the profound moments in *Polyeucte,* that other play, in the French theater, on the power of grace.

The concentration of this work on the problem of fear, the symmetry and proportions of its structure, the nobility of its language, make of the *Dialogues* a work that is both religious and dramatic. Mère Marie, the most courageous of the community, is not present when the sisters are arrested, and is absent from the guillotine. Bernanos seized upon the mystical meaning of this absence, because the place of Mère Marie is taken, at the last moment, by the sister who had suffered the most from the very idea of death and martyrdom. When Blanche is first received into the novitiate, the first prioress explains to the girl that God meant to test her weakness in her and that she had to learn the simplicity of the shepherd guarding his flock. She explains that once we have left the innocence of childhood, a long time may be necessary before we can recover it again. With her newly found "simplicity" and "weakness" (these words figure frequently in the text) Blanche is able at the end to face the "agony" of the guillotine. The mother prioress who dies early in the action of the play foresees to some degree the test that is to be made of Blanche de la Force, the heroic example that her fear prepares.

Bernanos has a deeper understanding than other writers of his age of the mystical power of humiliation, of the reflection of Christ on the Cross visible in the hearts of the humble in spirit, of all the wretched and terrified children of the world. The supernatural exchange of grace that *Dialogues des Carmélites* illustrates is felt at the moment when Blanche replaces Mère Marie and dominates her fear of death, when the weakest member of the community becomes the strongest. The mingled themes of heroism and holiness which are in *Polyeucte* and Racine's *Esther* and Claudel's *L'Annonce faite à Marie,* reappear in *Dialogues* with comparable intensity and a similar nobility of language.

The function that Debussy performed for Maeterlinck's *Pelléas et Mélisande* has been carried out by Francis Poulenc. His opera *Les Carmélites* (1955) closely follows the text of Bernanos. The play itself is never lost sight of in the transparency of the music. The psychological dilemma of Blanche and the characterizations of the other nuns are consistently developed. The great scenes of the opera are those of the play: the death scene of the prioress in the first act, and the final execution scene, which is one of transcendent beauty.

François Mauriac came to the theater with a tremendous reputation as novelist and essayist and religious writer. Four plays were produced between 1937 and 1951, the first of which, *Asmodée,* has been highly successful. It was first presented at the Comédie-Française, in a production directed by Jacques Copeau, in November 1937.

During the 1920's, when he was publishing his early novels at regular intervals, Mauriac spoke of the theater in various articles and referred to the seventeenth century (when Pascal was writing his spiritual letters to Mlle de Roannez) as the only period in French history when the theater could reach a high degree of perfection. "Every Frenchman," he stated, "is a casuist." (*Tout Français est un causuite. . . .*) Casuistry is today pursued in journalism and politics rather than in the domain of theology.

Mauriac claims he is a dramatist who happened to write

novels. His characters are presented at a moment of crisis in their lives and remain throughout the story in a state of crisis. This characteristic of his novels explains the swiftness and intensity of the action. Edouard Bourdet, when he was administrator of the Comédie-Française, encouraged Mauriac to complete the writing of *Asmodée,* for which the novelist claimed he only had characters.

The power of *Asmodée* seems to come from the fact that the play can have an almost edifying effect on convinced Christians, but that its supernatural intentions may pass unnoticed by non-Christians. There is no need for a theological disposition or knowledge in order to follow the play. An atheist might find some confirmation for his views in the unhealthy Catholicism the play reveals, and a communist would find in it confirmation for desire to terminate the reign of the bourgeoisie.

The central character, Blaise Couture, a contemporary Tartuffe, a former seminarian, has become the spiritual director of a provincial family in which he is employed as a tutor. He exercises an unusual power over women, and in particular over the lady of the house, Mme de Barthas, widowed for eight years and still young. A young Englishman, Harry Fanning, spreads dissension in the family so rigorously governed by Couture. The daughter of the family, Emmanuèle, aged seventeen, falls in love with Harry. Couture encourages this marriage in order to remain alone with Marcelle de Barthas. This is complicated by the fact that for a while mother and daughter are rivals for the affection of Harry, and also because of a possible religious vocation in the daughter.

The title of the play is drawn from the eighteenth-century novel *Le Diable boiteux* by Lesage. In the book, the devil Asmodius flies over Madrid and removes roofs in order to observe domestic scenes. Harry Fanning, on his arrival at the home of Mme Barthas speaks of this. He wanted to see French homes and possibly some of the dramas in these homes. (*J'imaginais ces drames inconnus,*

des passions funestes et cachées. . . .) Marcelle de Barthas assures him that he is entering a peaceful house
where he will come upon no dramas of passion. The truth,
of course, is just the opposite, and Harry becomes the
instrument of the crisis. Blaise Couture, a powerful and
sinister personality, holds together all the strands of the
varied relationships in the drama. He is not literally a
Tartuffe, because he is not a religious hypocrite. He quite
directly incarnates a force of evil. Marcelle, like many
heroines of Mauriac, represents a sense of solitude and a
marked weariness of life. She is easily the prey of such a
strong character as Couture. He recalls Molière's hypocrite
only inasfar as he has retained the manner, the speech,
and the subtleties of thought of a seminarian. The unfolding of Marcelle's personality dominates the lesser
dramas in the play: the rivalry between Emmanuèle and
her mother for the love of Harry, and the struggle between
divine love and human love in the heart of Emmanuèle.

Mauriac's second play, *Les Mal Aimés,* of 1945, is more
Racinean in form than *Asmodée,* more close-knit, more un-
relieved in its depiction of an intense human conflict. The
action of the play concerns four characters: M. de Virelade,
a slightly transposed figure of Couture, who mounts guard
over his elder daughter, Elizabeth, whose life is totally
devoted to her father. She is in love with Alain, the man
who married her younger sister Marianne, and she even
contemplates flight with this man. At the end of the play,
Alain returns to his unloved wife, and Elizabeth to her
unloved father. The concept around which the work is
built is expressed by Elizabeth when she says that we are
bound to those we do not love. (*Nous sommes livrés, les
pieds liés, aux êtres qui nous aiment et que nous n'aimons
pas. . . .*)

Many reasons account for the failure of Mauriac's third
play, *Passage du malin,* first produced in the fall of 1947.
All the critics spoke of the inadequacy of the cast, but more
seriously of weaknesses of theatrical devices, of comic

scenes, and deficiencies in composition. The theme of the play is the temptation of a character, in this case the directress of a school, to dominate another character, a young girl, and free her from the physical love she has for a young man who is an opportunist and thoroughly unreliable. Momentarily she succumbs to the seductiveness of the man, but at the end of the play she returns to her duties.

Le Feu sur la terre, of 1951, was inspired, according to Mauriac, by the spectacle of a forest fire in the Landes which he had witnessed in the summer of 1949. But the literal forest fire is far less important than the symbolic fire of passion which is the subject of this fourth play. The setting of the Landes, the family house, the possessive love of a sister for her brother are themes that recall the Mauriac novels. When the brother returns home from his studies in Paris, with a wife of his own choice, the sister's plans (she had chosen an inconspicuous girl for her brother) are thwarted. The main action is her effort to break the marriage. Her love was perhaps too glibly called "abnormal" by the early critics of the play. It is a demanding powerful sentiment, but to call it "unnatural" would be to contradict one of Mauriac's most tenacious beliefs: that there is no distinction between normal and abnormal. All men are driven by the same inclinations and desires. Only external circumstances alter the patterns of love and defeat in love.

Of these four plays, the first two seem the most assured of some continuing success. Dramatic technique is not so suitable as the technique of a novel to Mauriac's great skill in depicting and utilizing an atmosphere. The religious theme is almost absent from his plays. It has often been argued that the believer, as believer, is not a suitable character for the theater. There are few exceptions to this rule in the contemporary theater. The leading exceptions would be, not Mauriac's plays, but Claudel's *L'Annonce faite à Marie* and Bernanos's *Dialogues des*

Carmélites. Despite Mauriac's disavowal of the theme of abnormality in his plays, most readers and spectators will look upon each of these plays as centering upon an abnormal or at least unusual relationship, such as that between Marcelle and Harry in *Asmodée,* between Elizabeth and her father in *Les Mal Aimés,* and between the brother and sister in *Le Feu sur la terre.* And yet Mauriac has insisted that in this latter there is no incest because it is a nonreciprocal relationship.

Anouilh, in a famous quip, described life as a long family dinner. Mauriac's quip, if he were to answer Anouilh, might well be: life is family relationships, the setting where each member of the family watches over and even spies on all the other members. The playwright himself is a member of this family if we remember his oft-repeated statement that his characters, in the novels and plays, are born from the most obscure and the most troubled part of himself, that they are formed out of that part of his own substance which continues in spite of all his efforts to eradicate it.

Mauriac's Catholic sensibility is in the sometimes visible and sometimes invisible background of his plays. Even when they do not refer to Him, God exists for his characters as a reproach or a source of exaltation. It has been said, with some degree of justice, that Mauriac's heroes are less free and more directed and controlled than are the heroes of other contemporary French writers. This seems to come from the fact that in Mauriac's universe sin is a presence, and evil is someone. The playwright-novelist fully realizes his intermediate position of not pleasing the world and of displeasing the saints. Montherlant has recalled that each century of French literature has had to deal with one great Catholic novelist. This may well be Mauriac's position. His one possible rival, who did not receive the honors accorded to Mauriac—admission to the Académie Française and the Nobel Prize—was Georges Bernanos.

IV. THEATER OF IDEAS

1. Gide (1869-1951)

At Gide's death there were almost no favorable or sympathetic notices given by the critics in their first summary estimates of his life work. The one exception was the moving article by Jean-Paul Sartre in *Les Temps Modernes*. This was totally unexpected because Sartre had never been influenced by Gide in any way. He stressed in his article the consistency with which Gide had lived through the crucial experiences of modern times. Gide arrived at the elimination of religious belief through trials and errors of sensibility rather than of speculative thinking. Georges Bataille in *Critique*, on the other hand, was hostile in his estimate of Gide's importance. He claimed that Gide tended always to remain on the surface rather than enter into the heart of moral problems. Gide had finally become the leading exponent of a serene acceptance of contradictions and ambiguities.

Gide's work includes three plays: *Saül* (1896), *Le Roi Candaule* (1900), and *Oedipe* (1930). These have all been produced, but without any significant success. *Perséphone*, an opera text, was written in 1933, set to music by Stravinsky, and performed by Ida Rubenstein. A one-act comedy, *Le Treizième Arbre*, was written in 1935 and performed in 1939. The dramatic instinct in Gide is apparent in several of the shorter works not primarily written for the stage: in *Philoctète*, for example, and *Bethsabé*. His short work on the prodigal son, *Le Retour de l'enfant prodigue*, was adapted with very little change in the text, and performed in Paris. This work is a kind of miniature drama in four scenes, in which the tone of each character harmonizes beautifully with the tone of the entire work.

The prodigal son, from Gide's treatment of him, can be looked upon as a sinner only from a bourgeois viewpoint. The understanding that Christ always showed to sinners and outcasts was a source and justification for many of Gide's theories. No human problem is solved in *Le Retour de l'enfant prodigue*, but all the problems raised in this provocative parable are transformed into a Gidean pattern. The questions and answers in each of the four dialogues that compose the work give consistency to the characters and delineate the moral position of each of them. In the opening dialogue with his father, the prodigal son is kindness and subtlety. To the leading question: "Why did you leave?" the son answers: "Did I really leave you?" The older brother, in the second scene, is more stringent and more obdurate than the father. He represents the law of the house, the sense of hierarchy. He is both reasonable and narrow in his remarks. The dialogue with the mother is on simple practical things. She urges him to get married, and asks him to speak to his younger brother, who seems restless. This leads to the fourth and most significant dialogue in the Gidean sense. The adventure of the returning brother has stirred the imagination and the desires of the younger boy, who wants now to leave the house. He asks about the taste of the fruit in the desert. As he sneaks out of the house, his steps are guided by his brother. The complexity of Gide's moral issues is present in this final scene when the prodigal son seems simultaneously to be corrupting the child and helping him to self-realization and freedom.

Jean-Louis Barrault and Edwige Feuillère in Claudel's
Partage de Midi. (French Cultural Services.)

Pierre Brasseur in the main role of Sartre's *Le Diable et le Bon Dieu*. Scene from the original production, directed by Louis Jouvet. *(French Cultural Services.)*

Eugene Ionesco (front) and the cast of his play *Jacques ou la soumission*. *(French Cultural Services.)*

Jean Anouilh.   *(French Cultural Services.)*

Arthur Adamov.   *(Lipnitzki.)*

Maria Casarès (Left) in the title role of the T.N.P. production of *Phedre*, with Lucienne Le Marchand as Oenone. *(Varda.)*

Louis Jouvet in Claudel's *L'Annonce faite a Marie*.
(*French Cultural Services.*)

Monique Melinand and Yvette Etievant in Jean Genet's
Les Bonnes.   *(French Cultural Services.)*

The form of the medieval *sotie* attracted Gide, and he has applied this generic term to three of his works: *Paludes*, *Le Prométhée mal enchaîné*, and *Les Caves du Vatican*. The *sotie* was a dramatic form, a kind of morality play, developed in France in the fourteenth and fifteenth centuries, in which all the characters are fools. Gide's *Prométhée* of 1899 is not playable, but it demonstrates Gide's sense of drama and humor and dialogue, and the manner in which he uses these traits for the projection of his ideas. The dialogue carried on between Prometheus and his eagle is that between a young man and his conscience. Prometheus resembles Bernard in *Les Faux-Monnayeurs* and Lafcadio in *Les Caves*. They are aspects of the Gidean adolescent attempting to perform a gratuitous act, one that will be accomplished without a motive but with the exercise of one's full personality. At the end of his life Gide adapted for the stage his own *Caves du Vatican* with its famous scene in which Lafcadio pushes out of a fast-moving train an aged gentleman he had never seen before. To be in a state of gratuitousness is to remain faithful to one's first thought, because usually between the thought and the act one loses the best of oneself. When the hero in *Le Prométhée mal enchaîné* allows his eagle to feed on him, he is demonstrating a faithfulness to his conscience.

For the subject matter of his three plays, André Gide turned to the Bible and Greek mythology, and hence followed the tradition of the French classical theater. But the modern spirit and Gide's own sensitivity and understanding of personal morality are everywhere present in them. He observes the unity of action, but not the other unities of place and time. In his treatment of the three heroes: Saul, Candaule, and Oedipus, he shows little respect for them. He seems to be observing them critically and understandingly, and at times uses them as fools of a *sotie* rather than as characters of a drama.

Saül is the most serious of his plays, the most powerful.

The oblivion into which it has sunk is difficult to understand and explain. It was written in 1896, when Gide was
twenty-seven, and was published in 1903. Antoine planned
a production of it but was unable to carry it through. It
was not performed until 1922, at the Vieux-Colombier,
under the direction of Jacques Copeau. The play was
received with only mild interest. Gide himself has explained that *Saül* was conceived and written to offset *Les
Nourritures terrestres,* which he had just completed.
Whereas *Les Nourritures* is a dithyrambic treatise and
prose poem on a hedonistic view of life, an admonition to
welcome all desires and the advice never to fix on one desire or one choice, *Saül* is the tragedy of a man who has
accepted his temptations, who submits to them and refuses
all action that would be contrary to their indulgence. This
carefully constructed play is constantly illuminating the
central drama with which Gide is concerned, the drama
of man's will. The action of the play is in reality the slow
disintegration of Saul's will power. This is projected in the
many monologues of the King and in the speeches of the
demons who represent the temptations. They expose the
situation at the beginning of the play. Then they begin to
appear to Saul when he is alone. At the end of the play,
they are with him even when he is not alone.

The exterior action in the play is drawn largely from
the Book of Samuel. The fits of madness through which
Saul passes turn him into a figure of deep pathos who has
been abandoned by God and destined to a terrifying solitude. As Saul's obsession over David grows, his familiarity
with the demons increases and they begin to participate in
the articulated thoughts of the King. When Saul consults
the Witch of Endor, she recognizes him and tries to warn
him by saying that what he calls fear is really desire (*ce
que tu nommes crainte, tu sais bien que c'est du désir*) and
that whatever delights him is harmful (*tout ce qui t'est
charmant t'est hostile.*) From this moment on in the play,
Saul gives no heed to anything that might help him or save

him. He becomes a man unable to control himself. His character disintegrates gradually from scene to scene until he is a man inhabited solely by vice and desire, and is slain by a servant.

Written in 1900, *Le Roi Candaule* was first performed in 1901, under the direction of Lugné-Poë. The part of Candaule was played by Lugné-Poë himself, and that of Gygès by the actor De Max, to whom *Saül* is dedicated. Gide took many liberties with the story of Candaulus as related by Herodotus. The play is written in verse, but the lines do not follow any regular pattern. They vary in their number of syllables, but their scansion is more regular than the prose of *Saül*.

The King wishes to share the beauty of his wife Nyssia with his courtiers. At the banquet where she unveils her face, one of the guests bites into a ring in a fish he is eating. On the ring the words are inscribed: "I conceal happiness." The fisherman Gygès is sought. The King tries to befriend Gygès and has him live in the palace. He arranges for the fisherman to stay alone with Nyssia by putting the ring on the man's finger, which makes him invisible. At first his love for the Queen is offset by shame and remorse, but when Nyssia learns of the trick, she urges Gygès to slay the King and literally take his place.

The absence of jealousy in the heart of Candaule is a major difficulty in the play. His scandalous generosity is hard to motivate and explain. Nietzsche in speaking of the Candaule-Gygès story says that the King is generous to the point of vice. The play has the force of a parable, a warning, as if addressed to artists not to reveal the most intimate aspects of their lives. At the beginning of the play, Gygès is shocked by the exhibitionism demanded by the King. When he in turn becomes king, he will behave in exactly the opposite way.

In his preface to the first edition of *Le Roi Candaule* (*Revue Blanche*, 1901), Gide says that his play came from a reading of Herodotus (Clio VIII) and of an article that reproached the artists of today and the leaders of opinion for not offering to the masses exhibitions of beauty and thereby training their taste and educating them. In the preface to the second edition (1904), he quotes abundantly from a hostile press that seems to say that for the play itself to disappear from sight, the ring of Gygès will not be necessary!

Georges Pitoëff was responsible for the first production of *Oedipe* in 1932. The three-act drama was written in 1930. Pitoëff directed the play, designed the set and costumes, and played Oedipus. His wife Ludmilla played Antigone.

Gide's ideology is present throughout his *Oedipe*. It is drier, more intellectualized treatment of the Greek story than Cocteau's *Machine infernale*. All of the characters move far away from their traditional roles and assume a modern stance, a modern problem, a modern figuration. Oedipus announces his belief in progress and democracy, and underscores on several occasions the happiness of his life. When his life turns out to be constructed on lies, he pays up for his boastful optimism by losing his eyesight. Tiresias is the unctuous, intriguing priest who tries to strengthen his position in the kingdom by preaching the fear of God. Jocasta is a pious, almost bigoted woman, attached to the priest. Creon, brother-in-law of Oedipus, demonstrates vulgarity in his behavior and a shrewd prudence in his politics. He scorns the people and tries to stop their cries by advocating religious practices for them. Eteocles and Polynices, sons of Oedipus, have an incestuous interest in their sister Ismene. They are portrayed as two young present-day intellectuals who write in bold terms about the temper of their age, who describe and illustrate its "anxiety." Antigone has great moral purity and strength of conviction. She is close to the figure of Alissa in Gide's *La Porte étroite*.

As in *Saül*, Gide depicts in *Oedipe* the tragedy of extreme individualism. In his quarrels with Tiresias, Oedipus extols his personal ethics at the expense of the orthodox views. This is a familiar Gidean theme, but it is unwisely treated here because Gide seems to sympathize more with the traditions upheld by the priests than with the individual ethics of the king. In 1951, the part of Oedipus was played by Jean Vilar. He illuminated Gide's text by playing an Oedipus who was constantly watching and judging himself. The entire production brought a variety of tones and an animation to a text that is secretive and congealed.

These three major plays of Gide are among the hardest of the modern plays to perform, the hardest to project. They have tempted four of the best directors: Copeau, Lugné-Poë, Pitoëff, and Vilar. But they have not yet been produced in such a way as to bring out to the fullest their subtleties of argument, their high dramatic moments, their sardonic touches, and their lyricism.

2. Sartre (1905-   )

By the nature of the philosophy he expounds and by the forcefulness of his writing, Jean-Paul Sartre has divided the French intellectual public during the past fifteen years. Violent quarrels have punctuated the development of every phase of existentialism, the appearance of every book, and the early performances of every play. Political theory and political affiliation have had their part in these quarrels. Sartre has been denounced by Thorez and the extreme left as well as by the extreme right, whose exponents seem to be asking to have the writer burned alive. This atmosphere of argumentation and battle is not unusual in France. Every literary movement has tried— and usually in a belligerent way—to adopt and assimilate and illustrate a philosophy. Sartre's case represents this phenomenon in reverse order. He is a philosopher who uses literary forms for the expression of his philosophy. Almost at its inception as a highly technical philosophy, existentialism annexed literary genres: novels, plays, essays, in order to explain itself to an ever-widening audience. Its principal literary products are literary without any doubt, and can be approached as literature. They are also demonstrations. Critical writings on Sartre and existentialism have, on the whole, been a medley of philosophical explanation and literary judgment. And they will probably remain such a medley for some time to come.

M. Sartre, however, has said that it is not necessary to understand his philosophical system as such in order to read his novels and to attend performances of his plays. His doctrine, elaborate and meticulously constructed, is still unfinished. Any final judgment, either praise or condemnation, will have to be suspended, at least for a time. Meanwhile, Sartre belongs to literature in his multiple roles as novelist, dramatist, essayist, and polemical writer. His mind is as active and engaging as his pen is prolific. He has all the resources, all the capabilities of becoming a major writer. In fact, he is that already for many critics who have not hesitated to couple his name with that of Voltaire, and to compare his influence with that of Voltaire in the eighteenth century.

The style of his writing is always close to his thinking. In reading him, one has the impression of following his thought in all of its complexity and immediacy. Writing that remains so faithful to philosophical thinking is bound to appear verbose and overabundant. Is this prolixity or richness? Such a question often comes to mind in the presence of a Sartre text. God is deliberately and doctrinally omitted from his considerations, and there is an absence of spirituality in the usual sense of the word. But there is sincerity and conviction. His characters seem separated from him and often appear more as arguments than as living human beings. But he places them in a world, in an atmosphere that is very much his own creation. There is a Sartrean "world," recognized as such in many countries of the real world today, and this is the result of a vigorous productive temperament, of an intellect and a sensibility that have redefined and agitated some of the eternal problems of humanity.

Three terms or themes concerning man's fate in the world occur so often in the writing of Sartre that they can justifiably be taken as the pivotal points of his considerations. First is man's solitude, his aloneness and even, in its extreme form, his alienation. Each of us is a body, separated from all other bodies, irreparably alone, a world unto itself which can never be fully communicated to another world. There are passages in Proust's novel on the separateness of every human life to which I believe Sartre would fully subscribe. The second term is man's freedom, a power residing in each isolated body which may or may not be used. Freedom, in the Sartrean sense, is closely associated with the third term, responsibility, because it is usually defined as that freedom which man may use in assuming some kind of responsibility which is outside of him, an autonomous responsibility.

These three terms, with the emphasis given them by existentialist philosophy, place the work of Sartre close to that of other systematic thinkers in the twentieth century. They announce considerations that are central in the work, for example, of the humanist André Malraux and the Catholic Georges Bernanos. Sartre does not believe that there is any system or any philosophy that assures man of enduring comfort and security and peace. Bernanos has expressed very similar convictions about Catholicism, which he defines as a daily struggle and adventure, and not at all as peace found within an established order.

The feeling of aloneness, of man's solitude, is constantly being contradicted by his desire to assume responsibility as a human being, to join with some cause. In fact, it is more than a contradiction or a paradox; it is a tension that often grows into such proportions that it can be called anguish or destiny or absurdity. These are the familiar existentialist terms and they designate the principal problem upon which Jean-Paul Sartre has thus far based most of his writing. His approach to this problem seems more systematic, more rigorously organized than the more dramatic approach of Malraux (in *La Condition humaine*) or the more lyric approach of Bernanos (in *Sous le soleil de Satan*). And yet it would be erroneous to look upon the novels and the plays of Sartre as propaganda literature, as *pièces à thèse*. They have their own unity and independence, their own settings and themes. They emphasize, more than the works of other twentieth-century writers, the restricted and yet all-embracing world of the human conscience.

Traditionally in France, the theater is looked upon as a domain that the leader of a new movement is anxious to capture and utilize. This was true for Voltaire in the eighteenth century and for Hugo in the nineteenth. Without being a professional dramatist, in the sense that Jean Anouilh is a dramatist, Sartre has used the theatrical form with considerable ease and naturalness and spontaneity. His thought about the great problems that his philosophy raises, such as man's solitude, and freedom and responsibility, has a greater clarity in the plays than in the other forms of his writing. As a dramatist, in the highest sense of the term, however, he lacks some of those mysterious bonds that join the heroes of the stage with their creators, and he lacks the full power of poetic expression by means of which spectators are able to follow the deepest dramas in the souls of dramatic heroes and even to see the most subtle expressions visible on their faces. The overwhelming facility of Sartre and his disarming intelligence are almost impediments in his more purely literary works and especially in his plays. One feels that the writing of his dialogue has been accomplished without effort because it is dominated by the very clarity of the subject matter as he sees it. But this dialogue, in its freshness, spontaneity, liveliness, is dramatic in itself, and because of these very qualities. One follows so many ideas, as they multiply rapidly in scene after scene, that they hold our full attention and we end by not missing, in any serious sense, the psychological hesitations and subtleties, and the dramatic insights of poetic metaphor that are pervasively present in such playwrights as Shakespeare, Pirandello, and

Claudel. So substantial is the intellectual nourishment of a Sartre play, that we forget what it lacks.

When *Les Mouches* (*The Flies*) was first put on in 1943, under the direction of Charles Dullin, at the Théâtre Sarah-Bernhardt, Sartre was known to a fairly limited public for his volume of stories *Le Mur* and his novel *La Nausée*. He was writing at that time his treatise *L'Etre et le Néant*. His new treatment of the fable of Orestes seemed to the public of 1943 to bear a strong relationship to the moral dilemma of the Occupation. The Parisians went to the theater not only to see a new play but also to feel united one with the other in this interpretation of the daily drama they were living through. The theme of the Resistance was far less obvious to the public that attended the revival in 1951.

Some of the essential elements of the *Oresteia* are preserved in *Les Mouches*: Clytemnestra has married Aegisthus, who has usurped the throne and is tyrannizing the people. Electra, daughter of Clytemnestra and legitimate heiress, is impoverished. Full of hate, she sits at the door of the palace. Her brother Orestes returns from exile, brought back by fate and the persistent prayers of his sister. To these familiar elements Sartre has added the figure of an ironic Jupiter and a swarm of gigantic flies, evil-smelling and avenging spirits who hold the city of Argos in a mysterious plague. Orestes returns to the plague-ridden city of his birth, in obedience, as he explains it, to a need to return home, to feel himself one with his own people. (*Je me soucie bien du bonheur! Je veux mes souvenirs, mon rôle, ma place au milieu des hommes d'Argos. . . .*) Such speeches as this, in which a facile kind of comfortable happiness was derided, seemed to the public of 1943 to extoll the life of risk and peril that they were living through in Paris.

The newest theme of the play is that of Orestes as redeemer. After sixteen years of exile in Corinth, he returns to Argos and witnesses the poverty and wretchedness and fear of his city. Aegisthus maintains in the people of Argos, by means of a yearly evoking of the dead, an obsession with their past sins. In slaying his mother, Orestes will commit a crime far worse than all the other crimes of the city. He commits this deed of his own free will, as an act of justice, because he makes the discovery, in his dialogue with Jupiter, that the gods are not just. His crime will draw down upon him the swarm of avenging flies. As he leaves the city, the citizens of Argos are recovering their former lightness of heart and a conscience relieved of the obsession of guilt and fear. This concept of redemption, brought about by means of crime, is of course the opposite of the Christian concept of redemption, of sanctity and martyrdom.

The relationship between Orestes and the people of Argos is a moving dramatic situation in *Les Mouches,* and it is also the source of much of the existentialist philosophy in the play. Orestes makes a choice, and thereby exercises his freedom, when at the end of the play he takes on the fear and the guilt of his people and thereby experiences alienation. The reign of Aegisthus (which is also the reign of Jupiter) has made the people slaves to a dead myth. At the beginning of the play, Orestes wants to acquire the memories of the people and thereby fill the void of home-lessness in himself. But at the end of the play, by killing Aegisthus and Clytemnestra, he takes on the remorse of the people and frees them from their guilt. The people of Argos represent, for the existentialist philosopher, the old collective power that is enslaved and propagandized. By making his choice, Orestes exists and creates his self. Electra, who at the beginning of the play appears as a revolutionary, is terrified at the end by her brother's violence. When threatened by Jupiter, she quickly falls back into conformity and into the state of terror from which Orestes wanted to liberate her. She criticizes Orestes' freedom and thereby announces in *Les Mouches* the unexpected theme of misogyny.

At the beginning of the play, Orestes returns to his origins and to his city. He finds in the city of his origins a people ruled by the authority of Jupiter and Aegisthus. Moreover, he finds that his mother has become the consort of the tyrant-usurper. Althugh he expresses contempt for the people of Argos, he kills for the sake of the people. This is a social gesture that is quite in keeping with the program of existentialism. The antithesis that the play establishes between the people and Orestes would seem to illustrate the antithesis that Sartre the philosopher establishes between "being" and "existence." The people of Argos, representative of being, are part of a system into which they were born, which they had not chosen and which they accept passively and guiltily. Orestes, on the contrary, demonstrates the existentialist creed of "commitment." By choosing to act, he emerges into the transcendent state of existence. By this function of his active will, he passes from the nondescript state of being to that of a dedicated existence. We do not see in the play how this emergence takes place, and yet we realize that the hero has renounced the collective (which the philosopher calls essences and systems) and has accepted as the condition of his existence a state of estrangement and anguish.

This freedom, practiced by Orestes in *Les Mouches*, is defined by the philosopher as the need in each man to choose at each moment of his life the way in which he should see the world. Man's freedom is therefore his conscience, which functions only when it is thinking something. In himself man is nothing. In order to exist he has to create his own existence. As his conscience, in its free functioning, separates him from all things in the world, he feels exile. But exile in his freedom. Jupiter says to Orestes that he is not at home in the world, that he is an intruder, a splinter in the flesh, a poacher in the lord's forest. (*Tu n'es pas chez toi, intrus; tu es dans le monde comme l'écharde dans la chair, comme le braconnier dans la forêt seigneuriale. . . .*)

Man is therefore called upon, during the unfolding of his existence, to create the very meaning of that existence. This admonition of existentialist philosophy dominates all the plays of Sartre. Man's conscience has to be perpetually lucid, perpetually choosing. What may possibly be called the psychology of Sartre is his study of the various means by which man tries to evade the necessity of choosing and creating his existence. Man's dream is to become placidly immobile like a stone, insensitive. This is his fundamental cowardice, his desire to play the social comedy of conformity, to appear before all other men as one of them. One of the characters in *Huis Clos* describes the six mirrors in the bedroom. In them she used to enjoy seeing herself as other people saw her and that kept her awake. (*Il y a six grandes glaces dans ma chambre à coucher. Je parlais, je me voyais parler. Je me voyais comme les gens me voyaient, ça me tenait éveillée. . . .*)

Huis Clos (*No Exit*) was first performed at the Vieux-Colombier in May 1944, just before the liberation of Paris. Three characters, a man and two women, find themselves in hell, which for them is a living-room with Second Empire furniture. Each of the characters needs the other two in order to create some illusion about himself. Since existence, for Sartre, is the will to project oneself into the future—to create one's future—the opposite of existence, where man has no power to create his future, is hell. This is the meaning of the Sartrean hell in the morality play *Huis Clos*. Garcin's sin had been cowardice, and in hell he tries to use the two women, who are locked up forever with him in the same room, under the same strong light, as mirrors in which he will see a complacent and reassuring picture of himself.

This play, an example of expert craftsmanship so organized that the audience learns very slowly the facts concerning the three characters, is Sartre's indictment of the social comedy and the false role that each man plays in it. The most famous utterance in the play, made by Garcin, when he says that hell is everyone else, *l'enfer, c'est les autres,* is, in the briefest form possible, Sartre's definition of man's fundamental sin. When the picture a man has of himself is provided by those who see him, in the distorted image of himself that they give back to him, he has rejected what the philosopher has called reality. He has, moreover, rejected the possibility of projecting himself into his future and existing in the fullest sense. In social situations we play a part that is not ourself. If we passively become that part, we are thereby avoiding the important decisions and choices by which personality should be formed.

After confessing her sins to Garcin, Inès acknowledges her evil and concludes with a statement as significant as Garcin's definition of hell. She needs the suffering of others in order to exist. (*Moi, je suis méchante: ça veut dire que j'ai besoin de la souffrance des autres pour exister. . . .*) The game a man plays in society, in being such and such a character, is pernicious in that he becomes caught in it. *L'homme s'englue* is a favorite expression of Sartre. The viscosity (*viscosité*) of such a social character is the strong metaphor by which Sartre depicts this capital sin and which will end by making it impossible for man to choose himself, to invent himself freely. The drawing-room scene in hell, where there is no executioner because each character tortures the other two, has the eeriness of a Gothic tale, the frustration of sexuality, and the pedagogy of existentialist morality. The least guilty of the three seems to be Garcin, and he suffers the most under the relentless intellectualizing and even philosophizing of Inès. At the end of the play, Garcin complains of dying too early. He did not have the time to make his own acts. (*Je suis mort trop tôt. On ne m'a pas laissé le temps de faire mes actes.*) Inès counters this (she has an answer to everything, Garcin is going to say) with the full Sartrean proclamation: "You are nothing else but your life." (*Tu n'es rien d'autre que ta vie. . . .*)

No further argument seems possible after this sentence, and the play ends three pages later when the full knowledge of their fate enters the consciousness of the three characters and Garcin speaks the curtain line: *Eh bien, continuous.* . . . This ultimate line which, paradoxically, announces a continuation of the same play, was to be echoed ten years later in the concluding line of Samuel Beckett's *En attendant Godot.* The two plays bear many resemblances both structurally and philosophically.

In 1946, shortly after the *maquis* activities of the Resistance under the German occupation, Sartre's play *Morts sans sépultures* (*The Victors*) projected in a highly tragic form the drama of *maquisards* captured and tortured by other Frenchmen who were collaborating with the Occupation forces. Of all of Sartre's plays, this is the most classical in structure, the most concentrated in intensity, the most rewarding in psychological study. The action of *Morts sans sépultures* takes only a few hours. It begins very close to its denouement. At the time of the first performances, the tragedy was so close to the actual events that had inspired it, that the experience of the spectacle was almost too painful to witness. Now, after a decade, the play can be more easily considered outside of its immediate context. The horror of its action can still be felt, but as a more universal horror than in 1946. It reaches extremes in the feelings of pain and horror it arouses in the public, and in fact the play may be criticized for passing beyond the horrors that an audience can stand.

Five members of the *maquis,* one a woman, have been captured by the French militia. Their prison is an attic where they are handcuffed and trying to prepare themselves for questioning and the inevitable torture. After a scene with those about to be tortured, we see the torturers, whose markedly sadistic tendencies are made clear, and finally we see the two groups mingled: victims and executioners. Three events, or what classical dramaturgy would call three peripeteia, give to this situation a dramatic action.

The prisoners know that their jailers mean to extract from them the real name and whereabouts of their leader Jean. Their principal consolation is that they do not know these answers and that therefore no matter what torture is imposed, they will not be able to reveal the truth. This is the situation at the beginning of the play. The first change (or peripeteia) is Jean's being pushed into their group. He has been taken by soldiers who had no suspicion of his identity. This new capture changes the atmosphere. The prisoners know now that under torture they may reveal a valuable piece of information.

During the first round of questioning, when one prisoner kills himself by jumping from the window, the others do not talk. But one of them, fifteen-year-old François, is not questioned. He is shaken with fear and almost collapsing in the attic and the others realize that he will not be able to withstand the torture. The cause is at stake, and they do not hesitate long before they strangle the boy. This is the second change, one of horror and tragedy. The third is a stratagem arranged by Jean, who is about to be released. He plans to place papers in the pocket of a dead comrade whom the militia, when they come upon the body, will take for himself. The prisoners are therefore to reveal the hiding place of "Jean." But this is of no avail, for after the confession, the most sadistic of the jailers shoots one after the other.

The anguished moral debate that goes on in the mind of each prisoner makes of this play primarily a psychological drama. We follow the thoughts of these characters far more closely than their actions. The situation in which they find themselves is extreme. Their reaction to it constitutes the drama. The physical aspect of this struggle is at no point omitted or softened by Sartre. Physical suffering is at every moment joined with moral agony. The individuals of the group, each one of whom suffers in a different way, are related to the vast numbers of people they represent. We are constantly reminded of the reality of the cause for which the prisoners are being sacrificed. A play that might easily have emphasized the anecdotal and the horrifyingly realistic, is raised to a high degree of spirituality. The sacrifice of François, for example, in the third tableau, is carried out as a ritualistic act. The individual is sacrificed to the group, as the group is sacrificed to the people. The meaning of sacrifice enables the prisoner Henri to strangle the boy François, as it enables the others to turn their heads away as the deed is done.

The melodramatic effects and the lofty moral theme of *Morts sans sépultures* are present in Sartre's next important play, *Les Mains sales* (*Dirty Hands*) of 1948. The atmosphere again is one of suspicion, espionage, and the insignificance of a single individual life in terms of the cause or the party. In 1948 Sartre was an intellectual leader for a vast number of young Frenchmen. Since his play underscored a tyrannical comportment among the leaders of the party, and an almost stupid submission among the subordinates, the very orthodox Communists in France claimed that the play gave a false picture.

The action of the play takes place in a buffer state between Germany and Russia, and which resembles Hungary. Deliberately Sartre raises in *Les Mains sales* doctrinal problems of the day. He is one of the few contemporary French dramatists who have attempted to treat directly the political tragedy of the twentieth century. The plot has improbabilities and exaggerations. It describes a kind of underground Communism that it is hard to believe existed in one of Germany's satellite countries. Hoederer is the veteran Communist leader. Hugo is the young convert to Communism from his bourgeois background. To choose him as the assassin of the party leader, who is suspected of weakness and infidelity, is the outstanding improbability. The character and strength and passion of Hugo are well drawn. Raised by an adoring family, he has turned against them and against their indulgences. The picture of his background is stilted and his revolt against it seems far out of proportion to its significance. Those to whom he has turned, suspect him. He works hard to be accepted. He has learned the doctrines of Communism as a child learns his catechism. He believes every article of the doctrine and recites it uncritically.

He comes to Hoederer to serve as a kind of secretary and brings with him his wife Jessica. She is lively and talkative, but shrewd also. The contrast between Hoederer and Hugo is striking. Hoederer knows the rules of the game as well as the novice. He has served the party for a long time and has moved beyond the age of theory. Moreover, he is strongly patriotic and has no desire to see the Red Army take over his government for long. It will be enough if it withstands the invasion of the German army. This is the origin of the quarrel between Hoederer and the other party leaders whose hands are "clean." In speaking with Hugo and Jessica, he unbends somewhat and undertakes to explain to them the reason for his work, the reason why at times his hands are "dirty."

But Hugo has the intolerance of the young and the ardor of the convert. Twice he shoots at Hoederer. Once when a grenade is thrown into the room, which indicates the party's scorn for his delay in killing the leader. And the second time, a more theatrical device, when he enters the room and finds Hoederer embracing his wife. This time he does kill Hoederer. Not for a political crime, however, but because of a surge of jealousy. Later, in prison, Hugo learns that the party has given up its position and officially taken Hoederer's stand. But Hoederer had been murdered because of this stand, and Hugo realizes that he murdered a hero. This moment of the play, (which curiously enough has been criticized), when Hugo feels that his political faith has been betrayed, seems movingly tragic. It is the struggle of a purity in thought against the ways of the world, and surpasses even the intense

argumentative scene when Hoederer tries to win Hugo over
to his own political position.

The work of Jean-Paul Sartre was placed on the Index
at approximately the time of the first performances of
Le Diable et le Bon Dieu (*Lucifer and the Lord*) in 1951.
When it was learned that the play was set in sixteenth-
century Germany and that the hero was named Goetz von
Berlichingen, Sartre was of course asked whether he had
been influenced by Goethe's play of that name. He re-
plied in the negative in an interview in *L'Observateur* and
acknowledged some influence from a play of Cervantes
(*El Rufián Dichoso*). *Le Diable et le Bon Dieu* has been
called the opposite or the reverse of Claudel's *Le Soulier de
satin*. During the first half of the play, Goetz is constantly
deriding God. During the second half, he expresses religious aspiration, but this is impeded by men who do not
reward holiness and by God, who does not exist. Sartre's
philosophy redefines in this play man's fate as something
absurd.

The steady flow of language, filling four hours in performance, has all tones and modes: impiety, mockery,
atheistic existentialism: nothingness of man, the emptiness
of heaven, the power of evil and its persistent logic, the
impotence of the good and its ridiculousness. The play is
almost a parade, an assembly of characters and arguments.
It has an impressive majesty about it in the richness of
the ideas and their provocative violence. There are a few
truly dramatic scenes and others where the rhetoric of
dialectic dominates. To sustain such a long and vigorous
role, such an actor as Pierre Brasseur was needed in the
part of Goetz. There are few actors today with his
physical power and impeccable diction. Jean Vilar matched
him as the priest of good will who was forced to treachery
and casuistry.

The play is a chronicle and presented in the manner
of classical Spanish plays, in three acts and eleven tableaux.

Goetz, a captain, is fighting his brother Conrad, and besieging the city of Worms. This pleases the archbishop-prince who is dissatisfied with the bourgeois of Worms. Goetz wants to destroy the city, for the joy of massacre and pillage. He is on the side of evil and looks upon himself as contender against God. The wretched priest Heinrich fails to understand his duty and gives over the keys of the city to Goetz for a few religious imprisoned by the bourgeois. Then the unexpected takes place. Goetz cheats in order to lose. He chooses the good and distributes his lands to the peasants. But it is hard for him to do good, and Sartre demonstrates that he will win nothing and understand nothing about his experiment.

The generosity of Goetz is welcomed with suspicion and even open hostility. He tries to assume the suffering of the prostitute Catherine, who has been his victim. At one point, he deliberately wounds himself and pretends he has received the stigmata. He founds a new city (Cité du Soleil) dedicated to peace and nonresistance. The city easily succumbs to a general massacre. The defrocked priest Heinrich convinces Goetz that his reasons for doing good are the same reasons for his once doing evil. This leads Goetz to his conclusion that God does not exist. Here *Le Diable et le Bon Dieu* joins with an important theme of Sartre's first play *Les Mouches*. Crime appears as the condition for a true communism among men.

In a sense, the play is a vast elaborately staged demonstration of Sartre's atheism. (Catholics may easily wonder why Sartre worries so intensely about God who he decides does not exist!) At the end of *Les Mouches* some degree of hope for man's future is offered. Orestes had killed his mother and was leaving his native land, but at least he had been convinced that the gods are powerless when man learns that he is free. *Le Diable et le Bon Dieu* is on the theme of *Les Mouches*, namely the relationship between man and God, to which Sartre has given a more drastic answer. In the *Observateur* interview Sartre said that if God exists, good and evil have the same result. Goetz is responsible for general massacres when he is evil and when he is good. At the end of the play, Goetz accepts a limited human morality. The conclusion for man would seem to be social, but the play is confusing in its philosophical implications as well as in its structural organization. The strongest part of the text is in the opening tableaux, where Goetz appears as the incarnation of evil, as powerful as Lucifer and as convincing as Mephistopheles.

With these plays and with others not so successful (*La Putain respectueuse* [*The Respectful Prostitute*], *Nekrassov*, and *Kean*), Sartre emphasizes predicaments in which the characters find themselves. The situation is unusual and highly dramatic: a plague of flies in Argos (*Les Mouches*), a living-room in hell (*Huis Clos*), a torture chamber (*Morts sans sépultures*). The analysis of the characters in these plays is limited to the necessity they feel to adapt to the situation, to identify themselves with the situation, to choose the situation. There is a strong Corneillean tradition in this existentialist theater where will power is depicted at the heart of stricture and suffering. Whatever situation Sartre constructs for his characters, he is intent upon studying the conflict that takes place between the sincerity of the character in his effort to choose his own life and the power of his conventional world as it seeks to trap and distort him. The predecessors of Sartre, each in his own way, have analyzed this familiar struggle between convention and honesty. As studies of the conflict between sincerity and insincerity, Sartre's plays mark one moment in a literary theme that is both ancient and contemporary.

Such a lesson is almost ludicrously clear in *La Putain respectueuse*, where social morality is purely hypocritical and where the rights of men are in the hands of those in power. In the play the United States is satirized as representing a purely social morality. Behind such a play is an age-old quarrel over the source of evil: is it in an unjust unfair society, as Rousseau would claim, or is it in man himself, in the psychic life of man, as Pascal would say. Sartre, on the whole, takes the latter view. Whenever man is ruled solely by conventions that are hypocritical for him, he has failed in his own existence, failed in assuming his own rights.

One of the goals of literature for Sartre, defined in his elaborate theory of literature as commitment, is to reveal the petrification of man when as a coward he becomes fixed in a social pose. This immobilization is a glue, a stickiness, in Sartre's favorite image. Orestes in *Les Mouches* demonstrates the possibility of avoiding it. There is a danger at the beginning of the play that he will not change, that he will remain in a comfortable routine existence. When he learns of the crime that holds the city in its power, he has an intuition concerning his mission. If he perpetrates an act contrary to social conformity (in this case, the attitude of the people of Argos), he will liberate the city and create his own existence. In this choice of Orestes', Sartre very clearly defines the greatness of man as his willingness to accept responsibility.

If the realization of freedom is the first stage in Sartrean morality, the use of this freedom—its commitment—is the second stage, which will coincide with the discovery of reality. Orestes makes this discovery, and Hoederer, in *Les Mains sales*, represents in his life of action an acceptance of responsibility. Man, who before the realization and the employment of his freedom is nothing and is comparable to the immobile things around him in the world, becomes a "project." He becomes his own value. After killing Clytemnestra, Orestes explains to his sister Electra that he has committed *his* act, that he will bear its responsibility, and that henceforth he will follow his own road. (*J'ai fait* mon *acte, Electre. Je le porterai sur mes épaules comme un passeur d'eau porte les voyageurs. . . . Dieu sait où il me mène, mais c'est* mon *chemin. . . .*)

The plays of Sartre have the dynamics of existentialist exercises. In them he tracks down the alibis we make in our daily lives and flails the system of routines by which so much is carried out in history. The fear of standing alone forces us to these routines, exemplified in the plays by fear in the people of Argos (*Les Mouches*), by the static quality of hell (*Huis Clos*), by the goal of security in the bourgeois world (*Les Mains sales*).

3. Camus (1913-1960)

Albert Camus was born on November 7, 1913, in Algeria, the son of an agricultural worker who was killed in the first battle of the Marne, in 1914. He himself has discussed the principal experiences of his early years: poverty; a love of sports, from which he derived a sense of moral values; and a love for school and study. He received his *licence de philosophie* at the University of Algiers and began to prepare for the *agrégation de philosophie* when his work was interrupted by a serious illness.

Camus's passion for the theater developed during his early years in Algiers. Le Théâtre de l'Equipe was founded in 1936, with Camus as the head. The story of this little theater group is a fine example of individual abnegation for the success of a collective enterprise. Camus's work with L'Equipe was similar to his anonymous labors for *Combat* during the Occupation. All activity was carried out for the good of the group. The first production of the new Algerian company (first called Le Théâtre du Travail) was in May 1936. The play was an adaptation of Malraux's *Le Temps du mépris,* by permission of the author. This choice was not surprising for Camus. Although there are wide divergences in their styles, the works of the two writers have concentrated on the theme of the fate of man, on the collective destiny of mankind.

The actors in *Le Temps du mépris* were students and workers. The public was likewise made up of students and workers, and French citizens living in Algiers who followed the new manifestations of art and literature. The first play was followed by Copeau's adaptation of *The Brothers Karamazov* (in which Camus played Ivan); Gorky's *The Lower Depths; Prometheus Bound* of Aeschylus, in an adaptation by Camus which has never been published, in which a young Algerian worker played the role of Prometheus; Vildrac's *Paquebot Tenacity,* and Synge's *Playboy of the Western World.*

During the Occupation, Camus became well-known as editor of the clandestine newspaper *Combat,* and, in 1942, as the author of the short novel *L'Etranger,* and its accompanying philosophical essay, *Le Mythe de Sisyphe.* His first two plays, *Le Malentendu* and *Caligula,* were performed in 1944. *La Peste (The Plague)* was a full-length novel, published in 1947. His last two plays, *L'Etat de siège,* of 1948, and *Les Justes,* of 1950, were not so successful as the first two.

Today Camus's high position in French letters is due, not to his plays, but to his roles as polemicist and chronicler and thinker. His short novel *L'Etranger (The Stranger)* is far superior to his plays. His book of 1951, *L'Homme révolté (The Rebel),* demonstrates in his thinking an attainment to a kind of hope, an attitude that is almost serene. The plays represent, in the unfolding of his thought, a moment of tragic lucidity. They are quite literally the spectacle of his thought as it tried to comprehend that other spectacle of contemporary society lost in its political machinations.

L'Etat de siège and *Les Justes* testify to a definitive break on the part of Camus's own spirit with the lies and the compromises he discovered in the composition of our society. The lucidity of his accusations never turned

Camus away from his feeling of solidarity with mankind. He refused to tolerate the evils of society, but he felt one with all those who suffer in society. He saw the role of the writer to be that of witness, of the one who will cry out against injustice and fraud. The characters he has created for the stage do shout their complaints and their vituperations far more stridently than the characters of his novels and the style of his essays. This very stridency is difficult to listen to. It constitutes the principal weakness of the plays because it is endlessly repetitive and reaffirmative. The form of the essay, the more quietly modulated polemical writing, permitted Camus to control and develop his thought. It is difficult to discover in the plays the theme of fundamental hope which the essays reveal. *L'Homme révolté* and the editorial articles collected under the title *Actuelles* represent a philosophical position that is the opposite of the nihilism fairly apparent in some of the plays.

Today the meaning and what might be called the philosophical import of *L'Etranger* are inextricably bound up with the essay *Mythe de Sisyphe,* published a few months after the novel, in 1942. The essay is looked upon as the philosophical interpretation of the novel, and the novel is looked upon as the demonstration of the philosophical concept. The famous opening sentence of the essay: "There is only one really serious philosophical problem—suicide" (*Il n'y a qu'un problème philosophique vraiment sérieux: c'est le suicide . . .*), leads Camus to an examination of the meaning of life and to his conclusion that it is without meaning, that it is "absurd." The absence of any real reason for living lies at the basis of man's daily worry and useless suffering, according to Camus. We learn to deceive this fundamental absurdity with travesties of habit and sentiment. In Greek mythology, Sisyphus was condemned by the gods to roll to the top of a mountain a block of stone which inevitably rolled back down the mountain as soon as it reached the summit. This useless and hopeless activity symbolized for Camus the fate of man in an absurd world.

An anecdote inserted in the text of *L'Etranger* is the story of Camus's first play to be produced (although the second he write), *Le Malentendu (The Misunderstanding)*. This work is a further illustration of his philosophical thought. It was first played at the Théâtre des Mathurins, in 1944, with Maria Casarès and Marcel Herrand in the leading roles. Martha and her mother run an inn in a country district of Bohemia, in a rainy dismal landscape from which Martha longs to escape. To accumulate the necessary money for the voyage to a warmer, sunnier climate, she and her mother kill the travelers who stop at the inn, and dispose of their bodies after robbing them. After a long absence from home, Martha's brother Jan returns incognito in order to establish himself anew in the affection of his mother and sister. But he is murdered like all the others. This is the "misunderstanding" (*le malentendu*). Both the mother and Martha kill themselves. The play emphasizes the terrifying solitude of each individual, his incapacity of recognizing another individual. Our lives touch one another but do not communicate with one another.

The play, in its bareness, resembles a metaphysical demonstration. The characters lack a dimension that would make them into human beings. They are too closely associated with the idea that Camus decided each should represent, with the symbolism of the tragic fate devised by the playwright.

Camus's first play, *Caligula,* was first performed at the Théâtre Hébertot, in 1945, with Margo Lion and Gérard Philipe. Caligula is the handsome and young emperor, and yet a single grief, unexpected and swift, the death of a sister whom he loved, is sufficient to change the universe for him, and to reveal a truth, almost stupid in its simplicity: "men die and are not happy." (*Les hommes meurent et ils ne sont pas heureux. . . .*) Since Caligula is emperor, his powers are limitless, and he can claim the will to change the order of the universe. He defines the impossible, the will to cause laughter from suffering, to exchange ugliness for beauty, to mingle the sky with the sea. To perform the impossible is within the emperor's power. This is Caligula's lesson on freedom which he wants to teach his court. (*Réjouissez-vous, il vous est enfin venu un empereur pour vous enseigner la liberté. . . .*) This is the beginning of an experiment during which he ridicules the patricians, tortures countless victims, blasphemes, and strangles his mistress. Caligula performs these horrors and watches himself perform them. Before he is slain, he experiences a nameless solitude and the approach of hate and conspiracy.

When it was first performed *Caligula* stimulated interest and reflection, and revived the fresh memories of the Occupation. Today it resembles a philosophical drama of the type that Renan wrote at the end of his life. The dialogue is varied and direct and holds the attention of an intelligent audience. But the play is not a dramatic conflict. We do not see the moral crisis in the character of Caligula. We witness a rather elaborate spectacle commented on, which is the result of the moral crisis.

The "impossible," which appears as a kind of temptation for man, is a theme in both *Le Malentendu* and *Caligula.* A deep-seated will to revolt against injustice and humiliation and a fear of death creates the psychosis in both Martha (of *Le Malentendu*) and Caligula. The scorn they manifest for their fate is an almost Nietzschean will to power, will to move beyond man's fate. The "misunderstanding," when applied to more than an individual life, to a nation, for example, and to all of mankind, grows into a study of political tragedy. Caligula's action and death derived from a monstrous kind of logic, visible in the Second World War and in much of subsequent world history.

Camus's third play, *L'Etat de siège* (*State of Siege*),

was performed in October 1948 at the Marigny by the Compagnie Madeleine Renaud–Jean-Louis Barrault. A curious coincidence presided over this production. Since 1941 Barrault had wanted to organize a dramatic presentation around the theme or the myth of a plague (*une peste*). Camus had of course studied the same myth for the writing of his novel *La Peste* (1947). Both men collaborated in the writing and production of *L'Etat de siège*, which was an experiment in the combining of many theatrical forms (lyric monologue, dialogue, movement of large groups on the stage, farce, chorus, pantomime) to give a dramatic expression to the theme of pestilence.

The pestilence that comes to Cadiz and takes over the city is the incarnation of violence and tyranny which subjugates and tortures mankind. All the familiar instruments of tyranny are used: the firing squad, the concentration camp, hard labor, and the most modern of all forms: the record (*la fiche*)—police record, or pass, or rationing card. Camus stresses the new bureaucratic form of tyranny in its terrifying efficiency. The acknowledged goal of this system is to reach the maximum number of slaves and the minimum number of corpses. The corpses are means.

Despite some admirable elements, notably its strong lyric accent, *L'Etat de siège* was a failure. The characters are abstractions, and the speeches are a potpourri of ideas. The model seems to be the medieval morality play or a Spanish *auto sacramental*. The play has nothing of the solemn dignity of Camus's novel *La Peste*. It almost resembles the caricature of a musical review. The allegory is too transparent and the form too rhapsodic. An excessive verbosity spoils many of the effects: the pathos of the martyrs and the love scenes of Diego and Victoria (played by Barrault and Maria Casarès.)

In adapting, for the 1957 season, William Faulkner's *Requiem for a Nun* (*Requiem pour une nonne*), Camus produced another play on man's fate, on the tragic tensions of existence, on an implacable kind of destiny. The strong themes of schizophrenia and sexuality make the work seem, especially to the French public, a psychiatric study rather than a drama. Faulkner represents for Camus the great American writer, the only one in the tradition of the American nineteenth century—a creator of myths, a creator of a universe.

Camus never claimed to be a philosopher. He has written only about those themes he has lived directly or indirectly, on which he has meditated at length. His early preoccupation with the theme of the absurd and suicide, in *Le Mythe de Sisyphe,* was accompanied by the theme of murder in *Le Malentendu* and succeeded by that of revolt in *La Peste. L'Homme révolté* continues the analysis of revolt, and the distinction between revolt and revolution, and the hope for mankind—already present in *L'Etat de siège*—when political ideologies and machinations will be unmasked.

During the last years of his life, on several occasions, Camus expressed irritation with being considered the representative of virtues. He felt himself unworthy of such praise. The ideas of a man inevitably change or deepen with the passing years. Especially the kinds of concepts and ideas Camus examined and re-examined all his life.

The reasonableness of his mind was always being baffled by the rapture of his senses and by the dismay he felt on examining the universe. The country boy and the philosopher remained simultaneously present in him. He spoke of the two possible ways of living in our day: solitude and solidarity, and he advocated neither one. Sartre once called him one of the gifted heirs of Chateaubriand, and in that definition evoked the curious amalgam of traits that he demonstrated: the exotic, the idealistic, the quasi-Christian.

4. Green (1900-   )

When the first play of Julien Green was announced for
March 1953, something of the same curiosity was aroused
in Paris that had been felt at the première of Mauriac's
Asmodée. Green was highly esteemed for his penetrating
psychological novels, in which he always studied a human
being divided and tortured by irreconcilable or unrealiza-
ble aspirations. Because these books were marked by an
absence of any exceptional events, by an almost total
absence of exterior catastrophe, one wondered if M. Green's
talent was suited to dramatic form. In the second volume
of his *Journal,* he claimed that he was not representative,
and that he had always lived somewhat apart from his
world, in a kind of self-dedicated isolation. (*Je ne me
flatte pas d'être le moins du monde représentatif; je crois
même que dans une grande mesure, j'ai vécu et je vis
encore en marge de mon siècle.*)

For the public at large, *Sud* was first a perplexing play.
But on close study, it turns out to be a remarkable composition, one of the few really successful attempts in recent
years at creating the pure tone of tragedy: all the ambiguities of the characters; the richness of their inner life which
is communicated; the vigor, simplicity, and directness of

the writing. The action takes place on a South Carolina plantation on April 11, 1861, the day before the beginning of the American Civil War. Lieutenant Ian Wiczewski is visiting the Broderick family. Their niece Regina is struggling against a strong attraction to Ian, who appears as mysterious and haughty as a Stendhal hero. He is liked by everyone in the family save by an aged colored servant, who is blind and who plays a Tiresias part in trying to warn Mr. Broderick about Ian: *Je n'aime pas le son de sa voix, il est cruel.* . . . Ian meets for the first time a dinner guest, Eric MacLure, a young planter and neighbor of the Brodericks. The meeting takes place at the end of the first act. When the second-act curtain rises, the two men are in the same positions and the action continues. Ian proposes to the young daughter of the house, Angelina, but no one takes the proposal seriously. Eric is in love with Angelina, and Ian forces him to speak of his love, insults him, challenges him to a duel, and dies in the duel because he offers himself to the bullets.

The play is a tragedy on the theme of homosexuality, but it is also on a far more universal subject, and the public might well fail to recognize the immediate subject. Ian suddenly and hopelessly falls in love with Eric on meeting him, but he never confesses his love. The beauty and power of the play are precisely in this silence of Ian. It is quite possible that Ian had not been aware, or fully aware, of his nature. His meeting with Eric is a moment of illumination. And he recognizes this illumination as impossible. His passion is doomed from the start, as irrevocably as Phèdre's for Hippolyte and Oedipus' for Jocasta.

The title *Sud* is fully applicable to the tragedy of Ian Wiczewski. The background of the play is the national crisis about to break out, in which the South will eventually lose, and the foreground of the play is occupied by the fires of destruction and suicide in the young lieutenant. His sin is not in any literal sense his love—which he does not seek out and which is never realized—but rather in his suicide, which he plans and executes despite his conscience as a Catholic. The unity of the play is built on the action of a man discovering his real nature. *Sud* begins as an elaborate social tableau, with a good deal of military and political discussion. And then gradually two figures emerge: Regina, who is in love with Ian, and Ian himself, who treats her with some degree of cruelty as his own hopeless love propels him toward catastrophe.

The action of Julien Green's second play, *L'Ennemi* (1954), takes place in a lonely castle in Ile-de-France, just before the Revolution. At first, there are three characters: a young woman leading a desultory existence; her husband, whom an accident has made impotent; and his brother, who has become the lover of his sister-in-law. Everything changes with the unexpected arrival of the husband's half-brother, who has escaped from a monastery where he had been living without having taken final vows. He is diabolical in nature and easily seduces Elizabeth, to whom he speaks in mystical language. While she thinks he is speaking of the good, he is actually speaking of evil. Elizabeth had been waiting for just such messages as Pierre gives her and which add a new degree of complexity to the lives of the three people in the castle.

This curious religious drama is based on a mystical revelation, made to Elizabeth, by a man of obviously evil intent. He becomes the instrument of salvation by means of a reversed satanism. *L'Ennemi* for Pierre is the Prince of the world, Lucifer himself, but for Elizabeth he is God or the Enemy of her sin.

The third play of Julien Green, *L'Ombre*, performed in 1956, is—like *Sud* and *L'Ennemi*—a play in which the destiny of the characters is altered by the unexpected arrival of a man from the outside world. It is the story of an Englishman who becomes an accomplice in the assassination of his wife because he believes that she was the mistress of his friend, who is the assassin. Ten years later, he discovers that his wife had always been faithful to him and had repulsed the advances of the friend. Unable to live with the ghost of this woman, he takes his life.

In these last two plays Green evokes some of the mysterious forces that control human destiny. In his dramaturgy, as in his novels, he passes easily from the real world to the surreal world. A supernaturally evil atmosphere surrounds many of the scenes, and yet there is intense drama in the effort of the characters to resist their fate. Especially in *Sud,* Julien Green calls attention to one of the most tragic aspects of physical love in the modern world. The human problem is never described or analyzed, and yet it is seen in its religious context. For Ian, love is forbidden in that irremediable way that the French associate with the tragedies of Racine.

V. EXPERIMENTAL THEATER

1. The Little Theater

Le Théâtre Marigny, on the Champs-Elysées, was occupied between 1946 and 1956 by the Compagnie Madeleine Renaud–Jean-Louis Barrault. On January 13, 1954, a small theater, attached to the Marigny, was inaugurated. Le Petit Marigny was destined to perform new plays, lyric plays, texts that would have difficulty in finding the usual kind of theater. It was founded with the intention of showing the plays of Schehadé, *La Ville dont le prince est un enfant* of Montherlant (which as yet has not been performed in Paris), *Tête d'or* of Claudel, *L'Orestie* of Aeschylus in Paul Mazon's translation.

More than thirty-five years ago, Jacques Copeau addressed the Washington Square Players in New York on the subject of "The Spirit in the Little Theaters," and the text of this lecture was printed in the *Cahiers de la Compagnie Renaud-Barrault,* devoted to *Le Petit Théâtre.* Copeau was not sure that a new experimental dramatic form corresponded to a real need, but he was convinced that a new movement in the little theaters had begun, and he emphasized the importance of the "spirit" of this movement.

The little-theater movement in France and elsewhere is

not the struggle of a younger theater with the older established theater. In fact, the new movement is more traditional than revolutionary. It is more "moral" than aesthetic, an effort to renovate the theater in all of its aspects and to create a new life in it. Copeau did not hesitate to call this "spirit," one of love and freedom. The little-theater movement began in most of the Western countries in the twentieth century, but at different moments and without the dependence of one country on the other. Curiously, the movement started in each country in approximately the same way and because of the same needs and the same aspirations. In many instances the founders of a typical little theater were a playwright and an actor who bore little or no resemblance to the professional writer and the actor accomplished in those histrionic devices that almost always assure success.

Copeau's Vieux-Colombier was the most famous and the most fecund of the little theaters of the twentieth century. All subsequent little theaters have continued the example of the Vieux-Colombier in opposing what Copeau called the double plague of the theater: industrialization and *cabotinage*. The meaning of the first term is obvious. But the meaning of the second, which is purely French, is more difficult to define. It has to do with the art of the actor, which in its lowest manifestation can equal a degrading kind of parody. The *cabotin* is vulgar, vain, and even ferocious. The weariness of rehearsals and backstage intrigues, gossip, and desultoriness are able to sterilize the energies and moral character of an actor. *Le cabotinage* is a sickness that infects a good deal of the theater. It reaches, of course, the world outside the theater, because it is, in its fundamental sense, the malady of insincerity, of falseness. The person suffering from *cabotinage* ceases being authentic as a human being. He is not hypocritical because he believes that he is sincere. He never recognizes the malady in himself. In his training, the actor risks the complete mechanization of his personality. Copeau often spoke about the need for the actor of reaching a total *simplicity*. This word he used as the opposite of *cabotinage*. This simplicity in the actor would give to the work of art its maximum human quality, its power of pathos and poetry.

The little-theater movement was, for Copeau, precisely the means of reaching this simplicity. It was not so much the teaching of a new technique as it was training in ways of feeling and living and reacting. Copeau wanted his actors to be human beings. That is why he welcomed nonprofessionals in his company. (That is also why, of course, certain movie directors today, notably the Italian, use nonprofessional actors.) It is quite true that when Molière founded, with members of the Béjart family, L'Illustre Théâtre, he was an amateur. Copeau revindicated the place of the amateur in the theater, the unaffected unpretentious actor who has not been subjected to the hardening experience of professionalism. He deplored the tendency to overtrain the professional actor, to separate him from the normal contacts of daily life, and to make him into a virtuoso, a star.

The little theater is a corporation based upon a spirit of abnegation, of discipline and enthusiasm. It protects the dramatic masterpieces of the past and offers a place of refuge to the masterpieces of the future. It will not allow the overelaborate pretentious *mise-en-scène,* which, starting in twentieth-century Germany and spreading to other countries, has become today another form of *cabotinage.* The little-theater movement has always emphasized an almost rudimentary form of production as the richest in possibilities and because it is the sort that prevailed in ancient Greece and Elizabethan England. Such a theater allows a new dramatic poet, when he arises, to impose his own mode of interpretation, his own dramatic form.

In an important article published in 1953, Jean-Louis Barrault called for a new Cartel in France (*Cahiers de la Compagnie Renaud-Barrault,* No. 2).

When the first Cartel was formed among Dullin, Jouvet, Baty, and Pitoëff, the critics of the day, men like Brasillach and Dubech, claimed that a renaissance was taking place in the theater. It was the founding of a kind of "theater-family." Each one of the four brought to the group his own opinions and his own labors. The new directors since the war—Vilar, Barrault, Vitaly, Dasté, among others—have not formed an alliance comparable to the famous quartet. In the numerous small theaters of Paris, such as Les Noctambules, Le Babylone, La Huchette, where often a sold-out house means the sale of eighty tickets, the directors are united by a spiritual solidarity, and continue to produce plays by the experimental playwrights—Audiberti, Schehadé, Beckett, Ionesco, Adamov.

In early 1957 Le Théâtre Gramont produced *Lust, la demoiselle de Cristal,* taken from Paul Valéry's *Mon Faust,* which had always been looked upon as unplayable. A young actor from the Théâtre National Populaire, Yves Gasc, was responsible for this undertaking. This was not a theatrical production in the traditional sense, but a reading with several voices. This chamber-music effect was appropriate for this meditative work of Valéry, where in three acts the poet develops with humor and profundity his observations on the vanity of life.

The little-theater movement in England and the United States has encouraged the writing and the performance of verse plays, of what is often referred to as lyric theater. There are almost no examples in French of new plays written in verse. Henri Pichette's *Epiphanies* was in free verse and his *Nucléa* in regular Alexandrines. The example of Racine, who raised to such a degree of perfection the verse tragedy, has discouraged attempts in our day. The plays of Claudel are the leading exception. But the Claudelian verse is not traditional. The plays of Georges Schehadé have a poetic quality, a poetic atmosphere, but the text is written in prose.

The emergence of the new experimental theater in Paris is the consequence of a decline and even the death of another kind of theater. The kind of play which seems moribund today was born with the Second Empire, about 1850, and represents a form of playwriting often referred to as *le théâtre bourgeois*. The efforts of the great theater directors of the past eighty years in France—Antoine, Copeau, and the four directors of the Cartel: Dullin, Jouvet, Baty, and Pitoëff—were aimed at producing these plays and endowing them with as much life and vigor as possible. The plays bear almost no relationship to our world today. When they are performed (and they are still performed much more often than the experimental plays), they seem apart from the tempo and the problems of today. They can still appear as skillfully written plays and often serve as vehicles for stars (*La Dame aux camélias,* for example, of Dumas *fils*). Two major wars within less than thirty years have changed aspects of the social structure in France, and especially of the bourgeoisie. The majority of the Paris theaters continue to give plays from a repertory that has not evolved with the times. Those newer plays that reflect more faithfully the psychic and social problems of our day are still looked upon as experimental and are usually confined to the little theaters.

Since the liberation several new, youthful companies dedicated to the production of the new plays have occupied intermittently and usually for short runs such little theaters as Le Babylone, La Huchette, Les Noctambules, Le Studio des Champs-Elysées, le Petit Théâtre Marigny, Le Petit Théâtre de l'Alliance Française. This proof of new vigor in experimentation is also in evidence in the provinces, especially in such centers as Lyon, Marseille, and Nantes.

The new playwrights whose plays have been performed in the little theaters and are just beginning to be produced in the larger theaters, are first those interested in writing a poetic kind of play, lyric in tone, but not written in verse: Ghelderode (a Belgian), Audiberti, Pichette, and Schehadé; and a second group, more philosophical in intention: Adamov, Ionesco, Genet, and Beckett. It may well be that the three most important new playwrights in France are Adamov (of Russian origin), Ionesco (of Rumanian origin) and the Irishman Samuel Beckett. What all these writers have in common is a scorn for the traditional form of playwriting, for the well-made play that has flourished in France for almost one hundred years. In the work of these writers a new literary play has finally come into prominence, twenty or thirty years after the same revolution was realized in poetry and painting. This is normal in the history of the theater. Its revolutions occur twenty or thirty years late.

For these new plays a new kind of production has been evolved. Poverty was the material condition of the younger theatrical companies. They had no money, no stage equipment, and almost no stage. When they did secure one of the miniature stages, they had to construct sets that could be easily transformed. They learned how to build supple, lightweight sets. Jean Dasté has had a marked influence in this domain. His famous sets for *Les Frères Karamazov* and for *Le Cercle de craie* of Brecht were reduced to bare essentials. In reality they were as powerful and suggestive as the sumptuous, spectacular settings of the early twentieth century. Jean Vilar has continued the use of this kind of set in his productions at the Théâtre National Populaire.

2. Artaud (1895-1948)

Antonin Artaud's name is associated with a fundamental revolt against insincerity, and especially against insincerity in literature, where the written word corresponds to an attitude or a prejudice. His most cherished dream was to found a new kind of theater in French which would be, not an artistic spectacle, but a communion between spectators and actors. As in primitive societies it would be a theater of magic, a mass participation in which the entire culture would find its vitality and its truest expression. In January 1947, a year before his death, Artaud gave a lecture in Paris, in Copeau's old theater, the Vieux-Colombier. Among those present, and mingled with a youthful, fervent audience, were such writers as Gide, Breton, Michaux, and Camus. Artaud symbolized for all the generations in his audience an exceptional fidelity to a very great belief, a life devoted to a cause and an unflinching persistence in extolling the cause.

He was born in Marseille and spent his childhood in Provence and Smyrna. He studied in Marseille. At the age of eighteen, he was briefly cared for in a sanitarium for mental disorder. There were other attacks in 1916. In 1918 he went to a clinic for two years. In 1921 he acted for Lugné-Poë at the Théâtre de l'Oeuvre and for Dullin at the Atelier. He was engaged by Pitoëff in 1923. At this time some of his poems were published in literary magazines. He was one of the early followers of surrealism. In Paris he lived with his mother between 1924 and 1937. He was strongly attracted to the movies and played the role of the monk Massin in Carl Dreyer's *Passion de Jeanne d'Arc* of 1922. In 1927, for approximately one year he severed all connections with surrealism, and founded the Théâtre Alfred Jarry, which lasted for two seasons.

Of major importance in the evolution of Artaud's thought was the Colonial Exposition of 1931, where he was able to observe performances of the Balinese theater. These were the immediate origins of his conception of the Theater of Cruelty for which he wrote the First Manifesto in 1932 and the Second Manifesto in 1933. In May 1935 Artaud produced his play, *Les Cenci*, based upon a play of Shelley and a short story of Stendhal. Performances ran only two weeks. He spent a part of 1936 in Mexico. Between 1939 and 1943 he was in a sanitarium. The year after his release, in 1944, his most important writing on the theater, *Le Théâtre et son double*, was republished. Artaud died in 1948.

From this brief biographical sketch, it is obvious that Artaud's greatest activity in the theater fell approximately between the years 1930 and 1935. They were productive years for the Paris theaters in general. Jouvet produced three new plays of Giraudoux: *Electre*, *La Guerre de Troie n'aura pas lieu*, and *Ondine*. Dullin was responsible for a fine production of *Richard III*. Pitoëff put on three plays of Chekhov: *The Sea Gull*, *Three Sisters*, and *Uncle Vanya*. But even such repertories as these were unsatisfactory for Artaud. He wanted to go much further in dramatic experimentation, desiring for the theater the same kind of frenzy and moving violence that he found in the paintings of Van Gogh. He claimed that a new kind of civilization was needed, one that would consummate a break with the sensitivity and the logical mentality of the nineteenth century. Thunderingly he denounced his age for having failed to understand the principal message of Arthur Rimbaud.

Artaud summarized the classical tradition of the French theater, which he found still dominant, as that art which states a problem at the beginning of a play, and solves it by the end. It is an art form, he says, that presents a character at the beginning and then proceeds to analyze the character during the remainder of the play. Artaud questions the authority of this procedure. "Who says that the theater was created to elucidate a character and to solve a conflict?" He claims that already in France there have been signs of a new kind of theater, one that is characterized by freedom, by the surreal, and by mystery. He sees the beginnings of this theater in Mallarmé, in Maeterlinck, and in Alfred Jarry. He finds an instance of it in Apollinaire's *Les Mamelles de Tirésias,* which he opposes to the then popular plays of Bernstein and François de Curel. The most successful plays of recent years, those of Sartre and Anouilh, are closer to the traditional form of the French play, even to the form of a Bernstein, than to the experimentation of an Apollinaire or a Jarry. As yet, the theories of Artaud have rarely been put into practice.

In analyzing his particular mission in the theater, Artaud divides humanity into two groups: the primitive or pre-logical group and the civilized or logical group. The roots of the real theater are to be found in the first group. At the Colonial Exposition of 1931, where he saw the Balinese theater, he was struck by the tremendous difference between those plays and our traditional Western play. He felt that the Balinese dramatic art must be comparable to the orphic mysteries that interested Mallarmé. A dramatic presentation should be an act of initiation during which the spectator will be awed and even terrified—and to such a degree that he will lose control of his reason. During that experience of terror or frenzy, instigated by the dramatic action, the spectator will be in a position to understand a new set of truths, superhuman in quality.

Although Artaud was usually condemnatory of Christianity, he defined the goal of the theater in spiritual terms. Its "sacral" goal, he claimed, is to communicate delirium whereby the spectators will experience trances and inspiration. Dramatic art induces as strong a delirium as a plague does. A true play, according to Artaud's concept, will disturb in the spectator his tranquillity of mind and his senses, and it will liberate his subconscious. Aristotle had emphasized especially the ethical power of the theater. Artaud intends to release its mediumistic force. If the theater is able to exalt man, it will drive him back to the mysterious primitive forces of his being.

The method Artaud proposes by which this will be brought about is to associate the theater with danger and cruelty. "This will bring the demons to the surface," he says. Words spoken on the stage will then have the power they possess in dreams. Language will become an incantation. Here again Artaud draws upon the poetic theory of Mallarmé and Rimbaud. Action will remain the center of the play, but its purpose is to reveal the presence of extraordinary forces in man. The *metteur-en-scène* becomes a kind of magician, a holy man, in a sense, because he calls to life themes that are not purely human. To illustrate this kind of spectacle Artaud equates it with certain paintings of Grünewald and Hieronymus Bosch.

The one experiment in Artaud's theater of cruelty was *Les Cenci*, his adaptation of texts by Shelley and Stendhal. It initiated the fundamental notion of a "theater in the round," which has been especially developed in America, and which was destined by Artaud to establish a closer contact between actors and spectators than the normal theater could ever realize. In this production mechanical devices were used to create a visible and audible frenzy: strident and dissonant sound effects, whirling stage sets, the effect of storms by means of light, unusual speech effects. It was often difficult to distinguish between tragedy and the Grand Guignol.

Certain mass movements used by Jean-Louis Barrault in some of his recent productions are reminiscent of Artaud's *Cenci*. This production of 1935 marked a return in the French theater to a complicated stage production, which has been developed especially by Barrault (who had a part in the original performances of Artaud's play). The production was a failure, although some of the discerning critics, such as Jouve in the *Nouvelle Revue Fran-çaise*, praised the stage set of Balthus and the direction of Artaud.

Out of the financial failure of *Les Cenci*, Artaud emerged as a prophet in the theater. His madness, accepted by some as a real sickness, has been interpreted by others as the sign of his revolt. He became a martyr of illogicality by protesting against morality and rationality. To be an actor for Artaud is equivalent to suppressing in oneself traits that make one distinct from other men. It is therefore equivalent to a kind of suicide. The last long internment of Artaud was interpreted by the surrealists as purely arbitrary, as a sign of the persecution that society is constantly imposing on revolutionaries and dissidents. However one interprets the terrifying obsessions of Artaud, they allowed him to see into unusual depths of the human mind, where he claimed the eternal questions on life and death are clearly visible.

The principal tenet of *Le Théâtre et son double* states that reform in the modern theater must begin with the production itself, with *la mise-en-scène*. Artaud looks upon it as something far more than a mere spectacle: it is a power able to move the spectator closer to the absolute. The Oriental theater, which Artaud saw as a compact agglomeration of gestures, signs, postures, and sounds, constituted for him the language of production and staging. (*Le langage de la réalisation et de la scène. . . .*) The result of this kind of *réalisation* (which seems to be the more effective French word for our term "production") is the awakening of the spectator's thought, which will take attitudes that are "metaphysical in action." (*La méta-physique en activité. . . .*)

The real objective of the theater for Artaud is the translation of life into its universal immense form, the form that will extract from life images in which we would have pleasure in being. This is what he means by the word "double" (*Le Théâtre et son double*). The theater is not a direct copy of reality; it is of another kind of dangerous reality where the principles of life are always just disappearing from beyond our vision. He compares these principles to dolphins, who as soon as they show their heads above the surface plunge down into the depths. This reality is beyond man, with his habits and character. It is inhuman. If the theater is able to lead the spectator back into his world of dreams and primitive instincts, he will find himself "in a world that is bloodthirsty and inhuman" (*sanguinaire et inhumain*). Artaud has acknowledged that in this conception of the theater, he is calling upon an elementary magical idea used by modern psychoanalysis wherein the patient is cured by making him take an exterior attitude of the very state that he should recover or discover. A play that contains the repressed forces of man will liberate him from them. By plastic graphic means, the stage production will appeal to the spectators, and will even bewitch them and induce them into a kind of trance.

The Western theater has always been too dependent on a text. The Eastern theater is able to furnish a physical and not a verbal idea of theater. Theater in the West is associated with literature, whereas the Balinese productions that Artaud had seen were addressed to the entire being of the spectator and the words used in them were incantatory. Artaud wanted to see stage gesticulations elevated to the rank of exorcisms. In keeping with the principal tenets of surrealism, Artaud would claim that art is a real experience that goes far beyond human understanding and attempts to reach a metaphysical truth. The artist is always a man inspired who reveals a new aspect of the world.

3. Beckett (1906-   )

Samuel Beckett's first play has given a phrase to the French language: *j'attends Godot,* which means that what is going on now will continue to go on for an unidentifiable length of time. *A la Trinité* is one of the more classical French phrases to designate the implacable future. *J'attends Godot* is really equivalent to saying: "This is what it means to keep on living." But if the phrase has reached an exceptional degree of popular usage, the play itself still remains enigmatic. It has been translated into eighteen languages and has been performed in many countries. The public is held by the play—Beckett is a skillful dramatist —but the aftereffect is one of worry and wonderment. The French themselves still use, in speaking of *En attendant Godot,* two opposing terms which, when applied to a certain kind of writing, are almost indistinguishable: is the play a *canular* (hoax) or a *chef-d'oeuvre* (masterpiece)?

The known facts about Samuel Beckett's life are few in number: his Dublin birth in 1906, of Irish parents, his plan to become a French teacher, his post as *lecteur d'anglais* at the Ecole Normale Supérieure for two years (1928-30), his friendship with James Joyce in Paris (although he was never Joyce's secretary as has been falsely reported), his year's experience as French teacher in Dublin, his decision to give up this career, his travels in Europe, his return to Paris in 1938, and his life as a writer since that return. Beckett first wrote in English: poems and essays (notably one on Proust), and his first novel, *Murphy,* published in England in 1937. He remained in France during the war. To escape the Gestapo, he left Paris for Roussillon, in the southern district of Vaucluse.

During the years following the liberation, he wrote directly in French the works with which his name today is associated: *Molloy, Malone meurt, L'Innommable,* and two plays, *En attendant Godot* (1952) and *Fin de partie* (1957). In 1953 Roger Blin produced *Godot* in the Théâtre de Babylone. It ran for four hundred performances, and was continued at the Théâtre Hébertot.

The plan of the play is simple to relate. Two tramps are waiting by a sickly looking tree for the arrival of M. Godot. They quarrel, make up, contemplate suicide, try to sleep, eat a carrot and gnaw on some chicken bones. Two other characters appear, a master and a slave, who perform a grotesque scene in the middle of the play. A young boy arrives to say that M. Godot will not come today, but that he will come tomorrow. The play is a development of the title, *Waiting for Godot.* He does not come and the two tramps resume their vigil by the tree, which between the first and second day has sprouted a few leaves, the only symbol of a possible order in a thoroughly alienated world.

The two tramps of Beckett, in their total disposition and in their antics with hats and tight shoes, are reminiscent of Chaplin and the American burlesque comedy team. Pozzo and Lucky, the master and slave, are half vaudeville characters and half marionettes. The purely comic aspect of the play involves traditional routines that come from the entire history of farce, from the Romans and the Italians, and the red-nosed clown of the modern circus. The language of the play has gravity, intensity, and conciseness. The long speech of Lucky, a bravura passage that is seemingly meaningless, is strongly reminiscent of Joyce and certain effects in *Finnegans Wake*. But the play is far from being a pastiche. It has its own beauty and suggestiveness, and it makes its own comment on man's absurd hope and on the absurd insignificance of man.

The utter simplicity of the play, in the histrionic sense, places it in the classical tradition of French playwriting. Its close adherence to the three unities is a clue to the play's dramaturgy. The unity of place is a muddy plateau with one tree, a kind of gallows which invites the tramps to consider hanging themselves. This place is any place. It is perhaps best characterized as being the place where Godot is not. As the play unfolds we come to realize that M. Godot is not in any place comparable to the setting of the play. He will not come out of one place into another. The unity of time is two days, but it might be any sequence of days in anyone's life. Time is equivalent to what is announced in the title: the act of waiting. Time is really immobility, although a few minor changes do take place during the play: the tree grows leaves and one of the characters, Pozzo, becomes blind. The act of waiting is never over, and yet it mysteriously starts up again each day. The action, in the same way, describes a circle. Each day is the return to the beginning. Nothing is completed because nothing can be completed. The despair in the play, which is never defined as such but which pervades all the lack of action and gives to the play its metaphysical color, is the fact that the two tramps cannot not wait for Godot, and the corollary fact that he cannot come.

The rigorous use of the unities is demanded by the implacable interpretation of human life. The denouement of the play is another beginning. Vladimir asks his friend: *Alors? On y va?* And Estragon answers: *Allons-y.* But neither moves. And the curtain descends over their immobility. In scene after scene the permanent absurdity of the world is stressed. In the scene, for example, between the master and the slave, Lucky is held on a leash by Pozzo. He carries a heavy suitcase without ever thinking of dropping it. He is able to utter his long incoherent speech only when he has his hat on and when Pozzo commands him to think.

The unity of place, the particular site on the edge of a forest which the two tramps cannot leave, recalls Sartre's striking use of the unity of place in his first play, *Huis Clos*. There it is hell in the appearance of a Second Empire living-room that the three characters cannot leave. The curtain line of each play underscores the unity of place, the setting which is prison. The *Allons-y!* of Godot corresponds to the *Eh bien, continuons!* of *Huis Clos*. Sartre's hell is projected by use of some of the *quid pro quos* of a typical bedroom farce, whereas Beckett's unnamed plateau resembles the empty vaudeville stage. The two tramps in a seemingly improvised dialogue arouse laughter in their public, despite their alienation from the social norm and despite the total pessimism of their philosophy.

To trace the ancestry, and simply the literary ancestry of this thought, would be equivalent to a listing of those European and American writers who during the past century have written strong indictments against our civilization and especially its industrialization. *Godot* and the novels of Samuel Beckett are among the leading works of revolt in our age, with the novels of Jean Genet and the essays and manifestoes of Antonin Artaud. Behind them, in France, are *Une Saison en enfer* of Rimbaud and the entire writings of Lautréament. Such an anthology of revolt would have to include pages of Céline and D. H. Lawrence and Henry Miller, as well as Kafka and Pirandello. No one work in this list has affected so immediately its public as *En attendant Godot*.

Many ingenious theories have been advanced to provide satisfactory interpretations for the characters of Beckett's play. Religious or mythical interpretations prevail. The two tramps Estragon (Gogo) and Vladimir (Didi) may be Everyman and his conscience. Gogo is less confident and at one moment is ready to hang himself. Vladimir is more hopeful, more even in temperament. One thinks of the medieval debate between the body and the soul, between the intellectual and the nonrational in man. Certain of their speeches about Christ might substantiate the theory that they are the two crucified thieves. Pozzo would seem to be the evil master, the exploiter. But perhaps he is Godot, or an evil incarnation of Godot. The most obvious interpretation of Godot is that he is God. As the name Pierrot comes from Pierre, so Godot may come from God. (One thinks also of the combination of God and Charlot, the name used by the French for Charlie Chaplin.) The little boy, who would be an angel in the religious interpretation, ascribes a white beard to M. Godot. If Godot is God, he has no characteristics of the Christian God. He is inscrutable and indifferent, but his very existence gives a reason to human activity. It is impossible for Estragon and Vladimir not to wait for him. Their attitude toward Godot varies from respect to irritation. This could easily be interpreted as indicative of the vacillation of the ordinary believer.

Mr. Beckett himself has repudiated all theories of a symbolic nature. But this does not necessarily mean that it is useless to search for such clues. The fundamental imagery of the play is Christian. Even the tree recalls the Tree of Knowledge and the Cross. The life of the tramps at many points in the text seems synonymous with the fallen state of man. Their strange relationship is a kind of marriage. The play is a series of actions that are aborted and that give a despairing uniformity to its duration.

The second Beckett play, *Fin de partie (Endgame)*, was finished in July 1956. It was published in February 1957. The first production, again in the hands of Roger Blin, was put on in the Studio des Champs-Elysées in May of that year.

The title of the play is a term used in chess to designate

the third and final part of the game. This technical meaning is not recognized by most of the French. It was perhaps chosen for its indeterminateness, for its capacity to designate the end of many things, the end of life itself. The approach to "the end" is indeed the principal theme of all of Beckett's writings.

Two of the characters, Nagg and Nell, live in ash cans, the covers of which they raise from time to time in order to speak. But most of the dialogue is carried on between their son, Hamm, who is paralytic, blind, and confined to a wheelchair, and his male attendant, Clov. Even more than in the first play, Beckett in *Fin de partie* indicates with great precision, as if he were writing a musical score, the pauses between speeches. This is unusual for the French style of acting. If observed in the performance of the play, the effect may well enhance the painfulness of waiting, the emptiness of existence, the expectancy of a collapse, of a manifestation of total despair. The innumerable pauses between speeches when the stage is silent underscore the anguish in each of the four characters and the nudity of the words themselves when they are spoken.

Clov, throughout the action of *Fin de partie*, is constantly expressing a desire to leave. When Beckett was asked to summarize his new play, he stated that whereas in his first play, everyone expects the arrival of Godot, in the second play, they will be expecting the departure of Clov. He is terrorized by the thought of being left alone, of being the last man left on the earth. This is a familiar fantasy of terror which most men have felt at some time or other in their existence, and which Beckett has succeeded in casting into the reality of a play.

This second play is totally different from the first, although it bears the unmistakable mark of Beckett's style and manner of thinking. Whereas *Godot* was concerned with the theme of waiting, *Fin de partie* is on the subject of leaving, on the necessity of reaching the door. We have the impression of watching the end of something, the end possibly of the human race. All movement has slowed down. Hamm is paralyzed and confined to his chair. Clov walks with difficulty. Nagg and Nell are legless and occupy little space in their ash cans. The setting vaguely resembles a womb and the ash cans are wombs within the womb. The two windows look out onto the sea and the earth, which are without trace of mankind. No affection joins the four characters. Nagg and Nell depend on Hamm for food. Clov, the son-slave, would kill Hamm if he knew the combination to the buffet where the last crackers are stored. Each has the remains of a kind of dream or aspiration that he tries vainly to communicate to the others. Nagg and Nell speak of a boat ride on Lake Como and the accident that made them *culs-de-jatte*. Hamm recites from time to time a literary story. Clov keeps referring to his departure, which he really knows is impossible.

This is the game that man constantly plays and in which he is always checkmated. The fundamental tragedy or hopelessness of the situation is offset by a fairly steady tone of burlesque and farce. The text is full of surprises and formulas that keep it moving ahead toward its conclusion. The metaphysical conclusion of the play—and this is the same in *En attendant Godot*—belongs to each individual spectator who will interpret it in accord with his own sensitivity and his own philosophy. In Beckett's art the elements of time and of reason are rejected so that the playwright will be free to exploit the impotency of man. The drama is the lack of meaning which the spectacle of life provides and which is offered to the spectators seated in the theater although it may not be so comprehended by the characters in the plays. In the dialogue between the two tramps, as well as in the dialogue between Hamm and Clov, there is an inverted kind of desperate intellectualism. This becomes clearer to the spectators after they have left the theater and they are able on different levels to contemplate the mystery of life.

After the première of *En attendant Godot*, Jean Anouilh

stated that he felt the occasion to be as important as a Pirandello première. Such American writers as Tennesee Williams and Kenneth Rexroth have made similar claims for the significance of Beckett. In the space of a very few years, Beckett has gained the stature of an international figure. The reason would seem to be that his attack or his indictment against civilization is thoroughly simple and lucid. Similar indictments had been made by Rimbaud, Lautréamont, Hölderlin, and Artaud, but in each case such tension had resulted in madness or flight. Beckett's vision of man is comparably grim and absolute, but he seems to have maintained a personal serenity of outlook.

4. Genet (1909-   )

Concerning his play *Les Bonnes* (*The Maids*), Jean Genet
has said that it is "a tragedy of the confidants." In
a classical tragedy, the confidant listens to the hero discuss
his loves and his exploits. The subject of M. Genet's play
is the unfolding of the confidant's thought after he has left
the presence of the hero. There are two confidantes here,
two maids who devotedly serve their mistress, and who
gratefully receive Madame's castoff dresses. Their life
has been so reduced by this service, by the silence imposed
upon them, that the only way they feel they can exist in-
dependently and truthfully is by committing a crime. But
the planned murder of their mistress turns against them.

The sense of horror which this play creates seems almost
more intense and more menacing than the horror generated
in countless scenes of Genet's books. When performed
on the stage, with living actors, a story like *Les Bonnes*
reveals a violence that is almost unbearable. This is an
example of the theater of cruelty that Artaud spoke of.
It is not the revelation of scandal which hastily written
dramatic criticism has often called it. It is rather the
revelation of a moral distress able to turn human beings
into sufferers, whom we often live close to without recog-

nizing. These sufferers speak in words of sumptuous beauty because Jean Genet is a very great writer.

The first production of *Les Bonnes* was directed by Jouvet at the Athénée in 1947. More human, more bare, and more intense was the second production, seven years later, at the Théâtre de la Huchette, by Tania Balachova, who played the older of the two maids. In this new production, the action shifted from the struggle between Madame and the two maids who want to assassinate her, to the struggle between the maids themselves. They call themselves sisters, but it is more than likely that the term is euphemistic. A marked difference in age, which Genet insists on, was observed in the Balachova production. The main action is perpetrated by the younger of the two "sisters," the one who plays the role of the absent mistress and who at the end poisons herself.

The action of Genet's second play, *Haute Surveillance* (*Deathwatch*), takes place in a prison cell where a very precise and powerful hierarchy of seductiveness exists between three young men. Yeux-Verts (also called Paolo les Dents Fleuries) is the murderer of a girl. He expects that in two months' time he will be guillotined: *D'un côté de la machine j'aurai ma tête, et mon corps de l'autre côté.* . . . He dilates at such length on this situation of horror that it becomes something monstrous and fabulous. He loses himself in admiration over the magnitude of his own condemnation and fate. He is the *maudit,* but without the romantic halo of rebel and apostle. He is the exalted criminal. By his prestige he dominates a second prisoner, who in his turn dominates a third prisoner, a mere thief. This is the hierarchy of the cell, where seductiveness (essentially of a sexual nature) comes from the power of evil.

The heroes of *Haute Surveillance* walk back and forth in their close cell and provide thereby a picture of their obsessions, from which they cannot escape. Theirs is a self-contained world of damnation. Genet does not move outside of the world of the damned and gives to it the inverted vocation of evil. His subject matter is that which is condemned by society, and to it he gives, as an authentic playwright in *Les Bonnes* and *Haute Surveillance,* an infernal order, a presentation of evil conceived of in terms of a criminal hierarchy. Yeux-Verts, the protagonist of *Haute Surveillance,* has his own prestige and magnificence. He is the beneficiary of a perverted kind of grace and power. Baudelaire understood and felt the dramatic power of evil. And Rimbaud, on certain pages of *Une Saison en enfer,* describes the admiration that children can feel for criminals and pariahs. (*Encore tout enfant j'admirais le forçat intraitable sur qui se referme toujours le bagne. . . .*) Jean Genet has exploited methodically the appeal and the prestige that vice can have.

In his critical work *Saint Genet comédien et martyr,* Sartre has meticulously pointed out the strong relationship between the two plays. In writing for the stage, Genet was unquestionably drawn by the artifice of the theater, by its pretense and lie. In the text of *Les Bonnes,* he gives the formal direction that the two maids be played by adolescent boys in order to enhance even more drastically the ludicrousness of their appearance and the strangeness of their strategy. In the uniform structure of the two plays the important male figure is absent: the husband of the house in *Les Bonnes,* and the Negro criminal Boule-de-Neige, who obsesses the minds of all three prisoners in the prison play. There are three visible actors in each play. One of the actors, Madame in *Les Bonnes,* and Yeux-Verts, the head criminal in *Haute Surveillance,* serves as a kind of intermediary between the absent actor, whose power and authority have been somewhat transmitted to him, and the couple: the two maids in *Les Bonnes* and the other two prisoners, Maurice and Lefranc, in *Haute Surveillance.* In each play the couple is a weird pair of beings who are simultaneously drawn to one another and hate one another, and who dream of committing a murder. One play ends with a suicide and the other with a murder.

Genet calls this couple the eternal marriage between the criminal and the saint. (The sentence is in *Les Bonnes: le couple éternal du criminel et de la sainte*.) Maids and criminals belong to the order of evil, in Genet's conception. They represent an absolute of disorder which is the opposite of the order of society. On one side are servants and criminals, and on the other side are the masters. Genet found the subject matter of *Les Bonnes* in the notorious crimes of the Papin sisters. Each of the maids plays the part of Madame. At the beginning of the play, Claire is pretending to be Madame and insults Solange. We realize that this game of pretense is played every evening. The revolt of the maids against the order of the bourgeois world takes place only in their minds. By their repetitive antics they almost reach the state of schizophrenia, but it is clear that they wish to be enslaved, that they have no desire to change their state of subservience. Likewise, the young criminals of *Haute Surveillance* have no inclination to cease being criminals and hence lose the prestige of evil and martyrdom.

Most men are able to play some kind of role in society. By feeling thus integrated with a social group, they justify their existence. Jean Genet is concerned in his two plays, as well as in all of his books, with the type of man who is alienated from society. This man has been given a role outside of society and accepts it. He can discover no justification for it. Sartre can easily find in the writings of Genet examples of a gratuitous and absurd existence. The maids and the criminals in the two plays, in the acceptance of their alienation, have only one recourse. They have to play at being normal, at being integrated characters. So the maids play at being their mistress and the criminals form a hierarchical society in their cell. But the characters of Genet know what they are doing. They know that they are counterfeiting society. They know that the actions that they invent will not justify their existence. So in reality they are always playing their own alienated selves. We are therefore always watching simultaneously two actions in the plays of Genet: the invented actions of the characters playing at being something they are not, and the fatal drama of alienation.

In a new edition of *Les Bonnes* (*Les Bonnes et l'atelier d'Alberto Giacometti,* 1958), Genet has published an important letter on his play and on his opinion of the theater in general. On the whole, he feels repelled by the clichés and formulas of the Western theater. In the tradition of our theatrical performances, the actor identifies himself with a character in the play, and this, for Genet, is basically exhibitionism. He claims that our Western plays are masquerades and not ceremonies. What transpires on the stage is always childish. Genet wrote *Les Bonnes* through vanity, he says, because he was asked to by a famous actor, but he was bored during the writing of this work. He was depressed by his knowledge that it would be performed in accord with the conventions of the modern theater, where everything is visible on the stage, where the actions of men, and not of the gods, are depicted.

5. Adamov (1908-   )

La Parodie, Arthur Adamov's first play, was written in 1947 and performed in 1952, in Paris, at the Théâtre Lancry. In the second volume of his collected plays (*Théâtre II*), a preface by the playwright comments on his career, on the origins of his plays, on his dissatisfaction or satisfaction with them.

His real reasons for writing for the stage are not clear to Adamov. He had been reading Strindberg intensively and he believes that because of this reading he had been paying attention to chance street scenes that were theatrical in nature. He was impressed especially by the steady flow of walkers, by the solitude of each individual walker in the midst of such a crowd, and by the diversity of the conversations he overheard, the fragmentary remarks whose ensemble seemed to contain a profound symbolism. Then one day he witnessed an incident in the street, seemingly insignificant, but which appeared to him as a scene from a play: *C'est cela le théâtre, c'est cela que je veux faire.* . . . He observed a blind man asking for alms. As two young girls passed, they heedlessly bumped into him. At that moment they were singing a popular refrain: "I closed my eyes and it was wonderful." (*J'ai fermé les yeux, c'était merveilleux. . . .*)

From this scene, almost casual and banal in itself, the idea for Adamov's first play, *La Parodie*, came to him. He would try to demonstrate as blatantly as possible the subject of man's solitude, the impossibility of communication between men. *La Parodie* was the result of three years' labor and many different versions. Today Adamov looks upon the characters in *La Parodie* as marionettes, and this seems explicable to him by the fact that he took as a point of departure not real details but a general idea, a "metaphysical" idea. His basic philosophy says that all existences are equivalent, that the character N., in his refusal of life, and the character of the clerk (L'Employé), in his unthinking acceptance of life, come to the same end, namely total destruction. This first play was a sign of rebellion for Adamov. He had been strongly influenced by Artaud's *Le Théâtre et son double*, and disgusted with the so-called "psychological" plays of his day.

When the character N. in *La Parodie* says that everyone is dead (*tout le monde est mort, il n'y a pas que moi*), he summarizes two major characteristics of Adamov's world as reflected in his plays: everything moves toward death, and death has no reason. Adamov seems to be preparing the advent of tragedy and at the same time denying the authenticity or the competence of tragedy. In this sense, his world is a "parody." If fate is the same for everyone, then there is no fate.

For his second play, *L'Invasion*, performed in 1950, at the Studio des Champs-Elysées, under the direction of Jean Vilar, Adamov resolved to take a specific subject and create characters rather than types. But he intended to maintain the leading principle of *La Parodie:* no character understands or even hears any other character. He believed he was inventing a new stratagem in the theater by having a character heard by another but not having him say what he meant to say. Adamov later discovered that this kind of dialogue distinguishes the plays of Chekhov!

A dream was the basis of the third play, *La Grande et la Petite Manoeuvre*. In his dream Adamov was threatened with militaristic exercises that were to mutilate and finally kill him. The fear that he felt in the dream he wanted to communicate in the new play (first presented at the Théâtre des Noctambules, in 1950). Le Mutilé (Adamov in his dream) is destined to be destroyed, but le Militant is also destroyed. The Kafkaesque themes in this play are used in a fully theatrical way. The *mise-en-scène* is of primary importance. Noises and unexpected events are the physical destruction that really narrates the moral destruction of the hero. The revelation of the play, namely the belief that the failure of all human action is written down somewhere, is the result of the fear Adamov had experienced in his dream and his rationalizaton about human existence. These first three plays of Adamov were in reality demonstrations of a profoundly pessimistic philosophy, concerning the uselessness of man trying to oppose the forces destined to crush him. An action is accomplished only to be defeated, a passion is experienced only to be denied. Everything fatally results in failure.

Adamov interrupted the composition of his fourth play, *Le Sens de la marche*, in order to begin the writing of his fifth, *Le Professeur Taranne* (first performed in Lyon, in 1953). This, again, was the transcription of a dream, but this time Adamov claims he did not try to confer a general meaning on the drama. He believes that the satisfaction he still derives from this play comes from the fact that he used no parts of the dream as mere allegory. The speeches of Taranne are comparable to the speeches Adamov made in his dream. The writing of the play was accomplished immediately, within the space of two days. He had spent five years on *La Parodie* and *L'Invasion*.

Le Professeur Taranne is a brief play about a man unable to live up to his public role as university professor. He is accused of a number of things, among them appearing naked on a beach, where some young girls had seen him, and of plagiarism. As his imagination evokes the accusations, we see the changing sets and the accusers. This is a play about fantasies, of a very cruel order, and one of the most successful theatrical projections of Adamov's world. The protagonist appears completely within his tragic circumference. He has been condemned for exposing himself. This is the beginning of a long series of affirmations on the part of Taranne which are immediately turned against him and act negatively on his case. Every word he uses exposes him in the wrong way and ends by annihilating him. Every minute during the action of the play, Taranne is within the confines of the tragedy of his existence.

The central object around which the action of *Ping-Pong* revolves is the pinball machine, the dominant attraction for the clientèle of Mme Duranty's café. The characters are defined by their varying reactions to the machine, to the degree of obsession which the machine creates in them. This object, both fetish and symbol, permits the spectators, according to Adamov, to separate themselves from the characters. Although the playwright claims that he has left a certain amount of freedom to some of his characters in *Ping-Pong*, they appear more simply as victims of the pinball machine, namely of the inevitable structure of the tragic universe.

The première of *Paolo Paoli* took place in 1957, in Lyon, at the Théâtre de la Comédie. This very ambitious play of Adamov was performed in Paris in early 1958, by the same company, under the direction of Roger Planchon, at the Vieux-Colombier. The subject of this new play is the egoism and the narrow-mindedness of French society between the years 1900 and 1914. In the earlier plays Adamov's characters were general and allegorical, but in *Paolo Paoli* they are more real and more individualistic. The principal character, Paolo Paoli, the son of a bourgeois family in Cayenne, comes to Paris about 1900 in order to found an unusual business—selling rare butterflies. This highly poetic commerce is the center of the action: twelve scenes during which the injustice and cupidity of a society moving toward self-destruction are exposed.

Paolo Paoli, a cynic, employs at the lowest possible wages the convicts of Cayenne to hunt his butterflies. His principal client, Hulot-Vasseur, runs another business, equally poetic, the sale of hummingbird feathers and heron plumes for ladies' hats. He, too, is an exploiter of the women in his employ. Abbé Saulnier, a former chaplain at Cayenne, is a friend of Paolo Paoli; he represents a fanatical belief in the Church and in tyrannical supervision of the working classes. The action of the play is precipitated by the escape of a falsely condemned convict, Marpeaux, who comes for help to Paolo and Abbé Saulnier.

The play stresses the worst side of French civilization during the pre-1914 years, but this worst side, in its farcical, lively and wicked aspects, is admirably drawn in the theatrical medium. The story is both weird and plausible. Adamov himself, who is very harsh in the criticism of his early plays, sees a radical change in his manner, with *Ping-Pong* and *Paolo Paoli*. The characters of the last two plays are far less abstract than those of *La Parodie* and *L'Invasion*, but this second manner of the playwright is nowise a negation of the first. In Paolo Paoli we come into direct contact with small, limited men, concerned with small businesses. Paolo Paoli is an entomologist who sells butterflies, and Hulot-Vasseur is an industrialist selling aigrettes and colibri plumes worried over the new social laws among the working classes. The indignation scenes of Abbé Saulnier and the lamentations over the state of the world recited by Mme de Saint-Sauveur are simultaneously comical and biting.

This world of the play is a microcosm of the bigger world moving steadily and fatalistically into war. The false or the materialistic reasons for the associations existing between the characters of *Paolo Paoli* serve as premonitions for selfish alliances between peoples and nations. Between the various scenes or tableaux, quotations from newspapers and celebrities are projected on a screen. These relate to the important political figures of the epoch and to the world situation. This is a device that serves to maintain an equilibrium between the immediate parochial drama taking place on the stage, and the wider context of world politics and the doom of mankind.

In one of the most important articles yet to appear on the dramaturgy of Adamov, Maurice Regnaut asks whether *Paolo Paoli* may not be considered a tragedy. (*"Arthur Adamov et le sense du fétichisme," Cahiers 22, 23, de la Compagnie Renaud-Barrault,* May 1958.) M. Regnaut argues brilliantly that this question revolves around the character of the workman Marpeaux. At the end, no one can do anything for or against Marpeaux. The power of the world, no longer divisible into grievances and complaints, has turned against a man and is obliterating him.

6. Ionesco (1912-   )

In a recent interview, Eugène Ionesco pointed out the futility of wishing for a healthy, comfortable, and comprehensive theater. To achieve this kind of theater would be equivalent to killing it. To be in a state of crisis is not only characteristic of the theater, but the characteristic of humanity itself. Ionesco reminds us once again that man is a sick animal, the only animal in the universe which is dissatisfied with its condition. But this is why man has a history. The function of art, literature, and the theater is to express the permanent crisis of man. M. Ionesco does not believe, for example, that an economic crisis really affects the theater since it lives by and through much more serious crises. There is no minority theater, he claims, which cannot become a majority theater. It was once said that Anouilh's plays were accessible only to a bourgeois public. This has been disproved. He has had success in the popular theaters where also the experimentalists Audiberti, Beckett, Ghelderode, and Ionesco have been warmly received.

As is usually the case with a new playwright, the critics are divided over Ionesco in praise and blame. His admirers find in his writings the abstractions of a philosophy of language, and his detractors grant him no talent, no importance. At the performance of an Ionesco play, there is considerable laughter in the audience. The source of this laughter is as old as the theater itself. It is man laughing at his own vacuity, his own emptiness, his own intimate triviality. This kind of laughter had been excessively exploited by the surrealists and by those close to surrealism, by Jarry in *Ubu Roi,* by Cocteau in *Les Mariés de la Tour Eiffel,* by Desnos and Queneau and Michaux. Language and mime plunge the spectator into the very heart of his own foibles and imbecilities.

The text of *La Cantatrice chauve* (*The Bald Soprano*) is an example of the burlesque inventiveness of Ionesco, of the verbal fantasies he can create, but the laughter the text generates is not very pure. It covers up a rather serious worry of man, a *malaise.* This is a text made up of commonplaces very skillfully reconstructed, or placed just a bit out of context. We laugh because of the persistent disparity between the words as they are said and the behavior of the characters speaking the words. The spectacle that transpires on the stage (and which nowise resembles a plot or a story) is very close to the spectacle going on in us or around us almost all of the time.

La Cantatrice chauve, which Ionesco calls an "antiplay," was first produced in May 1950, at the Théâtre des Noctambules by a young director, Nicolas Bataille. The roof over the stage leaked that night and the rain fell directly on the actors. This added to the confusion of a puzzling text, and to an absurd title, referring to a bald soprano who never appears. A few of the spectators enjoyed themselves, but most were furious in the conviction that they were being made fun of. The theme of *La Cantatrice chauve,* which occurs often enough in the other plays of Ionesco to be called his principal theme, is that of the aging couple, of the husband and wife who have made a failure of living together, or who at least suffer from some feeling of guilt. There are many Freudian aspects to his writing, but centering about this feeling of guilt, which provides pathos as well as monotony. As the dialogue continues its clowning and the nonsensical answers are given back and forth, a pathos slowly emerges and the tragedy of the married couple is faintly sketched. This is not the young couple, in love with one another but quarreling and misunderstanding one another, that Molière, Marivaux, and Goldoni give us.

La Cantatrice chauve is a parody play on our conversations, on the so-called "dramatic situations" of our lives, on our incapacity to remain silent. Three scenes in particular are models of burlesque parody: the domestic conversation between Mr. and Mrs. Smith, the recognition scene of Mr. and Mrs. Martin, and the unexpected visit of the fireman. In the deepest sense, *La Cantatrice chauve* is a parody of the theater. M. Ionesco himself has acknowledged this intention. But a parody of the theater would also necessarily be a parody of human behavior. By a deliberate stark use of the banal, by a repetition of the worn-out clichés of language, Ionesco generates an unusual, fresh atmosphere, an atmosphere that seems so new that we are better able to understand the daily novelty of each existence.

At this first play, when no bald soprano appeared, the public was first irritated and then resigned to the trick. So when the second play, *La Leçon (The Lesson)*, was announced, the public knew that there would be no lesson. They did not know that Ionesco was going to be unpredictable from one play to another. The play turned out to be an authentic private lesson given by a teacher to a rather stupid girl, and this lesson lasts the length of the play. The teacher is nervous and tense, and grows more irritable as he continues to teach his young pupil, who is preparing the full doctorate *(le doctorat total)*. At the end, the teacher kills his pupil. Often in the plays of Ionesco the ending is punctuated by some irreparable gesture.

Already *La Leçon* has become throughout the world a

kind of classic of the new French theater. It has been performed in England, America, Germany, Turkey, and Japan. The first two plays are more simple than the subsequent plays, but they contain the essence of Ionesco's dramaturgy. They are filled with a ludicrous babbling and chattering. The speech of man seems unable to adapt itself to the sentiments and the truths that the language is attempting to express. The dialogue of Ionesco often resembles the monotonous whining of an animal unable to articulate the cause of its suffering, unable to make its suffering understood. The ritual of commonplaces can become so cruel that the laughter of the spectator is uncomfortable.

In *Les Chaises* (*The Chairs*) the obsessive theme of the husband and wife is fully developed. They are the only characters in this ingenious play. The setting is a bare circular room at the top of a tower that is surrounded by water at its base. After a long life of emptiness and mediocrity, the husband and wife, Le Vieux and La Vieille, attempt to justify their failure. They stage an imaginary reception, imagining a large number of guests who arrive to hear an important speech by the old man. They arrange the chairs and seat the invisible guests, talk with them and revive memories, dreams, mistakes. The bare stage becomes animated with pitiful dreams and repetitious memories. In her need to admire and protect her husband, the woman wishes above all to express maternal tenderness. And the man is determined to play the part of a misunderstood intellectual who has had a great message for the world, a message of freedom. These two characters are not deceived by the sinister game they are playing, and rather than wake up from the game, when it becomes too complicated and burdensome to continue, they jump out the window into the water below. Throughout the ceremonial of the reception and the speech, Ionesco has succeeded in maintaining a balance between madness and tenderness in the two characters. The audience laughs a great deal, but it is quite aware of the deep undercurrent of pathos. This picture of man's enisled fate describes his frustration over trying to communicate and to be remembered, but it does not depict any tragic dimension.

In *Amédée ou comment s'en débarrasser,* the bitterness between husband and wife is more marked. Amédée is a playwright, but in fifteen years he has written only two speeches. His wife, Madeleine, a typist, considers this a small output. Love is over between them, and in its place a feeling of guilt grows. They feel the presence of a corpse in the apartment—obviously the corpse of their love. It begins growing in a rapid geometrical progression until it fills the apartment and threatens to break through the walls. Mushrooms grow everywhere. Amédée gets the corpse out of the apartment and disappears into the air. This kind of play depends on considerable stage trickery. The existence of the body in the next room which feeds on the quarrels between husband and wife helps to establish a mood of anguish and emptiness.

The origins of these strange plays of Ionesco are not visible. The traditional theatergoer is bewildered by them because he is unable to place them within a historical literary context. *Victimes du devoir* (*Victims of Duty*) is the most complex of the plays, the profoundest perhaps, and the one with which Ionesco has expressed the most satisfaction. The subject of the play is mythological and even oneirocritical in its relationship with primitive mystery: the son in the dual role of slayer of his father and of redeemer. The action is oppressive and nightmarish. A policeman forces his way into the home of the Chouberts on the pretext of gathering information concerning a certain Mallot. During the course of the conversation, Choubert plunges so deeply into his memories that he confuses reality and looks upon his wife, Madeleine, and the policeman as his mother and father. The policeman in his role of father forces Madeleine to drink poison. Under the power of the maternal force in this household, both father and son attempt to justify their existences. But the will to destruction and disintegration is the dominant force. This familiar theme in contemporary literature is celebrated in *Victimes du devoir* almost as if it were a ritual.

In the text of the play itself, Ionesco makes a profession of faith about the theater and at the same time sets off a violent attack against the traditional psychological theater of his day. One of the characters says: "The theater today is still a prisoner of old forms. It has not moved beyond the psychology of a Paul Bourget. It does not correspond to the cultural status of our age. There is no correspondence between it and the spiritual manifestations of our time." To underscore his attack, Ionesco uses Bourget, the psychological novelist of a generation ago who seems today to be timid, inaccurate, and superficial. The old principles of unity and identity of a character no longer apply in the treatment of Ionesco. And yet the feeling of guilt does remain as a central obsession.

In the short play *L'Impromptu de l'Alma*, a parody reminiscent of Giraudoux's *L'Impromptu de Paris*, Ionesco answers his most vehement critics. The three doctors who surround Ionesco at his writing table closely resemble Molière's doctors at the bedside of a healthy man whom they have decided to have die in accord with all the known rules of medicine. With some justice, Ionesco attacks the critics who refuse to judge his plays in themselves but always in terms of well-established traditions in playwriting. One of the recent plays, *Le Nouveau Locataire* (*The New Tenant*), was a theme in *Les Chaises*. In the newer play there is almost no dialogue. A man is furnishing his apartment and the moving men keep placing furniture in chalk-marked places until the pieces mount around the tenant and he is no longer visible. He is buried in a tomb of odd pieces of furniture, and the moving men at the end of the scene turn out the light and leave.

In *La Nouvelle Revue Française* of February 1958 Ionesco published an important article on his experience with the theater. In autobiographical manner, the writer describes his early dislike for the theater. He attended the theater rarely because everything about it disturbed him: the acting of the players, the arbitrariness of the so-called dramatic situation, the artificiality and the trickiness of the productions. He found no magic in the theater, but on the contrary an intricate system of tricks and deceptions and patterns. These he calls *les ficelles*. The art and the activity of the actors seemed inadmissible to him. The living presence of men and women on the stage, playing parts foreign to their nature, was an unpleasant spectacle for him. He could not accept the art of the actor, as defined by Diderot and refined on by Jouvet and by Brecht in his theory of "distance," the art of the actor who is in full possession of the character he is playing.

Ionesco remained attached to some of the great dramatic texts of the past: Sophocles, Aeschylus, Shakespeare, but this was a literary attachment. The comedies of Molière bored him, and he found the greatness of Shakespeare's plays seriously diminished when they were performed. Ionesco was the opposite of what might be called an amateur of the theater. His judgments on playwrights are briefly stated in this article, but they are negative: Corneille is tiresome, Marivaux frothy, Musset thin, Hugo laughable, Giraudoux already unplayable, Cocteau artificial, Pirandello outmoded. Only Racine escapes total condemnation when Ionesco claims that he is played today not because of his psychological understanding but because of his poetry. By comparison with music and painting, the art of playwriting has accumulated very few masterpieces that have lasted. Twenty or thirty, at the most. As a tentative theory to explain this paltry figure of enduring successes, Ionesco wonders whether the playwright's habit of writing for his own time, of trying to remain close to his immediate audience, does not account for the dismally small number of dramatic masterpieces.

Not until M. Ionesco began writing for the theater and seeing his own plays performed, did his dislike for it turn to love. He relates how, at the first performances of his first play, *La Cantatrice chauve*, at the Théâtre des Noctambules, he felt terrified at seeing characters of his own imagination walking about the stage. The director of the play, Nicolas Bataille, played the part of Martin and Ionesco confesses to having found something almost diabolical in this incarnation.

In these early experimentations with playwriting and with the productions of the plays, he discovered that the essence of the theater for him was in the exaggeration of its effects. Rather than trying to conceal the various artificialities and conventions of a performance (*les ficelles*, in Ionesco's language), he believed that they should go as far as possible in grotesqueness and caricature. Ionesco recalls theories of Antonin Artaud when he advocates a theater of violence where the psychological study of characters will be replaced by metaphysical themes. He does not recognize any clearly marked distinction between the comic and the tragic. He deliberately calls his plays "comic dramas" or "tragic farces." In *Les Chaises* he purposely disguised the tragic element by means of a comic treatment. These two elements of the comic and tragic are not fused; for Ionesco, they coexist. Each stands as a criticism of the other.

No predetermined plan, no prearranged set of ideas guides Ionesco in the writing of his plays. Artistic creation appears to him essentially spontaneous. Yet this creation of a possibly new theater is associated in his mind with the coexistence of contradictory principles: tragedy and farce, the poetic and the prosaic, fantasy and realism, the familiar and the unusual. His texts seem to indicate a belief that the playwright remains more separated from his characters than the novelist, and that he is therefore a more accurate observer of their lives. In his greater detachment, he can perhaps be a more authentic witness.

In February 1960 Barrault presented Ionesco's new play, *Le Rhinocéros,* at the Théâtre de France. The parable of the new work is fairly simple. The inhabitants of a small provincial town are transformed into rhinoceros. Bérenger, the type of average man, grows into the stature of protagonist because he is not influenced by words and speeches. He struggles against the exaltation of friends and colleagues, against an overwhelming force that isolates him. At the end of the play he is totally alone, after observing, without always fully understanding it, a clinical study of conformity and contamination. This solitude of man is at the center of all of Ionesco's plays, and it is always manifested in the same way, with the same admixture of irony and burlesque and humor. For the first time in his career, Ionesco has conquered a large public easily and quickly. In the addition of allegory Ionesco has lost some of the theatrical purity he reached in *Les Chaises* and *La Leçon,* where no didactic element blurred the simple functioning of the infernal machine.

7. Schehadé (1910-   )

In 1951, when Georges Schehadé's first play, *Monsieur Bob'le*, was performed, a hostile press did all it could to close the theater. But a certain number of poets, in particular men like André Breton and René Char, who believed in the poetry of Schehadé, came to his defense. Two drama critics, Thierry Maulnier and Jacques Lemarchand, spoke in his favor. This controversy has even been referred to as *la bataille de Monsieur Bob'le*.

The text of the play had been ready for some time when Georges Vitaly chose it for his company at the smallest theater in Paris, La Huchette. There were forty-seven performances in all. The actor R.-J. Chauffard, who played the part of Monsieur Bob'le, has written in one of the *Cahiers de la Compagnie Renaud-Barrault* of his experiences in this play. He speaks of the sadness all the actors felt at the time of the last performance. But in the perspective of a few years, he knows that they were wrong. Bob'le continues to live. People now speak of the play in France and abroad; it is often written about. In public places Chauffard is often approached by someone who saw him play the part. This stranger sometimes speaks to the actor and offers him a drink. In speaking of the play,

Chauffard realizes that the stranger is not confusing him with the *part* of Bob'le. What has happened is one of the mysteries of the theater. Bob'le has become a real personage, a character of the theater. He is separated from the actor who played him and exists in the minds of the spectators.

Who is this character in the play of Georges Schehadé? A curious character, both lovable and mysterious. On all those who approach him, he exerts a very subtle influence. The entire action of the play gravitates around him, and yet he speaks less than some of the other characters. Whenever he does speak, it sems to be with the purpose of destroying the image or the interpretation of him which has just been established. He has been happy in the small village of Paola Scala, where he chose to live. And yet he has decided to leave it. The reason he gives for this departure is money. He is leaving Paola Scala in order to get money elsewhere, and yet everyone knows that Bob'le scorns money. Everyone knows of the purifying and illuminating influence he has had on all the villagers.

This man is a poet, but he is also a man of action. His speech is often difficult to understand, but his friends know that it corresponds to what is in his heart. They trust what he says, and derive images from it, and assurances of contentment. Miraculously he is able to create a sense of security around him. The villagers have accepted all the paradoxes that Bob'le's character demonstrates. He lives alone, but he is loved by everyone. He prays to the Virgin, and yet at times he doesn't seem to believe in God. He easily speaks about himself, but no one knows anything about his past. He does not seem attracted to women, and yet he inspires love in everyone. It is more painful for him to say good-by to his dog Excelsior than to his ward, the young boy Michel, who may well be his own son.

After he has left Paola Scala, his faithful friends live in expectation of his return. He sends them strange, mysterious messages that continue to direct their lives almost as if he were there in person. They ask for his return, and on his way back he falls ill and dies. The story has the simplicity of a village myth. It is the story of Monsieur Bob'le, of his departure, of his absence, and of his death. He is a sage or a poet who gives life to a small village and who dies far away from it.

At the beginning of 1954, Jean-Louis Barrault chose Schehadé's second play, *La Soirée des proverbes,* for the opening of the Petit Théâtre Marigny. He directed the play and acted in it with the members of his company. The dramatic and poetic qualities of the text had guided his choice.

The theme of *La Soirée des proverbes* is the natural purity of youth, of its faith, of its enthusiasm and its dreams, of its rightful ambitions. The complementary theme of the play is old age, which continues to live although it is really dead, and which appears as a mask without personality. In the first act (*"L'Auberge du Cygne Blanc"*) we see the community of old people. Comedy and fantasy are fused here in the many characters. They leave the inn and come to a forest in the second act (*"Dans le bois"*). In the third act (*"La Soirée des quatre-diamants"*) they are inside a house whose façade was visible in the forest. There the *soirée* begins. The guests are caricatures of what they once were. They have grown pathetic and ridiculous. A young fellow, Argengeorge, upsets them with his verve and enthusiasm. He is pure in heart, a kind of Parsifal in the midst of the aging whose hearts have lost their purity.

When the hunter Alexis kills Argengeorge, it becomes obvious that the hunter and the hunted are the same man. Alexis is really Argengeorge grown old. But this vision is unbearable, and Argengeorge prefers to die and hence remain young and pure. He does not defend himself against Alexis, because of his despair at recognizing that purity is not of this world. The other characters, clearly and diaphanously delineated in the art of the playwright, collaborate in this sacrifice of Argengeorge. The sacrifice is of course a liberation.

The third play of Georges Schehadé, *Histoire de Vasco*, was first performed in Zurich, in 1956, by the Renaud-Barrault Company, under the direction of Barrault. The action of the play takes place about 1850, in an unnamed country, during a time of war. Vasco is a simple, innocent man, a barber in the village of Sosso. He dislikes warfare. But General Mirador chooses Vasco to carry a message into enemy territory. He is loved by a young girl, Marguerite, whom he has never met and who tries through several campaigns to catch up with him. She travels in company with her vagabond father, César, a vendor of stuffed dogs. When Vasco the barber is in the midst of the enemy, we see him successively metamorphosed as poet and lover and hero. In the last act he is captured and killed. Vasco dies before he is able to become the hero that General Mirador has counted on making him. His innocence is reminiscent of Argengeorge and Monsieur Bob'le, and it is the kind of innocence that cannot last very long in the world.

When Barrault finally played *Histoire de Vasco* in Paris, in 1957, at the Théâtre Sarah-Bernhardt, the work instigated a battle that raged for some time. Two dramatic critics in particular, and both very important authorities, were harsh in their criticism: Robert Kemp in *Le Monde* and Jean-Jacques Gautier in *Le Figaro*. An editorial writer in *L'Aurore* called it an antimilitarist play and demanded that it be censored because at that very time French soldiers were being killed in Algeria. Although Kemp's article had been nonpolitical, he was accused of disliking the play because of its antiwar theme. *Le Monde* published a letter by René Char who agreed with Kemp and attacked the play as mediocre poetry. The *Observateur* then concluded that Char was jealous of Saint-John Perse and Jules Supervielle, who had spoken highly of Schehadé's poetry! Strong demands were made for the censoring of *Vasco*.

The poetic qualities of Schehadé's plays are reminiscent of Giraudoux. When *Monsieur Bob'le* was first performed in 1951, some of the faithful theatergoers remembered the poetic eruption of *Siegfried* in 1928. Schehadé is a Lebanese whose poetry has also been extolled by such poets as Max Jacob, Paul Eluard, and André Breton. He joins the ranks of the few French poets of modern times who have tried to write for the stage: Claudel, Apollinaire, Audiberti, Supervielle. He is a practitioner of words, sensitive to their profound meanings and to the power of their images. He is shrewd and wise in his creation of the innocent hero who is saintlike: Bob'le, Argengeorge, Vasco. With the vision of a seer, of the original kind of *vates*, he establishes communication between worlds that are usually closed off from one another, between life and death, between old age and the past.

With the poetic theater of Georges Schehadé, and to some extent in the two plays of Henri Pichette, *Les Epiphanies* and *Nucléa* (the latter written in Alexandrines), dramatic writing moves farther away from the "bourgeois theater" than do the experimental plays of Beckett and Ionesco and Adamov. This kind of play is perhaps the hardest of all to re-establish in France. The nonpoetic theater has had a long history and seems deeply entrenched. It speaks of what is immediately apprehended: a scene of adultery, a scene of history, a problem in psychology. When a poet's language is used on the stage, the action of the play becomes the action of language where an effort is made to explain as profoundly as possible the multiple relationships that the characters establish among themselves. The pure verbal invention of the poet, as in the art of Schehadé, takes hold of the action as an ivy clings to a tree. The language embellishes and stylizes the action. Because of this embellishment, we are able to follow, with a new intensity, the story of man's fate.

The efforts of Schehadé and Pichette, of Audiberti and Supervielle, are perhaps the first steps in an important revindication. Throughout the history of the theater, the suffering of man, his *pathos,* has been *inextricably bound* up with lyricism. The most noble way man has devised for the translation of his suffering is the theater: in the art of narrating, of mining, of dancing, and of acting. The life struggle of Dionysus and his defeat cannot be separated from the solar serenity of Apollo and the creation of a poetic form.

VI. CONCLUSIONS

1. Molière Today

The permanence of Molière in the repertory of the French theater is one of the characteristics, if not one of the surprising traits, of the twentieth century. A history of the brilliant productions, from those directed by Copeau in 1913 to those of today, directed by Jean Vilar and Jean Meyer, would itself constitute a long volume. Studies and monographs on Molière have never ceased to appear, until today his bibliography is one of the most voluminous on any major French writer. More significant than the multiple modes of interpreting Molière on the stage, more important than the countless erudite interpretive books on Molière, is the pleasure still afforded to spectators of Molière performances. The universality of his art is still enjoyed abroad. New translations are constantly appearing. One of the most recent is Richard Wilbur's excellent verse translation of *Le Misanthrope*. Although the rhythm and vigor of Molière's language cannot be translated into another tongue, the situation and characterization of his plays are sufficiently basic to the comic and the psychological spirit to assure some degree of success in skillful translation.

What elements of this art have assured its survival?

Why was Jouvet approved of by the Paris public when he claimed that Molière is the youngest of the French playwrights? Louis XIV once asked Boileau who in the critic's estimation was the greatest writer of his reign, in which one of the great writers of Paris and Versailles would his reign be best remembered. The answer was: "Molière, Sire." Bolieau's prophecy is fully justified in the twentieth century, when no playwright is more frequently performed in Paris, when the slightest deviation from the traditional interpretation of a Molière character is lengthily commented on and easily instigates a literary quarrel.

The uniqueness of Molière has become with time lucidly apparent. Other French playwrights were first writers and then writers for the theater. Their plays were first published texts and then texts to be performed on a stage. Molière's case was different from all others. He was first and always an actor. He was in addition the director of a theatrical company and hence responsible for the prosperity of the entire group. He was, thirdly, a writer and even a poet who furnished his actors with some thirty plays written over a period of fifteen years. Even Shakespeare in this respect cannot be compared with Molière. If Shakespeare was an actor as well as playwright, he did not direct the company nor feel responsible for the destiny of those who acted in his plays.

Some of the recent critical writing about Molière, Jouvet's, for example, and especially René Bray's, has presented a Molière having reality only on the stage of his theater, when he was speaking from the footlight row of candles, bedecked in the farcical costume of Mascarille or the green-ribboned jacket of Alceste, and repeating the mimicry and the grimaces that delighted the soldiers and the bourgeois standing in the pit as well as the nobles and the *précieuses* seated in the loges. Molière's total devotion to his calling is seen today as the leading trait of his character, so strong that it can explain his revolt against his father's trade of royal tapestry maker and the social ostracism that this young bourgeois accepted and never attempted to change during the thirteen years spent in the provinces on the precarious tour of the Illustre Théâtre, and the subsequent fifteen years in Paris and Versailles. The prestige of the theater was so intact for him, and his vocation of actor so irresistible, that this son of the merchant Poquelin learned willingly to live with the hazards, the jealousies, the endless risks of the world of the theater.

Early in his career Molière learned the varying unpredictable demands of the public. This was the monster he had to placate and cajole nightly. Valéry's general precept, in which he defines the public as the ever-present, ever-impure element of literature, *Il y a toujours dans la littérature ceci de "louche," la considération d'un public . . .*, applies more poignantly to Molière than to other writers. The care with which he directed rehearsals, the willingness with which he changed the text being rehearsed, his own skill as actor and particularly his comic talent, were commented on frequently during his own day. These traits of Molière as actor in his own plays, and as playwright for his own company, have received particular study in recent books of scholarship. His debt to the great Italian actors in the Paris of his day, and particularly to Tiberio Fiorelli, usually called Scaramouche, is as important as his more general debt to the style of the *commedia dell'arte.* The stylized burlesque acting and the principle of improvisation, characteristic of the *commedia,* are visible in Mascarille of *Les Précieuses ridicules,* in M. Jourdain of *Le Bourgeois gentilhomme,* in *Monsieur de Pourceaugnac.*

For the twentieth century, Molière has become first the actor who incarnated a large number of roles and imposed them on the public, and who secondly was a playwright, the intellectual member of a company of actors, who wrote and produced thirty comedies during the fifteen seasons of his Parisian career. He is unique in the annals of the French theater in that he was a poet who had an intimate and extensive experience with the stage. Molière wanted and needed the applause of a wide general public and not only the approval of a few intellectuals and critics. His goal was to afford pleasure to the spectators, to please his public. Success was the measure of his play's value. To reach this success and prolong it, he used every theatrical device and stratagem known to him. There are countless bravura passages, for example, which Molière unquestionably wrote as histrionic vehicles, as means of demonstrating an actor's virtuosity and hence stopping the show with applause: the famous portrait scene in *Le Misanthrope,* or Sganarelle's long moralistic speech to his master Dom Juan, whom he wants to save from damnation. Molière appreciated the value of plays written for one star, dominated by one leading character. In fact, he enjoyed being the star himself. This would be true of *L'Ecole des femmes,* in which he played the elderly Arnolphe. Out of the thirty-two scenes in the play, Arnolphe appears in thirty-one. *Le Misanthrope* is another star play, in which Alceste, originally acted by Molière, occupies seventeen of the twenty-two scenes.

From traditional farce, out of the heritage of Scaramouche, Molière borrowed a basic simple structure for his plays which explains to a large degree their momentum and dynamics and brio. Important scenes in many of the plays are sketches or skits, literary renditions of plots reminiscent of the *commedia dell'arte* and broad farce. These skits occur even in the highest comedies, the opening sonnet scene of *Le Misanthrope,* for example, and Monsieur Dimanche's scene in *Dom Juan,* but they are especially prevalent in the more general comedies, such as *Le Bourgeois gentilhomme,* where the music lesson of Act I and the philosophy lesson of Act II are set pieces for the virtuosity of the star. In such compositions, where sketches are fragments of the whole, the function of

Molière as poet seems to be subordinated to the talents of Molière as actor and Molière as director.

The basic structure of the comedies is usually very simple. *Le Misanthrope* is a succession of *contretemps*. Alceste wants an explanation from Célimène, and he makes four or five unsuccessful attempts to extract this explanation before succeeding. The work is constructed on a pattern and cadence not unlike a ballet choreography. The form of the comedies lends itself to an abundant use of *lazzi* or traditional comic gestures observed by Molière in the art of the Italian players he had seen in Lyon and Paris. His text calls for these gestures so naturally that there was little need to indicate them. They are often clownish and even scatological, as in the first-act ballet of *Monsieur de Pourceaugnac*.

Certain types recur in Molière's plays with the frequency of the types of the *commedia dell'arte*. The character called Scaramouche in *Le Médecin malgré lui* is fated to be tricked and deceived. This type, which is incorrigible, reappears with only slight variations as Harpagon in *L'Avare*, as Arnolphe in *L'Ecole des femmes*, as Jourdain in *Le Bourgeois gentilhomme*, as Chrysale in *Les Femmes savantes*, as Orgon in *Tartuffe*, and even as Alceste in *Le Misanthrope*. The recognition of stock characters is part of the classical tradition. In constantly rewriting the same play, Molière was elaborating on the lesson of Scaramouche, on the eternal game going on between the real world and the unreal world, or that world existing solely in the mind of a character.

Certain prevalent characteristics of Molière's plays, not always favored in other generations, have received particular commendation in our own. The tableau scenes, for example, where all or almost all of the characters appear together (such as the opening scene of *Tartuffe*) are justly admired today for their extraordinary dynamics, for the complicated and yet always clear rhythm of the many parts whose speech is acted and not declaimed. For a long time the denouements in Molière comedies have been castigated by academic criticism and looked upon as unimportant and sloppily put together by the poet. But such an astute contemporary scholar as Jacques Schérer finds in the denouements, which are usually tableau scenes of recognition and marriage, high moments in the dramatic art of Molière where situation and language reach a marked fullness and demonstrate a strong and necessary culmination. Jouvet, in his capacity as actor and director, agrees with Schérer that the form of the Molière comedy derives from pure theatrical convention, that every aspect of this form is directed by the playwright-actor's need to organize and project the plot and the characters. ⎿ 261

The position of Racine and the development of tragedy in France are vastly different from the achievement of Molière and the fate of comedy. Tradition, rules, and models were inherited by Racine who, with his poetic genius and his understanding of tragedy, was able to perfect the form and create a work that is still unrivaled in French. For Molière there was far greater freedom, a far greater necessity to create a form rather than to perfect one. The rules of Molière's comedies owe little to Aristotle and Horace. Because of propriety and custom he could hardly use Aristophanes, Terence, and Plautus as models. Molière was always closer to Scaramouche and the Italian tradition than to the classical. And yet Molière's art is literary and the *commedia dell'arte* was art based on spontaneity in performance, improvisation, fluidity of movement and speech.

The authenticity of Molière's speech, a trait that perhaps explains why he is the most universal French writer, is due largely, of course, to his genius. But it is also due to the literary form he elected. His diversity and his vision and his sense of humanity are perhaps less important to the world than Racine's poetry and sense of tragic intensity. But Racine's very perfection prevents his being appreciated to any large extent outside of France. The universality of Molière is doubtless due to his imperfections. In any strict sense, he is the least classical of the classical writers of Louis XIV. He risked too much, ranging too far from buffoonery to a high comedy that is almost tragedy. His extraordinary sense of the theater and of the public made it unnecessary for him to labor with the rigors of a Racine.

And yet he seems to possess for us today that precision of form which dramatic and literary critics of the nineteenth century denied him. An art that was once looked upon as perfunctorily thrown together is now seen as artfully conceived as a composition of Bach or Mozart where the entrances and the climaxes are meticulously timed. From various sources—rough medieval French farces, comedies of intrigue largely Italian in origin, burlesque Spanish models—Molière created French comedy and raised it to an aesthetic level that has not been surpassed, to a level of seriousness that Corneille had reached in the form of tragedy a generation earlier. Molière drew his subject matter from literary models to some extent, but especially from the human society he had observed, from family life, from his own knowledge of impostors, of *précieuses*, of affected fops, of cranks.

Since Molière's time, every new comedy of any worth has been compared with his. His influence has been far more extensive than Racine's, who so perfected the classical form of tragedy that since the time of his ineffectual imitators in the eighteenth century, almost no playwright has attempted to recreate the pure genre of tragedy which *Britannicus* represents. Molière's descendants live today. His method of selection of incidents that succeed one another and culminate at decisive moments is still the prevalent method used by the French playwright. Two or three well-chosen incidents are sufficient to outline and highlight the traits of a character. This brief reduced selectivity in Molière's art is in strong contrast with Shakespeare's.

A Shakespeare character is studied from so many different angles that we have the conviction of knowing everything about him, even the most subtle and the most subconscious traits of his personality. An American or an Englishman, familiar with the plays of Shakespeare, will be struck by the bareness and sparseness of Molière's delineations. Tartuffe, for example, one of Molière's most remarkable characters, is probably less fully drawn than Horatio is, not to mention Hamlet. Tartuffe does not appear until Act III (although the comedy is about him), and from that time to the end of the play we learn only three things about him: the falseness of his religious pretensions, his desire to seduce the wife of his friend, and his yearning for power, for control over the entire family in whose midst he lives. Molière's art lies in the fact that nothing in the play is said about Tartuffe or by him which is not related to one of these three points. Molière's art, and classical art in general, reveals not the complexity of human nature, but its intensity. And yet the essentials of Molière's characters are so relentlessly drawn that we feel their power as dramatically as we feel that of the characters of Shakespeare.

The doctrine of Molière's common sense, so laboriously annotated and repeated in the nineteenth century, does not account for the effects of grandeur, of near tragedy, of sublimity which characterize his achievements for twentieth-century audiences. The arrogance of Dom Juan's intellect, the repulsive spirit of Tartuffe, Philaminte's belief in the elevation of learning (*Les Femmes savantes*) demonstrate a few of the many sides of Molière's genius. The dramatic action of *Le Misanthrope* is beautifully relevant to the age of Louis XIV, but relevant also to any other age. This, of all of his plays, is perhaps the most successful, because in it his art seems equally compounded of lucidity of thought and profundity of observation. To portray a man in love with a coquette, with a Célimène, is not unusual. But to portray a misanthrope in love with a coquette is a master stroke. This is a play on the theme of disillusionment, with one of the sparest plots possible. Alceste, the suitor-misanthrope, tries unsuccessfully a few times to have a definitive conversation with the woman he loves. But Célimène lives in a *salon*, where she is surrounded by friends and admirers. The play ends when Alceste does have his definitive conversation. Between the opening scene, in which Alceste declares his rule of sincerity, and the final scene, when he announces his giving up of the world, the spectators are held by an extraordinary sequence of scenes depicting human conduct in many forms, and of lessons on the illusions and disillusions of the human heart.

Molière, at the head of the list as the principal source, and after him such writers of comedy as Marivaux, Beaumarchais, Musset, and in our own day, Jules Romains, Anouilh, and Roussin, are instructors of French ideas and French manners. They offer instruction in one of the pleasurable ways for which the French have always had a predilection: an evening spent in the theater. Viewed from an orchestra seat (*fauteuil d'orchestre*) or from a *strapontin* (a board filling the aisle space between orchestra chairs), or from a high, hard balcony seat, the pleasure is a plunge into human consciousness when the eyes and ears are enchanted, when all that is mental is externalized. Henry James, in an article called "The Parisian Stage" and dated 1872, describes the experience of a "cultivated foreigner" at the Comédie-Française. "He leaves the theatre," writes James, "an ardent Gallomaniac. This, he cries, is the civilized nation, *par excellence*. Such art, such finish, such grace, such taste, such a marvellous exhibition of applied sciences, are the mark of a chosen people, and these delightful talents imply the existence of every virtue." In 1955, when the Comédie-Française came to New York for the first time, Eric Bentley, writing about a performance of *Le Bourgeois gentilhomme*, declared: "The comic sense of life was more highly developed in Molière, it would seem, than in any other human being that ever existed, and he gave this sense the purest expression one can ever imagine its having."

To define Molière's art in terms of academic categories is futile, because he always exceeds them and overflows their limits. His exuberance and breadth seem to belie the formal aspects of his plays, which are in harmony with academic rules. He is of the academy and of something else that is solely Molière. He is a necessity of life, not a mere luxury, for the French. They recognize themselves in Molière and in a form acceptable to their taste for arrangement and swiftness. The morality of the plays is palatable to them because of the laughter and the controtions with which it is served. Molière is not a playwright of frivolity, and the French theater is not solely a source of amusement. It is a process of action and response to action, an institution that exists for the good of all and thanks to the support of all. The principal theater of France is rightfully called *la maison de Molière* and its actors the "children of Molière." When the theatrical season is poor in Paris, producers have simply to revive a comedy of Molière and the vitality of the French theater is once again restored. Molière is one of the common memories of the French, of their childhood, of their classroom, of their first visit to Paris and the *matinées classiques* on Thursday at the Théâtre Française. He is their common memory and also their standard of a kind of balance according to which they learn to live—a balance between vehemence and discretion, between passion and self-control.

As in almost every aspect of the modern French theater, Jacques Copeau pioneered in initiating the revival of Molière. Between his opening production at Le Vieux-Colombier, of *L'Amour médecin*, in October 1913, and *Le Misanthrope*, in March 1919, Copeau revived six comedies (*L'Avare*, December 1913; *La Jalousie du Barbouillé*,

February 1914; *Les Fourberies de Scapin,* November 1917; *Le Médecin malgré lui,* November 1918). Copeau's fundamental theory of the stage was easily illustrated in his treatment of Molière. He looked upon the stage as being first the action of the play, the space that materializes the form of the action. (*Le tréteau est déjà l'action; il matérialise la forme de l'action. . . .*) Then, as soon as the stage is filled by the actors, filled by their movement, it disappears as stage. (*Lorsque le tréteau est occupé par les comédiens, lorsqu'il est pénétré par l'action même—il disparaît. . . .*) A Molière text is admirably suited to Copeau's belief that the essential phase of a *mise-en-scène* is the reconstruction of the movement of the play. The production is a visual synthesis (as opposed to a literary emphasis) when the stage takes on its full meaning at the moment it ceases to be a stage.

Dullin's production of *L'Avare* was his most successful (and most famous). In it he deliberately went against the established and false tradition of the nineteenth century. He refused to force the character of Harpagon, which he himself played, but rediscovered for it the fundamental simplicity and even coarseness of the miser. He treated the play as a farce in which the leading character faced a series of oppositions which never altered his basic disposition, his basic reality. Dullin's acting was always carefully planned and precise, but every detail of his acting Harpagon contributed to what he had decided upon as the unalterable temperament of the character.

Louis Jouvet went further than Dullin in his separation from the traditional style of a Molière performance. Jouvet, more perhaps than any single person in the twentieth century, is responsible for the focus on Molière-as-actor rather than Molière-as-writer. His goal, forcefully defined in a lecture (published in *Les Annales* of June 1936), was to strip Molière of all trappings of literary naturalism and to restore to him his rightful "surreality." Jouvet disclaimed all credence in the familiar tag, "Molière's philosophy of common sense." Molière is pure theater, whose genius is visible in the scenic power of the performances. Jouvet taught that the actor has to find for himself the fictional character he is incarnating, and once this is discovered, the dramatic situation will unfold in rhythmical forms and movements.

Christian Bérard designed the set for Jouvet's production of *L'Ecole des femmes*. The *mise-en-scène* and the set as well were closely allied with Jouvet's interpretation of Arnolphe. The garden that opened out was both the place where Arnolphe tried to conceal Agnès and the trap where he was finally caught. Jouvet believed that the plays of Molière have remained youthful although they have been emasculated and distorted by academic prejudice and scholarship. In a text published in *Conférencia* in September 1937, Jouvet claims we must forget Molière the moralist and rediscover Molière the dramatist. He finds the dominant trait of the comedies to be the unreality or the surreality of the subject.

Three of Jouvet's productions were seriously criticized. His *Fourberies de Scapin*, which he directed for Jean-Louis Barrault at the Marigny, perhaps overemphasized the Harlequin mannerisms of Scapin, who is usually conceived of as being a tougher and more virile character. His *Tartuffe*, played by Jouvet himself in his own company, depicted a sincere character and hence seemed to contradict Molière's text itself. His *Dom Juan*, refurbished in an excessively Spanish style, was a courageous attempt to give a theatrical coherence to the most difficult of all of Molière plays.

Barrault played Scapin in the production directed by Jouvet for the Marigny. Although the fundamental conception of the role was criticized as diverging too widely from the text, its verve and remarkably sustained Dionysian quality made the performance into an intricately constructed ballet. The lyricism of Barrault's gesturing and caperings brought out the Italian sources of Molière's art. The style of acting that Barrault had been favoring throughout his career was given full expression in *Les Fourberies de Scapin*. It was more Italianate than Gallic, and for that reason perhaps it seemed foreign to the Paris public, too remote from the Molière they acknowledged as their own.

Amphitryon was given by Barrault an elaborate and handsome production. Here, too, there was exaggeration in the stylized acting. Barrault emphasized the lyric tenderness of the central scenes. The preciosity of the tone reminded the spectators more of Marivaux or Giraudoux than of Molière.

The Molière productions of Jean Vilar both in Avignon and in Paris have been adapted to a large stage (such as that of the Palais de Chaillot). The mixed popular elements of the large audiences for whom the Théâtre National Populaire was founded have also counted in Vilar's direction of *Le Médecin malgré lui, L'Avare,* and *Dom Juan.* For the latter play, one of Vilar's most notable successes, he devised a complex movement for the scenes between Dom Juan (played by Vilar himself) and Sganarelle (played by Sorano). The setting and the *mise-en-scène* were the opposite of the reduced Italianate type of stage. They were expansive symbolic sets.

Under the direction of Pierre Aimé Touchard, the Comédie-Française has offered in recent years several revivals and completely refurbished productions of Molière. *Le Misanthrope,* directed by Pierre Dux, and *Monsieur de Pourceaugnac, Le Bourgeois gentilhomme,* and *Les Fourberies de Scapin,* directed by Jean Meyer, are only a few of the more notable successes. It must be said that in all these productions the basic principle of the Comédie-Française remains the same: the declamatory element is still uppermost. The emphasis is always on what the voice can produce. The text of the play is recited and projected by the many possible intonations of the human voice. Gesture and action are so subordinated to the voice that at times they seem a mere commentary.

Molière criticism began a new phase with Jouvet's *Conférencia* article. This text of the actor-director represented the first major attack on Molière looked upon essentially as moralist, on the Molière explicated by the scholars, who had always failed to consider Molière as essentially the director-actor. Pierre Brisson's study of 1942, *Molière, sa vie dans ses oeuvres*, is, as the title suggests, an interpretation of the comedies in terms of the anecdotes of Molière's life, in terms of the not always trustworthy biographical material on the playwright. In the following year the university world seemed to make a determined traditional reply in Professor Daniel Mornet's book, *Molière*, which is primarily an apology of Molière as the French writer who best illustrates the philosophy of *le naturel et la raison*, of natural man and rationalism.

A few years later, in a study of French classicism, *Morales du grand siècle* (1948), Paul Bénichou claimed that Molière follows no coherent system of philosophy. He analyzed what he considered the central theme in all of the comedies. It is a moral problem, an effort to bring about a union between the natural instincts of man and his will as it adjusts to the various norms of society.

Soon after the appearance of Bénichou's work, an English critic, W. G. Moore, published his *Molière: A New Criticism* (1949), which incorporates and expands the ideas of Jouvet. Mr. Moore treats Molière primarily as a man of the theater, less interested in ridiculing the bourgeois, the hypocrites, and the libertines than in discovering the comic power in their characters. The leading character, in many instances, tries to have himself considered by others something that he is not. Tartuffe, for example, pretends religious piety in order to conceal his sexual desires. Arnolphe, in *L'Ecole des femmes*, gives himself the airs of a tyrant to disguise his obsessive timidity. Mr. Moore reinterprets the traditionally criticized denouements when he sees them as skillfully organized scenic effects in keeping with the French tradition of presenting together at the end of a comedy all the characters for the unfolding of the plot-situation and for their final bow to the audience.

The most detailed analysis of the structure of the comedies and of the dramatic forms invented or developed by Molière is to be found in *La Dramaturgie classique,* by Jacques Schérer (1950). In this important work, the emphasis is exclusively on the technical skill evident in the composition of the comedies and derivative from Molière's experience as actor: that the star of the play can, with the right kind of text, project the play and endear it to the audience. René Bray, in his study *Molière, homme de théâtre* (1954), also emphasizes the dramaturgy of Molière and derives all aesthetic consideration from Molière as actor and director. His book provides a vast documentation on the actual performances of the plays in Molière's lifetime, on the actors and on the roles they played, and on the success of the plays.

The claim is usually made for comedy that it is more concrete, more close to life than other dramatic forms. It is said to be an easier form, more flattering to the public and hence reaching a wider one, and is looked upon as the expression of common sense, of everyday simplicity. Molière is not easily adaptable to these criteria. The continuing power of his comedies on the stage places him apart from the usual categories and outside of the usual rules. The meaning and the interpretation of each of his great comedies, *Tartuffe, Le Misanthrope, Dom Juan,* have been the subject of controversy and even of embittered argument. They hardly present Molière as a champion of reason and simplicity. It is quite true that these three comedies provide an array of familiar human "types" borrowed from life itself, and in this sense they belong to "comedy." But the traits of these characters and the problems that harass them are presented without the clarity and the simplification of traditional comedy. The wisdom of Molière cannot be contained within a narrow set of rules of conduct. It has to do first with behavior at court, with courtly civilization, but the court is only the symbol or the microcosm of society itself. Moreover, the rules of court etiquette are not unique to the age of Louis XIV. They go back in the history of France to the courtly spirit of the twelfth century, to the romances of Chrétien de Troyes. Every age of French civilization, but especially the twelfth century and the seventeenth, the ages of courtly love and preciosity, has tried to establish some equilibrium between the heart and the ceremony of love, between tenderness and pomp, between the religion of love and the cult of heroism.

To sustain his comedy, Molière draws upon the prosaic bourgeois types or the affected insincere types of his society. These, shockingly and comically, when contraposed to the innocence of Agnès or the love of Alceste, create the form of his plays. It is erroneous to say that Molière satirizes preciosity. He does this, in truth, when preciosity intellectualizes the desire for love and atrophies it. But he defends preciosity when it affirms the rights of love. Twice in his career, at the beginning and at the end, Molière treats the subject of love and preciosity in a direct fashion. In *Les Précieuses ridicules* he satirizes those girls who stupidly and effectedly sacrifice everything in life to the problem of love. In *Les Femmes savantes* he satirizes those women who sacrifice a simple instinctive love for the attraction of learning and pedantry. The debate is not easy to define, but Molière's position seems to be close to that of courtly literature, a compromise between an apology for the instinct of love and its condemnation.

Molière's relationship to preciosity is one of many instances where it is impossible to define him or explain him in terms of a system or a movement. He saw beneath the superficial aspects of reform a maze of contradictions. Preciosity both extolled love and condemned it. Without trying to solve it, Molière used with varying emphases the gigantic problem of woman's freedom. The problem stated bluntly would be: is it possible for woman to achieve a combination of sexual happiness and intellectual equality or intellectual dignity with man? And because Molière demonstrated various aspects of this question without presenting one solution, he is as contemporary with the twentieth century as he was with the seventeenth.

The mode of human conduct imposed upon man by such a highly artificial society as the court of Versailles is the immediate source of the problems and the actions in *Le Misanthrope.* In passage after passage, Alceste defines his opposition to court morality. He finds no compatibility, no virtue in himself that will permit him to succeed at court either in matters of business or in matters of love. He is unable to play the flatterer, the courtier who conceals his real thoughts and his real sentiments. He is unable to play the suitor who will tolerate a coquettish lady. By nature and even by his language, Alceste claims that he belongs to an earlier, more simple period in history. In the opening scene of the play, Philinte refers to the medieval rules of conduct by which Alceste lives and which are in strong contradiction with the prevailing morality.

The "surreality" of Molière's art, as Jouvet liked to call it, is fully attested to in *Le Misanthrope,* and especially in the central drama of Alceste. He has become both a famous figure in the French theater and a character in French history. Each age has watched him and listened to him, and found the moral and even the political preoccupation of the age reflected in him. On the simplest level, the misanthrope is a man who opposes the world and flails the relaxed morality and the compromises he finds prevailing in his own day. But Fénelon, in a celebrated passage against political despotism (*Lettre à*

L'Académie, VII), sees Alceste as the champion of an earlier and less rigid monarchical system than that of Louis XIV. Rousseau and the French Revolution defended the social theories of Alceste as against the conciliatory thesis of Philinte.

We are today three centuries away from Molière and more hesitant, as the newest witnesses of his comedies, than ever before at defining the playwright's moral attitude and the symbolism of his social problems. The pleasure afforded by these comedies in the theater itself continues unabated. Whatever debate is raised in an individual comedy receives a solution in the form of the play, in the denouement of the intrigue. The thought concerning human destiny is infinitely more decisive in a Racine or in a Pascal, more absolute than the thought of Molière. The comic playwright softens human anguish and with each comedy resolves it by means of the dramatic form. But this human anxiety does recur in some manifestation in each comedy, only to play itself out by the last curtain.

2. Mallarmé and the Aesthetics of the Theater

In addition to Mallarmé's principal work, the poems and prose poems, there exists a body of doctrine on poetry, ballet, theater, and music. This doctrine was undoubtedly expounded during the famous "conversations" on Tuesday evenings, between 1880 and 1898, when Mallarmé received in his Paris apartment and discussed in solo fashion in the presence of the leading writers and artists of the day theories and ideas that were closest to him. Some of this doctrine is to be found in the articles and chronicles that Mallarmé published during the last years of his life. It would be impossible to make out of what exists now in print a complete system of aesthetics. General principles can be fairly well established, and some of the details concerning poetry and the theater, in particular, offer rich suggestions about the essence of the theater and its future.

Mallarmé had the intelligence of a great critic. He was not primarily a thinker and his ideas are always expressed in terms of his art. His prevailing dogma was the reality of art. It alone exists. The profession of poet he looked upon as sacerdotal by nature. He never ceased reflecting upon the subject matter of art and on the characteristics of genius. Everything in his life was a pretext for investigating a bit further the aesthetic problem: concerts, plays, books, ballets at the Opéra, lectures. A few of the major texts concerning his doctrine—"*Lettre à Verlaine,*" of 1885, the preface to René Ghil's *Traité du verbe,* of 1886, the short articles grouped under the general title *Variations sur un sujet*—show Mallarmé to be a poet deeply conscious of the meaning of his craft and of its philosophical implications.

In an essay published in *La Revue Blanche* in 1895, on the subject "*Le Livre, instrument spirituel,*" Mallarmé acknowledges a major statement of his belief, which had been used for and against him. This is the famous remark that everything exists in the world in order to end in a book: *tout, au monde, existe pour aboutir à un livre.* . . . The purpose of poetry is therefore to explain the world. If to this cardinal belief one adds Mallarmé's often reiterated precept that things count only because of their symbolic meaning, one has a schematized view on the French poet's idealism. All parts of reality are signs, and the purpose of poetry is to express man, not in his isolated individuality, but in his infinite relationships with everything. When Mallarmé capitalizes the word "book," *Le Livre,* he endows it with an absolute meaning.

The usual book of poems Mallarmé called a *grimoire,* a conjuror's book. Verse has an incantatory power. The act of writing verse is the adding of black to the white page, the adding of a human mystery to the immaculateness of white. A volume of verse is something definitive, a figuration of eternity. It is fixed forever in its form, and yet it is the source of an infinite number of suggestions. The reader never reaches the end of their meanings. This spiritual object, the book, moves the reader toward a secretive inner life. The effect upon a reader of such a book is the opposite of the effect of the performance of a play on the spectator. Mallarmé argued with himself about these problems and these differences, and seemed to reach the

significant conclusion that the highest form of poetry will
be that written for dramatic presentation before a public.
The ideal Book, *Le Livre,* is a complicated system of
hieroglyphics and the symbol of everything. But the
Theater is that form of art which will have a direct effect
upon the public and initiate it to the greatest of the
metaphysical problems.

In 1886 Mallarmé served as dramatic critic for *La Revue
Indépendante.* In general, he attended the theater in-
frequently, and his articles, grouped under the title
"*Crayonné au théâtre*" in *Divagations* of 1897, are not
dramatic criticism in the usual sense. The performance of
a play was for Mallarmé an occasion to meditate upon the
meaning of the theater and to enrich his mind concerning
his theory of the absolute theater. He seemed to enjoy
circus performances and fairs more than the legitimate
theater. At the circus the large crowds, eager for entertainment and expressive of their feelings, gave him a sense
of being alone and withdrawn. In the theater itself he
contemplated the center chandelier, *le lustre,* which
curiously had attracted Baudelaire also. He was fascinated
by the shining crystal reflecting the lights and the spectators. Mallarmé's meditations on the theater prolong his
meditations on the Book. To be present at the première
of a play is comparable to cutting the pages of a book
and reading it for the first time. If everything in the world
exists in order to end in a book, Mallarmé seems to add,
in his pages on the theater, that the Book in turn ends by
reaching a dramatic form. The power of the Book is the
infinite number of suggestions which reading generates,
and the Theater's function is to exteriorize this power of
suggestion.

As an initial parenthesis for one of his essays in "*Crayonné au théâtre,*" Mallarmé makes the claim that the
theater is the highest form of literature: *Le Théâtre est
d'essence supérieure.* (*Le Genre ou des modernes.*) This
claim is deeply embedded in his essay on *Hamlet,* where

the poet uses the verb "exteriorize" in explaining how Hamlet is the projection on the stage of the single character in an intimate, secret tragedy: *Hamlet extériorise, sur des planches, ce personnage unique d'une tragédie intime et occulte.* The very name of Hamlet, Mallarmé continues to say, exerts a strange power of fascination on him and on the rest of us. This fascination is closely allied to anguish. The principal theme of the essay is the poet's attempt to explain this feeling. He feels it to be a universal experience and one that is precipitated in us as we watch the solitary drama of Hamlet, "the walker in the labyrinth of unrest and grievance." (*Ce promeneur du labyrinthe de trouble et de griefs. . . .*)

When Hamlet appears on the stage, each of us sees in him the adolescent that we once were. This adolescent has disappeared, and yet he haunts us because of the suit of mourning he insists upon wearing. Hamlet exteriorizes the struggle that each of us carries on daily: the suffering we feel in *appearing* before the world, in *seeming* to be the character the world expects us to be. Mallarmé calls him *l'adolescent . . . qui se débat sous le mal d'apparaître . . .* , and such a sentence recalls Hamlet's words to the Queen: "Seems, Madame, nay it is. I know not seems."

Mallarmé sees Hamlet as "the latent Lord," the adolescent who is struggling to achieve himself, to become someone else: a more mature man. Hamlet is the juvenile ghost in us. Before he analyzes this struggle specifically, Mallarmé broadens this first observation into a very general and all-inclusive theory. He claims that there is no other subject for man, and then he states what he considers the general conditions for tragedy: the antagonism that exists in man between his dreams and the fatality meted out to his existence by disaster. Shakespeare's play is so constructed as to provide the central drama of man's mind. Tragedy is therefore the losing fight that the spirituality of man (dreams, ambitions, ideals) wages against the mortal realities of the world.

Hamlet was one of Mallarmé's lifelong obsessions. In his first letter to Henri Cazalis—written in May 1862, when the poet was twenty—he compares himself to Hamlet in his habit of remaining days on end inactive and passive. "A ludicrous Hamlet," he writes, "who doesn't even realize his collapse." (*Ridicule Hamlet qui ne peut se rendre compte de son affaissement. . . .*) In the celebrated clown sonnet, *"Le Pitre châtié,"* of which the first version was probably written in Tournon in 1864, he compares the clown who has escaped from his tent, to a bad Hamlet denying his vocation. In his final poem, on which he was working just before he died, *"Un Coup de dés,"* there is in the elaborate shipwreck scene a fairly obvious reference to Hamlet as the "bitter prince of the reef" (*prince amer de l'écueil . . .*) and to the feather of his cap as it disappears in the foam (*. . . la plume s'ensevelir aux écumes. . . .*)

The prose poem *"Réminiscences"* (first called *"L'Orphelin"*), without referring specifically to Hamlet, alludes to one of the most significant aspects of the Hamlet drama for Mallarmé, the son's search for his father. An orphan child approaches the son of a circus acrobat. The circus grounds and the circus family are briefly sketched. As the acrobat's son practices his leaps and pirouettes, he asks the orphan about his parents. When he learns that the boy has none, he expatiates on the joy of having parents who are entertaining. The drama of this brief prose poem is in the orphan's search for a father. This is carried on subconsciously at first, and then, with the conversation, becomes a conscious problem. The orphan is Hamlet, and the drama is the son's world in need of a father. This illustrates the antagonism that Mallarmé refers to: between the drama of man and the harsh fatality of his life and his condition.

Mallarmé is referring either to France alone or to Europe generally when he says that "our one splendor is the stage." The various arts used in play productions have given the stage a religious or official character, and Mallarmé adds to this definition the belief that the end of the century has shown little concern for this conception of the theater. The criticism that the poet levels at the theater of his day centers about its negligence of metaphysics. He sees the action of the characters on the stage so constructed and organized as to avoid very deliberately any metaphysical problem. He speaks somewhat favorably of Maurice Maeterlinck, whose *Pelléas et Mélisande* he looks upon as a superior variation, in its numerous brief tableaux, of the lusty old type of melodrama. In their avoidance of the metaphysical, Mallarmé reproaches the modern playwrights with presenting a false picture of man. Hence, the theater of his day has become incapable of subtlety.

This general criticism of the theater is similar to Mallarmé's criticism of the poetry of his day. Both arts, dramatic and lyric, had grown heavy with conventions. The actual poems of Mallarmé were to act as a liberation from the stereotyped romantic and Parnassian forms. In his critical pages on the theater, he expresses the hope that a comparable liberation will take place for that literary genre. The program for this liberation he sees in the example of Wagner, in the behavior and aspiration of large public assemblies on holidays, and finally in the performance and the significance of the Catholic mass.

It would seem that Mallarmé had very little knowledge of Wagner before the year 1885. *La Revue Wagnérienne* was founded in that year by Edouard Dujardin, and Mallarmé contributed to the issue of August 8, 1885, his article *"Richard Wagner: Rêveries d'un poète français."* In a letter to Dujardin, Mallarmé himself characterized this piece as "half article, half prose poem." He had not seen at that time a performance of a Wagnerian opera. In the years that followed, Wagner and the meaning of Wagner's art were habitual subjects of Mallarmé's conversations. His sonnet on Wagner celebrates the advent and the triumph of a new art.

Wagner seems to represent an important stage in the evolution of Mallarmé's thought concerning the supreme art or the final art, which he will define as the theater. His first interest in Wagner was undoubtedly the consequence of his admiration for Baudelaire. For Baudelaire, Wagner had emphasized the unity of myth as the ideal subject for the poet. (*Le mythe est le poème primitif et anonyme du poète.*) In the subsequent years, when Mallarmé regularly attended symphony concerts in Paris and became familiar with Wagner's music, he did not continue to comment on his impressions. But at this time of his most fanatical belief in Wagner, about 1885, Mallarmé expressed reservations about Wagnerism and Wagner's conception of the theater.

The French poet looked upon the Wagnerian synthesis of the arts as depriving each individual art of its full power of expression. He was hostile to the concept of adding up the arts and simply fusing them. In the light of his final theory of the theater, Mallarmé would criticize the use of anecdote and even legend in the Wagnerian drama, and the use of actors, and the use of a realistic setting. Mallarmé had no technical competence to judge the music of Wagner, but as a poet deeply concerned with the art of the theater, he did have serious reservations on the works of Wagner as syntheses of poetry, music, and dramatic action. His notations on the Catholic mass clarify and help define the kind of synthesis he believed the theater should represent.

A brief but significant article on *"Plaisir sacré,"* first published in *Le Journal* of December 5, 1893, is one of Mallarmé's most lucid texts on the role of the spectators in the theater. He is speaking of the first Paris concerts in the autumn. At the very time when the foliage disappears from the trees, and when the Parisians return from their vacation, the resumption of life in the city is symbolized by the raised baton of the orchestra leader at the first concert of the season. The sparkle of the candelabra, high above the heads in the center of the hall, reflects the eagerness of the spectators. All social classes have gathered here, but not, according to Mallarmé, for purely aesthetic reasons, not for the simple reason of listening to music, but for deeply embedded religious reasons. For the general public of our large metropolitan cities, music has replaced official and religious celebrations. It is a form of worship, a cult seemingly aesthetic, but in reality primitive and religious. The modern poet has not been able to assemble such a large crowd of spectators because his art has not sustained the ineffable and the pure quality of music. These people gathered in the concert hall, are, once outside, preoccupied with politics and the multiple problems of daily existence, but they have felt the need to come into the presence of the ineffable and the pure, this wordless poetry called music!

Mallarmé ponders over this mystification. This Sunday assembly of people who have chosen the particular pleasure of music have made it into a *sacred pleasure* (*Plaisir sacré*). Mallarmé calls it a religious service (*un office*). The members of this public are the guardians of a mystery. And this mystery is their own because it has taken the place of their religion. The attention they pay to clothes is more than a superficial habit. The elegance and the jewels of the women represent more than mere fashion. The spectators form a collective greatness and fidelity, as indispensable to the occasion as the music itself and the musicians!

Mallarmé first attended these concerts *par badauderie*, that is, dilatorily and without profound purpose. But gradually he became aware of something secretive, significant, and concealed which inhabits such a crowd of spectators. The subconscious, mysterious reason for these autumnal and winter gatherings first directed Mallarmé's thought concerning the role of the theater. The miracle of music is to create a reciprocal penetration—of spectators and of myth. They are literally an element of the spectacle —whether the spectacle is play or music or ballet. Whatever is being performed moves from the stage to the public and then back to the stage. The performance is controlled and animated by the spectators.

When Mallarmé said that "our one splendor today is the stage," he acknowledged that this is due in large part to the religious or official character of the theater. (*Le Genre ou les modernes*). The source of the modern world —Mallarmé calls it the "incubation" of the modern world— is the Middle Ages. This statement is found in the brief essay *"Catholicisme,"* which Mallarmé first published in *La Revue Blanche* in April 1895, and which contains most of his thought on the significance of the mass as it relates to the theater.

The mass is the prototype of all ceremonials because the sacrament of the mass—the consecration of the Host— designates communion. The sacrament is one, and yet it is partaken of by everyone. By extension, Mallarmé establishes the parallel with tragedy, which also is one and is experienced by everyone in the theater. The mass centers about the "Real Presence." God is present in one substance at the consecration of the mass, and yet He is diffused also and enters the body of every communicant. The actor is a single living presence on the stage, and as he performs his role he is assumed into every spectator by his gesticulations and movements and by the authenticity of the text he recites.

Mallarmé himself never expressed any personal belief in the dogmas of the Church. He even appeared somewhat hostile to Catholicism. Hence, his doctrine on the drama of the mass and his comments on the behavior of the faithful during the celebration of the mass are all the more striking. Catholic liturgy and the singing of hymns, responses, and motets impressed Mallarmé, and the responses from the congregation—in Latin, which they often did not understand—seemed to him expressions of exaltation. Mallarmé was able to look upon himself momentarily as a believer and realize that the drama of the mass was so profound that it voided or subsumed all other dramas. At each mass, for the believer, the supreme drama of the world is re-enacted, namely, the Incarnation of God. At the most solemn moment of the mass, when silence falls over the priests and the people, and when the ringing of a tiny bell is entrusted to a child, the silent gestures of the celebrant remind Mallarmé of his ideal theater, where one character suffices for the action, as in the tragedy of *Hamlet.*

These comments on the mass are closely related, for Mallarmé, to his aesthetic beliefs. The creation of art is of no use, he would say, unless it ends by saving mankind. The people subconsciously demand this of the poet. In *"Plaisir sacré"* Mallarmé raises the question of social snobbery as the reason for people attending the autumn concerts, but he gives a negative answer to this query. More religious reasons motivate their attendance. Art would seem to be for Mallarmé, if we interpret his pages correctly, a way of achieving a collective salvation. This element of his aesthetics would seriously invalidate an aesthetics of the void or of absence or of despair, which has often been proposed as Mallarmé's aesthetics.

The truth of a poetic or dramatic text, discovered by the poet, is preserved by the public. In a strictly theological sense, the mass can be celebrated by one priest without anyone else present. But Mallarmé, in the analogy he establishes between the celebration of the mass and the performance of a play, is thinking of the successive assemblies of people who assure the continuance of a work through time. A play, for its projection, demands the real presence of an actor, and the mass is centered around the "Real Presence." A tragedy, for Mallarmé, is not simply a secular counterfeit of the mass, because the god is present in the actor as he mimes the gestures of the god and diffuses his spirit throughout the audience. As the spectators are penetrated by this mimed action, they are transformed and begin participating in life different from their daily life, and one that is in accord with a new truth.

Mallarmé attaches a mystical power to the aspirations of the public. In reality the public is an actor participating as much in the action of a tragedy as the faithful participate in the mass. And Mallarmé without difficulty can extend the analogy of these kinds of participation to the reading of a book. A book, too, is a communion because each reader is able to read it in its totality without diminishing it. Hence the ideal Book and the ideal Theater are analogous. But only in the theater will poetry, in its complete liturgical form, be celebrated. A poem in a book is comparable to a private prayer said at home, whereas a poem enacted in the theater is comparable to the mass. The consequence of this thought is obvious to Mallarmé: no poet can afford to remain indifferent to the theater. The work, when it is triumphant, will bring about the disappearance of the poet as a human being. But it will, simultaneously, create and consecrate, so to speak, the public.

In speaking of the ideal form of writing for the theater, Mallarmé alludes consistently to aspects of the Wagnerian music drama and to the Catholic mass. This ideal form he names on several occasions the "ode." The ode and the ideal play represent a synthesis of poetry and music. This kind of poetry cannot be separated from holidays and feast days that all the people celebrate together. The ode is a kind of dramatization of heroic scenes in which several voices may be heard. It has the power of uniting the people around it, with a view toward celebration. This theory of Mallarmé is obscure and extremely difficult to follow. It is possible that its clue, its elucidation, is to be found in *"Igitur,"* and, to some slighter degree, in *Héro-*

diade and in the final poem *"Un Coup de dés jamais n'abolira le hasard."*

It would seem that drama for Mallarmé arises out of a conflict between two protagonists: the hero (or Igitur) who is capable of producing a work, and chance (or Le Hasard), which seems to represent a synthesis of all the forces in the world bent upon opposing the hero in the creation of his work. Igitur, in the tale of that name, triumphs over Le Hasard and demolishes chance. This work seems to be for Mallarmé the revelation of what the ideal theater is to be and what it is to include. There is one character, hero and protagonist, and one antagonist, complementary to the hero, who represents all the circumstances of life.

It is not difficult to claim that in the realm of poetry the work of Stéphane Mallarmé raised all the leading questions of aesthetics and offered answers that form a coherent poetics. In this system, such problems as the meaning of life and the meaning of reality are not absent. Nor is the poet himself neglected as a psychological phenomenon. Mallarmé believes that the genius of the poet derives from an exceptional freedom and boldness. He is the martyr of his conscience and its hero as well. He is the man, typifying the artist to a supreme degree, who in the creation of his work passes from the known to the unknown, if the point of departure for the poet is a familiar object or a familiar experience, his art culminates in an awareness of the boundless, the unmeasurable, the original terror that primitive man felt for the mysteries of nature and the mysteries of the unseen. In this basic conception of his poetics, as well as in his few scattered notations on the theater, Mallarmé pointed the way to a revision of values in the art of the dramatic poet.

3. The French Theater and the Concept of Communion

The absolute meaning of tragedy may well be impossible to ascertain. No concept in the domain of human existence has been so insistently explored. It would seem that by defining pure tragedy, man would move into the center of a new understanding of himself and of life. In its eternal joining of life and death, and in its constant concern with life after death, the concept of tragedy is perhaps unique in its power of illuminating the entire cycle of life-death-life.

Today the term is most frequently used in its literary application. The more general uses: "the tragedy of an existence," "the tragedy of an event," seem to have some connection, however vague, with the literary genre. And yet without the single domain of the literary genre, there are at least two extreme forms, and multiple variations of tragic intensity and expression between the extremes. On the one hand, tragedy tends toward the grandiloquent. It offers a moving spectacle of the sublime. This may involve a human sacrifice for the social good, a hero's death on the battlefield, a military tragedy. It is the form often conceived with official pomp and discourse, where the sentimental life of the hero is generalized and universalized. More appealing to the masses than other forms of tragedy, it can arouse a collective enthusiasm by means of its half lyric, half moralizing style. Both Hugo and Rostand knew the art of offering to a vast public the sublime in its more recognizable and simplified form of sentimentality. The tragic flaw of character receives in their dramas a more elementary illustration in the social ostracism of the hero or in a physical lack of beauty.

At the other extreme, in the art of Racine, tragedy may be stripped of its grandiloquence and of its sacrifice for the good of the social group. It may be here the art of very intense intimacy, where man is seen in his essen< as the victim of the most basic passions: love, jealousy, anger, pride, suffering, death. In this form, which has seldom been successful outside of the Sophoclean and Racinean tragedy, the private world of the hero counts far more than the outside world of men. In Racine, tragedy is immutable, inevitable, fixed at the very heart of a world that is its opposite, a world in flux, submitted to chance and variation. Hugo and Racine admirably illustrate these two extremes: the one, exaggerated in its simplicity, in which the poet sings the sentiment of misfortune; the other, exaggerated in its secrecy, in which the poet sings the tragic fate.

Of literary provenience, without any doubt, tragedy cannot be separated from its speculative-philosophical meaning. Between Aristotle, whose precepts are still studied and questioned, and Bergson, who defines tragedy as the glorification of the individual (in the last chapter of *Le Rire*), philosophers have never ceased meditating on the tragic destiny of man as illustrated by the great literary tragedies of the world, on the meaning of tragic emotions performed on the stage thanks to the art of the poet, and aroused thereby in the spectators themselves. The history of the theater and its accompanying philosophical inquiries seem to provide the surest guide to the meaning of tragedy.

The origins of the sacred dances of India are so obscure that it is impossible to explore them with any degree of historical accuracy. But the origins of the Greek theater in religious rite—in the Dionysian festivals that in Athens took place at the beginning of winter and which celebrated the death of the god—have been made more accessible to the modern scholar. The winter death of the vine plant was only a temporary death. It was death bound up with the hope of resurrection. Friedrich Nietzsche studied in the very name itself of tragedy—the song of the goat— its sacrificial meaning, its religious solemnity. He traces, in *The Birth of Tragedy,* the subtle and all-pervasive relationship existing between tragedy and dithyramb, between an altar sacrifice and a bacchic song. The transformation from a dithyrambic poem to a tragic poem is the transformation of a tale or a recital into an action. In the spring festivals, when the god, after his winter death and immobility, emerged from the cask of wine, the joy of resurrection was surely sung and performed with comic improvisation—such as were to exist later in the medieval marketsquare performers, in the *commedia dell'arte* of the sixteenth century, and even in the more purely literary comedies of Molière and Marivaux.

The attention that the origins of tragedy have received during the past one hundred years has accented the religious activity and hence has pointed out the religious value or meaning of all tragedy, which continues to contain some analogy with the exercise of worship. It is quite evident that a tragedy of Sophocles was for an Athenian citizen of the fifth century before Christ a participation in a public act of worship. The medieval theater in France, while bearing no resemblance in a literary sense to Greek tragedy, represented a continuation of the Catholic mass and religious devotion. The earlier writings were purely liturgical, interpolated in the mass itself at the great festivals of Christmas and Easter, and performed at the altar. As the interpolations grew longer and more autonomous, they were performed outside the church, at the portals first, and then on temporary stages (*tréteaux*) on the square. But the medieval *mystères* and *miracles* were performed under the patronage of the Church and supervised by the clergy. From the twelfth to the beginning of the sixteenth century, this was the only form of serious theater in France, a form that during its long evolution became diffuse and at times even obscene, but that never lost its affiliation with its obvious religious origins.

Then, quite abruptly, with the edict of Parlement (1548) forbidding performances of the mystery plays (to amuse and hold the public the actors had added improvisations that were often not only obscene but even blasphemous), the French theater made a completely new start in 1552 (*Cléopâtre* of Etienne Jodelle) with an imitation, in form and content, of Greek tragedy. In the French tragedy of the sixteenth century, the more purely profane elements of the Greek plays were incorporated and the more primitive religious character was so diminished that it became practically nonexistent. Even in the tragedies of Robert Garnier, where the subject matter is borrowed from the Bible (*Les Juives*), and which are the forerunners of the religious tragedies of Corneille (*Polyeucte*) and Racine (*Athalie*), there is little trace of religious celebration. Likewise in the Elizabethan theater the religious element is absent. Only in the Spanish writings of Lope de Vega and Calderón is there a marked trace of the religious origins of tragedy.

In the perfected form of the Racinean tragedy, more than one hundred years after the first example of classical French tragedy, the poet composes tragedy in terms of the bond existing between the destiny of man and the destiny of the universe. A profoundly religious sentiment is present in Racine, even if the exterior form of the tragedy is foreign to any religion. Hellenic and Racinean tragedy have in common a vision of man's fate in its passionate nature and in the fortuitous aspect of his adventures. For Greek tragedy the laws of a man's life, his fate, guide him as directly to catastrophe as the fatal play of passion in Racine's tragedy orientates his hero to the same end. In his preface to *Phèdre*, Racine states this claim, which his theater fully illustrates: Phèdre is predestined to commit a crime she abhors, in the same way that Oedipus (in Sophocles) is predestined to the crimes of patricide and incest, both of which he did all in his power to avoid. This entire theory of fate is as difficult to explain as it is mysterious in its unfolding. Its secret may well belong to the mystery cults of Eleusis, referred to in Plato's dialogues. The rite of tragedy, in its most primitive and significant meaning, is the rite of man in conflict with his most dangerous passions. It is the celebration of man consecrated to catastrophe, and a celebration of such an order, of such dignity in an aesthetic sense, that the society watching it may become aware of itself and live more profoundly with itself and its final end. Oedipus and Phèdre enact the mystery of their fate, which is a power beyond themselves, and each is sacrificed before a society that derives from that very sacrifice, acted as a play, a liberation that bears some analogy with the liberation of death portrayed on the stage. It would seem that the tragic hero with his desire, so compelling that it is total, approaches the status of the gods and hence arouses their jealousy. Prometheus is exalted by a divine power and hence finds himself a rival of the gods.

The epic hero, who today finds his counterpart in the novel and the film, is not purely the type of tragic hero because his actions are more familiar to his audience. The tragic hero is more separated from society, more alone, more untouched by the manifold ways in which society daily tries to assuage suffering. The hero of the modern novel and the film has to be close enough to the ordinary man in their vast audiences so that the reader and the spectator can identify himself with the hero. The identification between spectator and hero of a tragedy exists to a far less degree because the latter must appear more significant than the ordinary man, more capable of resisting an unmerited fate, more glorious in his final capitulation before it. The world depicted in Greek tragedy was always that of the gods and heroes. There is still something of the greatness of that world in *Hamlet,* in *Britannicus,* as well as in the contemporary tragedies of Giraudoux and Montherlant and Sartre. The whole meaning of catastrophe depends somewhat on the greatness of the character of the man who is going to suffer from it. The tragic hero must represent more than an existence of an ordinary citizen. He must be, in some sense or other, a prince, a representative, an archetype, a single man sufficiently profound to assume the lot of others. The hero of a novel or of a film is not defined by this degree of magnitude. If he were, it would alienate him somewhat from the tremendous public of the movies, the public accustomed to the form of tragedy depicted by a Chaplin or by a typist whose speech and whose pathos are fully recognizable by the average man and woman and child. And if, on the other hand, a tragedy written for the theater concerns an average man as hero (cf. the plays of Arthur Miller and Pagnol), an unusual degree of discomfort is felt by the audience because of the disproportion between the character of the hero and the absoluteness of the catastrophe. There is more time in a novel and more precision in a film, because of the rapid eye of the camera, to offset a tragic force by the depiction of the myriad forms of existence which daily surround tragedy and diminish it, than in a pure tragedy for the theater, where there is little time outside of that consecrated to the preparation and enactment of the tragic event. If tragedy in its pure form is the inevitable and deliberate unfolding of fate, the novel and the film are both closer to the documentation, preparatory for the possible unfolding of fate, a documentation close to the chaotic mode of daily existence, where rules of society and behavior interpose themselves between man and himself or man and his fate.

The first form of the Catholic mass, which evolved sometime between Sophocles and Racine, bears unquestionably a strong relationship with primitive tragedy. The celebrant-priest incarnates the hero-Christ who is going to die. The deacon and the subdeacon are subordinate actors, and the whole drama of consecration is carried out with the spectators, the faithful, answering the priests. When the actors and the spectators, in their combined parts, forget their own individual selves, they participate in the tragedy of redemption with something of the religious fervor that must have characterized the theater of Dionysus in Athens. The deepest meaning of this literary form is perhaps best stated in the mystery and the oxymoron of the phrase: tragedy of redemption. The two terms, so eloquently used by Nietzsche in his *The Birth of Tragedy,* "Apollonian" and "Dionysian," help to explain the evolution from a recital of a story, the epic of Apollonian content, to the dramatization, the tragedy or Dionysian form. Thus a myth of a historical event may be transformed into a drama. The poet, in his tragedy, identifies himself in some degree with his heroes as they experience the dramatic action. He lives their action as the spectators in their turn will participate in its enactment. There is always a narrative element in a tragedy which preserves an ancient affiliation with the epic, with the recited story, with the Apollonian element. The Dionysian element, or the action of fate on a human existence, cannot be realized in tragedy without this co-operation and fusion. Likewise, in the life of a religious, pure contemplation is seldom unaccompanied by the action of grace, the violent modification of the individual.

The need of tragedy, of its composition and its performance, must come from the fact that man, despite all the constraints and protections of civilization (marriage, work, diversion, etc.) needs to see the picture of his love, hate, jealousy, death. The deeply rooted drive in man toward his own destruction is surely one of the major explanations of tragedy in its literary manifestation. When the violence of tragedy is cast into a poetic form and played on a stage, the very violence of destruction appears miraculous. This is of course predominantly true of the mass and true always in some degree of a secular play because of the element of redemption inherent in tragedy. The final words of Hamlet and the final words of Phèdre are striking examples of this redemptive force that tragedy releases and which permits the spectators to follow the drama of destruction. Just before their deaths, Hamlet and Phèdre participate in an experience compounded of horror and sacredness. What had been inaccessible to them up until that moment is suddenly made accessible, and they contemplate it with a new emotion. Tragedy seems to culminate in that moment when the protagonist is able to sense both the terrifying and the ennobling aspects of his fate.

In recent years, especially since 1945, many attempts have been made in France to appraise and describe the "situation" of the theater. Lectures, symposia, books, and articles have offered analyses and interpretations of a state of affairs which by its very nature is provisional and tentative and changing. The theater has far less stability than the other arts. Any estimate of its present-day achievements and problems will probably be inaccurate and even ludicrously wrong as soon as the estimate is drawn up.

The theater is best characterized by a search at all times for an understanding, an *entente*, between actors and public. This search is preceded by an even more subtle one, which is endless too, the search for understanding between the poet and the actors. The theater is the history of a human concord or harmonization that is perpetually being established, only to be lost again. Each evening, each season, each decade, all the questions concerning the theater are raised, discussed, and solved. As soon as the situation of the theater is fixed and defined, we may be sure that it is no longer that.

In a word, it is impossible to define the situation of the theater in a fashion comparable to the situation of poetry or architecture or music of a given moment in history. The principal roles in the theater are held by poet, actor, and spectator, and the major power or control seems to move from one to the other. The poet has his day, and then the actor his, and even the spectator may have his triumph. The theater is probably the most ancient of the arts, and the gestures that we still see today on the stage, and which we call theatrical gestures, are probably the most ancient gestures of mankind. We read daily about the imminent collapse of the theater. We read how it is being killed off by the movies, by the radio and television, but we fundamentally believe that these newer arts will destroy themselves rather than destroy the theater, which despite momentary defeats and setbacks, will continue as long as mankind continues. In terms of its past, the future of the theater seems assured. The theater continues to live by the conviction that tomorrow will witness the première of a new *Cid* or a new *Hernani*.

Jouvet once wrote that the real situation of the theater is the dramatic situation of the individual play and that the kinds of such situations are innumerable: good and bad, perishable and imperishable, exciting and tiresome. There are dramatic situations created by Molière and Racine, by Musset and Giraudoux. Each one reflects to some degree its period, its moment in civilization. Hence we are tempted to characterize a play by the literary movement of its period and to call it realist or symbolist or existentialist. We state our preference for the *théâtre noir* or the *théâtre rose;* we tend to choose between the plays of Claudel or Sartre, between those of Mauriac or Cocteau. Erroneously we tend to establish the politics of the theater, to define the party lines and the doctrine.

Such activity, which goes on constantly, is futile. In a very fundamental sense, there is good theater and bad theater. Bad theater is usually characterized by commercialization and the need for excessive gesticulation. Good theater is characterized by the importance of a community, by the establishment of a communion that it propagates. It is the means of creating an incomparable spiritual bond between people. In our daily lives we unconsciously or consciously use elements of the art of the theater, but this is only natural since the theater itself is the stylization and the interpretation and the projection of life and human activity.

A single proof of the theater as major human activity was recently provided in the concentration camps of Europe, where performances of both serious and comic plays put on by the prisoners helped to revive in them hope and memory, and to restore them to themselves as they once were. The theater was reborn in the concentration camps and revived the understanding and the experience of human tenderness. This is the noble history of the theater from generation to generation, from century to century, from Aeschylus in antiquity to Lope de Vega and Shakespeare in the Renaissance, from Racine in the age of Louis XIV to the playwrights of today. With each successful performance of a significant play the spectators experience some kind of liberation. They discover some further knowledge about themselves and about the world. When the theater is purely itself, and not an instrument of propaganda, it can, like other arts, like music and painting in their purest forms, help to break down national barriers and effect an exchange of understanding and friendship and love.

During the past twenty years in France the theatrical seasons have on the whole been memorable, not only in the creation of new plays but also in productions of plays from other countries and in many new interpretations of classical plays. The new and old plays produced in Paris during and since the Occupation have represented an art closely related to the immediate and continuing problems of society. Each one has been an opportunity offered to the inhabitants of a city to witness and to participate in some exemplary adventure and to experience in the community of the theater a unifying emotion created by the play. Whether it be a tragedy of Racine or a comedy of Molière or a drama of Claudel, the play is a mirror in which each spectator is able to see himself and his period. The theater is an art that through the centuries has produced comparatively few masterpieces. Some of the best plays produced in Paris since 1945, those of Giraudoux, Montherlant, Sartre, Julien Green, Samuel Beckett, may not be enduring masterpieces, but they have been forms of art which have stirred and upset the spectators and have doubtless contributed to the formation of the contemporary conscience. Albert Camus's *Caligula* is the study of a mind obsessed by the absolute; *La Folle de Chaillot*, by Jean Giraudoux, is a poet's revolt against the domination of money; Jean Genet's *Les Bonnes* treats the theme of the identification of one character with another; *Les Epiphanies*, by Henri Pichette, is a complicated dramatic poem whose action is a refusal of the world as it is.

Just after the First World War, Jacques Copeau, founder in 1913 of the experimental theater Le Vieux-Colombier, summarized the meaning and the result of his undertaking with the words, "Le Vieux-Colombier is a small avant-garde theater." (*Un théâtre d'avant-garde pour petite salle. . . .*) He acknowledged not having reached a large public. At the close of the Second World War some of the most classical and conservative elements of the

French theater—the Beaux-Arts, the Comédie-Française, the Conservatoire—joined forces in order to restore and renew the vigor of the theater, in the hope that an increasingly wide public would be reached. At the turn of the mid-century a national popular theater was subsidized by the government and put under the direction of Jean Vilar, and recent reorganizations are aimed at similar goals.

The major preoccupation of the various theatrical movements—university groups, regional companies, the Comédiens-Routiers of Léon Chancerel, Vilar's Théâtre National Populaire, the Comédie-Française, the new Théâtre de France—is a will to find in the theater a collective expression: to express a public spirit and to find in the masses an adhesion, an enthusiasm that might resemble the mass enthusiasm created by the medieval mysteries. Theater directors like Jean Vilar, and like Jacques Copeau in the previous generation, seem to base their hopes for the resurgence of the theater in a unity of faith which the theater can provide. The more philosophically minded critics, Henri Gouhier, for example, have elaborated other theories to explain the theater, its persistence through the centuries and the role it is to play in our contemporary civilization.

The word most commonly used by all those who write on the theater today—directors or *metteurs-en-scène* like Vilar and Barrault, actors like Jouvet, aestheticians like Gouhier, critics and spectators—is the word "communion." Each tries to explain by this concept of communion dramatic art throughout its history and the current problems of dramatic art and theatrical presentation. They look upon a play when performed before an audience as an art of communion. Men and women have gathered in a theater in order to be together in listening to and seeing a drama. This physical gathering constitutes a kind of community. The question constantly being raised is whether this community in the theater is something more than that, whether it is, in reality, a communion, namely, an assembly of people united in the same vision. The major question that is always debated, and which remains debatable, is what the vision is, or around what reality the communion is formed.

We commit ourselves by our presence and by an act of our will to the anger of Alceste on the stage far more than we do to a scene of anger we might happen upon in everyday life. By taking our seat in the theater we yield to the wills of many people: the playwright, the producer, the director, the stage manager, the stage designer, the actors, and even of the stagehands. We are united with the other spectators who form the public and who sit together in order to grant existence to Tartuffe or Hamlet or Violaine. At the same time we reserve our critical judgment on the way a Jouvet plays Tartuffe, or a Barrault plays Hamlet, or a Pitoëff plays Violaine. As spectators in the theater, we believe in the existence of Ruy Blas, although we remain free in our judgment on the interpretation that Gérard Philipe gives to him.

Henri Gouhier defines as a "drama communion" (*communion dramatique*) that which the author and the actors demand of us who are spectators and which is something different from what others have called a spiritual unanimity in the theater. He somewhat opposes the dream of Copeau and Vilar, who believe that great theater arises at great periods of history when one religious belief unites all the spectators in the theater. Men like Vilar and Barrault look upon Paul Claudel as the one contemporary playwright of great stature. The discovery, in recent years, of Claudel as a major dramatist is an important factor in the history of the French theater, but spectators witnessing a play of Claudel are able to believe in it, to believe in the existence of Claudel's characters, without necessarily accepting the author's religious convictions. It would be difficult today, with our diversity of religious beliefs and the absence of religious belief, to reach in the theater a communion such as existed in antiquity in the public of

Athens watching a tragedy of Aeschylus, or in the Middle Ages, in the audiences that attended the lengthy mystery plays. It is beyond doubt that the first form of the theater was ceremonial and religious. But the theater through the centuries has become secularized as, since the Reformation, spiritual unanimity diminished in the West, until today the only possible communion in the theater is that created by the drama itself. The modern repertory includes tragedies of Sophocles and Shakespeare as well as dramas of Claudel and Jean-Paul Sartre. The variety of plays produced today, as well as the pluralism of religious and philosophical belief, substantiates Gouhier's belief in the dichotomy that has grown up between ceremonial theater and dramatic theater. And yet Gouhier believes that a degree of magical incantation and fervent spirituality exists in every form of dramatic writing and dramatic presentation.

A play comes to life only in the presence of a public concentrated on watching it. One evening at the Vieux-Colombier, when the performance was going badly and when the public was particularly uneasy and malicious, Copeau said: "It's not a public tonight, it's people." (*Ce n'est pas un public, c'est des gens. . . .*) By this statement he meant that the public had been decomposed into its elements. The public in the theater, when it is really constituted, acts almost as a single being that will last as long as the experience of the drama lasts. This simplification or unification of feeling endows a theatrical public with a primitive character that makes it submissive to the imagery of the language, and to whatever mysterious or miraculous events are enacted on the stage. The more unified the public grows, the more receptive it becomes to the same sentiments and emotions.

Jean Vilar is seeking to reach today, not the tremendous masses of people who come together for horse racing or baseball, but a large audience composed of people who are essentially simple, and who are capable of great enthusiasm when moved by the performance of a significant play. Despite the varieties of spiritual belief in a contemporary audience, the productions of Vilar have reached a quasi-mystical ideal where a collective being is formed by the poet, the actors, and the spectators. The actor is not so much a master of ceremonies capable of uniting and exciting the entire public as he is a man performing a sacramental act that will give to all the spectators the presence of something unknown and mysterious. Behind the actor the genius of the playwright succeeds in providing his characters with a reality such that those spectators who do not accept his fundamental philosophy will recognize their opponent's viewpoint and even be moved by it in terms of the dramatic conflict. The miracle of the modern theater might be defined by the communion it is able to establish within a large company of people who are divided among themselves and who are even hostile to one another. When dramatic art is realized, it creates a collective participation and unifies forces that are in conflict with one another. Of course, the dramatic situation in the play itself is often a conflict of similar forces, and hence the microcosm and the key to the bigger drama of the city or the nation. Even if initially, in our desire to attend the theater, there is an element of evasion from our daily reality, the art of the theater, when we are exposed to it, begins in us a recovery of some of the power of understanding and experiencing the world—both the reality that is ours and that which belongs more privately to the fictional characters who move on the stage.

The plays recently directed by Vilar and performed at Avignon emphasized the ceremonial aspects of the works by using the architectural background of the medieval city. The public was well-disposed and appreciative, the press was excellent, the entire undertaking was looked upon as successful, and yet Vilar speaks today of a disappointment he finds it difficult to analyze. He believes that there was at Avignon a ceremony, in the theatrical sense, but that there was no real communion established between spectators and actors. Something was lacking. Vilar believes that was the religious spirit that existed in the people of the Middle Ages who attended the *mystères*. What Vilar calls "ceremonial subject" is no longer conceivable because of the absence today of unanimous religious fervor. Catholic writers—like Claudel in *Partage de midi,* Mauriac in *Asmodée,* and Green in *Sud*—do not propose works of edification. However, Vilar advocates neither a theater for the people nor a theater for the elite. In fact, he confesses to no understanding of such terms. He invokes a celebrated formula of Stanislavsky when he urges a campaign for the creation of a theater "accessible to all."

The form of tragedy and the history of its theory have been ardently studied in our day by French philosophers, aestheticians, and literary critics, as well as by men of the theater. An increasing emphasis in this research is being placed on the religious origins of tragedy, on the filtration between tragedy and the dithyramb, and on the ritual significance of the Dionysian festivities. But modern tragedy is the work of literary men, and the very serious theater of playwrights like Montherlant, Anouilh, and Sartre shows almost no religious preoccupation when contrasted with Hellenic tragedy or with medieval mystery plays.

The concept of tragedy has been explored and redefined by such theorists at Thierry Maulnier, Segond, Gouhier, and Touchard. These critics discover a principle of purification, of appeasement immanent in the drama throughout its unfolding. With its appearance at the end, at the moment of epiphany, in accord with the ancient ritual of tragedy, the work is fully constituted and the spiritual atmosphere worthy of it is created. Tragedy is not therefore a faithful picture of reality, but a transfiguration of it. It is not a *tranche de vie,* as the realists called it, but a transfiguration or spiritualization of life. After the experiment of a narrow and limiting form of tragedy, the *pièce à thèse,* France discovered in the plays of Claudel, Cocteau, and Montherlant a more ancient and a more profound form, according to which sadness is majestic in its powers of transcendence. The meaning of tragedy in each period translates the meaning of civilization. When there is a communion between the tragic superman and the public, the total image of man can be recognized in the formula of the superman. The theater is one of the most persistent human activities. Quite possibly it is the supreme activity. This it owes to the importance of a community, of a communion on which it lives and which it sustains.

Selected Bibliography

PLAYS

Arthur Adamov

    Théâtre I. Gallimard, 1953: contains *La Parodie*
    (1947), *L'Invasion* (1949), *La Grande et la petite*
    manoeuvre (1950), *Le Professeur Taranne* (1951),
    Tous contre tous (1952).

    Théâtre II. Gallimard, 1955: contains *Le Sens de la*
    Marche (1953), *Les Retrouvailles* (1953), *Le Ping-*
    Pong (1955).

    Paolo Paoli. Gallimard, 1957.

    Les Ames mortes. Gallimard, 1959.

    (*Ping-Pong,* tr. Richard Howard, Grove, 1959.)

Jean Anouilh

    Pièces noires. Calmann-Lévy, 1945: contains *L'Her-*
    mine (1931), *La Sauvage* (1934), *Le Voyageur*
    sans bagage (1936), *Eurydice* (1941).

    Pièces roses. Calmann-Lévy, 1945: contains *Le Bal*
    des voleurs (1932), *Le Rendez-vous de Senlis*
    (1937), *Léocadia* (1939).

    Nouvelles Pièces noires. La Table Ronde, 1947: con-
    tains *Jézabel* (1932), *Antigone* (1942), *Roméo et*
    Jeannette (1945), *Médée* (1946).

Pièces brillantes. La Table Ronde, 1951: contains *L'Invitation au château* (1947), *Colombe* (1950), *La Répétition* (1950), *Cécile* (1949).

Pièces grinçantes. La Table Ronde, 1956: contains *Ardèle* (1946), *La Valse des toreadors* (1951), *Ornifle* (1955), *Pauvre Bitos* (1956).

L'Alouette. La Table Ronde, 1953.

L'Hurluberlu. La Table Ronde, 1959.

Beckett. La Table Ronde, 1959.

(*Selected Plays*, Vol. 1, Hill & Wang, 1958: contains *Romeo and Jeannette*, tr. Miriam John; *The Rehearsal* [*La Répétition*], tr. Lucienne Hill; *The Ermine* [*L'Hermine*], tr. Miriam John; *Antigone*, tr. Lewis Galantière; *Eurydice*, tr. Kitty Black. *Selected Plays*, Vol. 2, Hill & Wang, 1959: contains *Ardèle*, tr. Lucienne Hill; *The Lark* [*L'Alouette*], tr. Lillian Hellman; *Restless Heart* [*La Sauvage*], tr. Lucienne Hill; *Time Remembered* [*Léocadia*], tr. Patricia Moyes; *Mademoiselle Colombe* [*Colombe*], tr. Louis Kronenberger. *The Lark* also tr. Christopher Fry, Oxford, 1956. *Thieves' Carnival* [*Le Bal des voleurs*], tr. Lucienne Hill, in *The Modern Theatre*, Vol. 3, Anchor, 1955. *Medea*, tr. L. and A. Klein, in *The Modern Theatre*, Vol. 5, Anchor, 1957. *Ring Round the Moon* [*L'Invitation au château*], tr. Christopher Fry, Methuen, 1950. *Cécile*, tr. L. and A. Klein, in *From the Modern Repertoire*, Vol. 3, Indiana, 1956. *The Waltz of the Toreadors*, tr. Lucienne Hill, Coward-McCann, 1957.)

Guillaume Apollinaire

Les Mamelles de Tirésies. Editions Sic, 1918.

Jacques Audiberti

Théâtre. Gallimard, 1948.

Samuel Beckett

En attendant Godot. Editions de Minuit, 1952.

Fin de partie. Editions de Minuit, 1957.

Acte sans paroles. Editions de Minuit, 1957.

Tous Ceux qui tombent. Editions de Minuit, 1957.

La Dernière Bande. Editions de Minuit, 1960.

Cendres. Editions de Minuit, 1960.

(*Waiting for Godot*, tr. author, Grove, 1954. *Endgame* [*Fin de partie*], tr. author, Grove, 1958.)

Georges Bernanos

Dialogues des Carmélites. Editions du Seuil, 1951.

Albert Camus

Le Malentendu. Gallimard, 1944.

Caligula. Gallimard, 1944.

L'Etat de siège. Gallimard, 1948.

Les Justes. Gallimard, 1950.

(*Caligula and Three Other Plays*, tr. Stuart Gilbert, Knopf, 1958.)

Paul Claudel

Théâtre complet. Pléiade, 1949: contains *Tête d'or* (1890), *La Ville* (1893, 1897), *L'Echange* (1893), *Partage de midi* (1906), *L'Otage* (1911), *L'Annonce faite à Marie* (1910, 1912, 1948), *Le Pain dur* (1918), *Le Père humilié* (1920), *Le Soulier de satin* (1928-9), *Le Livre de Christophe Colomb* (1933).

(*Tête d'or*, tr. J. S. Newberry, Yale, 1919. *The City*, tr. J. S. Newberry, Yale, 1920. *The Hostage* [*L'Otage*], tr. John Heard, Luce, 1945. *The Tidings Brought to Mary*, tr. J. M. Sill, Yale, 1916. *Crusts* [*Le Pain dur*], tr. John Heard, Luce, 1945. *The Humiliation of the Father*, tr. John Heard, Luce, 1945. *The Satin Slipper*, tr. John O'Connor, Sheed and Ward, 1931. *The Book of Christopher Columbus*, Yale, 1930.)

Jean Cocteau

Théâtre complet (2 vols.). Grasset, 1957.

(*Orphée*, tr. Carl Wildman, Oxford, 1933. *The Human Voice* [*La Voix Humaine*], tr. Carl Wildman, Vision, 1951. *The Infernal Machine* [*La Machine infernale*], tr. Carl Wildman, Oxford, 1936. *Intimate Relations* [*Les Parents terribles*], tr. C. Frank in *From the Modern Repertoire*, Vol. 3, Indiana, 1956. *The Typewriter* [*La Machine à ecrire*], tr. Ronald Duncan, Dobson, 1947. *The Eagle Has Two Heads* [*L'Aigle à deux têtes*], tr. Ronald Duncan, Vision, 1948.)

Jean Genet

Les Bonnes. L'Arbalète, 1948.

Haute Surveillance. Gallimard, 1949.

Le Balcon. L'Arbalète, 1956.

Les Nègres. L'Arbalète, 1958.

(*The Maids, Deathwatch, The Balcony, The Blacks*, tr. Bernard Frechtman, Grove, 1954, 1958, 1960.)

André Gide

Théâtre complet (8 vols.). Ides et Calendes, 1947-9.

Théâtre. Gallimard, 1942: contains *Saül* (1896), *Le Roi Candaule* (1900), *Oedipe* (1930), *Perséphone* (1933), *Le Treizième Arbre* (1935).

(*My Theater*, tr. Jackson Matthews, Knopf, 1952: contains *Saul, Bathsheba, Philoctetes, King Candaules, Persephone*.)

Jean Giraudoux

Théâtre complet (4 vols.). Grasset, 1959.

(*Four Plays*, Hill & Wang, 1958: contains *Ondine, The Enchanted* [*Intermezzo*], *The Madwoman of Chaillot, The Apollo of Bellac*, tr. Maurice Valency. *Judith*, tr. John K. Savacool, in *The Modern Theatre*, Vol. 3, Anchor, 1955. *Siegfried*, tr. Philip Carr, Dial, 1930. *Amphitryon 38*, tr. S. N. Behrman, Random House, 1938. *Tiger at the Gates* [*La Guerre de Troie n'aura pas lieu*], tr. Christopher Fry, Oxford, 1955. *Electra*, tr. W. Smith, in *The Modern Theatre*, Vol. 1, Anchor, 1955.)

Julien Green

Sud. Plon, 1953.

L'Ennemi. Plon, 1954.

L'Ombre, Plon, 1956.

Eugène Ionesco

> *Théâtre I.* Gallimard, 1954: contains *La Cantatrice chauve* (1948), *La Leçon* (1950), *Jacques, ou la soumission* (1950), *Les Chaises* (1951), *Victimes du devoir* (1952), *Amédée, ou comment s'en débarrasser* (1953).

> *Théâtre II.* Gallimard, 1958: contains *L'Impromptu de l'Alma, ou le caméléon du berger* (1955), *Tueur sans gages* (1957), *Le Nouveau locataire* (1953), *L'Avenir est dans les oeufs, ou il faut de tout pour faire un monde* (1951), *Le Maître* (1951), *La Jeune Fille à marier* (1953).

> *Le Rhinocéros.* Gallimard, 1959.

> (*Four Plays,* Grove, 1958: contains *The Bald Soprano, The Lesson, Jack or the Submission, The Chairs,* tr. Donald M. Allen. *Three Plays,* Grove, 1958: contains *Amédée, The New Tenant, Victims of Duty,* tr. Donald Watson. *The Killer,* tr. Donald Watson, Grove, 1959. *Rhinoceros,* Grove, 1960.)

Alfred Jarry

> *Ubu Roi.* Mercure de France, 1896.

> (*Ubu Roi,* tr. Barbara Wright, New Directions, 1951.)

François Mauriac

> *Asmodée.* Grasset, 1937.

> *Les Mal Aimés.* Grasset, 1945.

> *Passage du malin.* La Table Ronde, 1947.

> *Le Feu sur la terre.* Grasset, 1949.

Henry de Montherlant

> *Théâtre.* Pléiade, 1955.

> (*The Master of Santiago and Four Other Plays,* tr. Jonathan Griffin, Knopf, 1951: contains *Queen after Death* [*La Reine morte*], *Malatesta, No Man's Son* [*Fils de personne*], *Tomorrow the Dawn* [*Demain il fera jour*], *The Master of Santiago.*)

Henri Pichette

> *Les Epiphanies.* K. Editeur, 1948.

Nucléa. L'Arche, 1952.

Jean-Paul Sartre

    Les Mouches. Gallimard, 1943.

    Huis Clos. Gallimard, 1945.

    Morts sans sépultures. Marguerat, 1946.

    La Putain respectueuse. Nagel, 1946.

    Les Mains sales. Gallimard, 1948.

    Le Diable et le Bon Dieu. Gallimard, 1952.

    Kean. Gallimard, 1954.

    Nekrassov. Gallimard, 1957.

    Les séquestrés d'Altona. Gallimard, 1959.

    (*No Exit and Three Other Plays,* Vintage, 1955: contains *No Exit* [*Huis Clos*] and *The Flies* [*Les Mouches*], tr. Stuart Gilbert, and *Dirty Hands* [*Les Mains sales*] and *The Respectful Prostitute* [*La Putain respectueuse*], tr. Lionel Abel. *The Devil and the Good Lord and Two Other Plays,* Knopf, 1960: contains *The Devil and the Good Lord* [*Le Diable et le Bon Dieu*] and *Kean,* tr. Kitty Black, and *Nekrassov,* tr. George and Sylvia Leeson.)

Georges Schehadé

    Monsieur Bob'le. Gallimard, 1951.

    La Soirée des Proverbes. Gallimard, 1954.

    Histoire de Vasco. Gallimard, 1956.

Michel Vinaver

    Les Coréens. Gallimard, 1956.

CRITICISM

Albérès, R. M., *La Révolte des ecrivains d'aujourd'hui,* Corréa, 1949.

    Jean-Paul Sartre, Editions Universitaires, 1953.

    An excellent introduction to the philosophy of Sartre. The plays are constantly referred to and used in the definition of theory.

Ambrière, Francis, *La Galérie Dramatique,* Corréa, 1949.

    A collection of reviews of Paris productions between 1945 and 1948. The articles on Salacrou place him among the most important contemporary playwrights.

Artaud, Antonin, *Le Théâtre et son double*. Gallimard, 1938. (Tr. by M. C. Richards, *The Theatre and Its Double*, Grove Press, 1958.)

Barrault, Jean-Louis, *Réflexions sur le théâtre*, Vautrain, 1949.

Bentley, Eric, *The Playwright as Thinker*, Harcourt, Brace, 1946.

In Search of Theatre, Knopf, 1953.

What Is Theatre?, Beacon, 1956.

There are many significant pages on the French theater in these three books. His critical writing reflects an extensive knowledge of the theater of many countries.

Bidal, M. L., *Giraudoux tel qu'en lui-même*, Corréa, 1952.

Brasillach, Robert, *Animateurs de théâtre*, La Table Ronde, 1954.

The first edition of this book, published in 1936, contained only the excellent chapters on the great theater directors: Copeau, Jouvet, Dullin, Pitoëff, and Baty. This new edition has added Brasillach's criticism of Paris productions between 1936 and 1944. A chronological repertory of plays produced by Jouvet, Dullin, Pitoëff, and Baty is also included.

Brisson, Pierre, *Propos de théâtre*, Gallimard, 1957.

A collection of articles about the theater, written during the past twelve years. Especially recommended are the chapters on Sartre, Mauriac, and Jouvet.

Brodin, Pierre, *Julien Green*, Editions Universitaires, 1957.

Chiari, Joseph, *The Poetic Drama of Paul Claudel*, Kenedy, 1954.

A reserved critical view on Claudel as dramatist. Mr. Chiari looks upon Claudel as a poet who happened to write plays.

Dussane, *Notes de théâtre*, Lardanchet, 1951.

A history of the Paris theater between 1940 and 1950. An excellent treatment of the Comédie-Française.

Fergusson, Francis, *The Idea of a Theater,* Princeton University Press, 1949.

One of the key contemporary books in dramaturgy and textual interpretation. Chapter Seven emphasizes the Paris theater and discusses *La Machine infernale* of Cocteau and *Noë* of Obey.

Fowlie, Wallace, *Claudel,* Bowes and Bowes, London, 1957.

A Guide to Contemporary French Literature, Meridian Books, 1957.

Gautier, Jean-Jacques, *Paris sur Scène,* Vautrain, 1951.

A collection of reviews of Paris productions between 1941 and 1951, which appeared in *Le Figaro.* Gautier is a ruthless critic. He attacks far more than he praises.

Grossvogel, David I., *The Self-Conscious Stage in Modern French Drama,* Columbia University Press, 1958.

A serious philosophical inquiry into the meaning of certain French and Belgian playwrights: Jarry, Apollinaire, Cocteau, Giraudoux, Claudel, Sartre, Anouilh, Crommelynck, Ghelderode. Briefer notice is given at the end of the volume to Ionesco, Adamov, and Beckett.

Gouhier, Henri, *L'Essence du théâtre,* Plon, 1943.

Le Théâtre et l'existence, Aubier, 1952.

L'Oeuvre théâtrale, Flammarion, 1958.

These three books on the theater, by a professor at the Sorbonne, are the works of a philosopher and the most profound studies written in our day on the aesthetics of drama.

Hobson, Harold, *The French Theatre of Today,* Harrap, 1953.

This is an English view of the French theater. After three chapters of general consideration, Mr.

Hobson studies the plays of Sartre, Montherlant, Salacrou, and Anouilh. The final chapter is a detailed commentary on several books about the French theater which Mr. Hobson considers significant.

Houlet, Jacques, *Le Théâtre de Jean Giraudoux,* Pierre Ardent, 1945.

Jouvet, Louis, *Témoignages sur le théâtre,* Flammarion, 1952.

The death of Jouvet interrupted the revision of the manuscript of this book. It is the handbook and the creed of an actor-director, a testimonial to his belief in the art of the actor. The passages on Molière and Giraudoux are original and refreshing.

Kemp, Robert, *La Vie du théâtre,* Albin Michel, 1956.

A generous collection of drama reviews that appeared in *Le Temps* and *Le Monde* between 1938 and 1956. In republishing these articles, M. Kemp did not alter them. His judgments should not be looked upon as verdicts but as the first impressions of a very penetrating critic.

Laprade, Jacques de, *Le Théâtre de Montherlant,* La Jeune Parque, 1950.

A close study of the traces of Jansenism in the plays of Montherlant. The religious aspect of the work is analyzed at the expense of other aspects.

Madaule, Jacques, *Le Drame de Paul Claudel,* Desclée de Brouwer, 1947.

This book contains a careful and lengthy analysis of each of the major plays of Claudel. A companion book to the earlier study of Madaule, *Le Génie de Paul Claudel.* Madaule is the most fervent of Claudel's defenders.

Mallarmé, Stéphane, *Oeuvres Complètes,* Pléiade, 1945 (pp. 293-422).

Oxenhandler, Neal, *Scandal and Parade: The Theater of Jean Cocteau,* Rutgers University Press, 1957.

This is the fullest and most satisfactory study in English of Cocteau's plays and films.

Pucciani, Oreste, *The French Theater since 1930,* Ginn, 1954.

Six French texts are included in this anthology: *La Machine infernale, La Guerre de Troie n'aura pas lieu, Le Voyageur sans bagages, La Reine morte, Le Malentendu, Les Mains sales.* The general introduction and the specific notes on each play and each dramatist condense a vast amount of critical interpretation and make this volume into something far more than a textbook.

Touchard, Pierre-Aimé, *Dionysos, apologie pour le théâtre,* Editions du Seuil, 1949.

An analysis of the dramatic genres tragedy and comedy, and a thesis that the theater today is beginning an era of greatness.

Vilar, Jean, *De la Tradition théâtrale,* L'Arche, 1955.

This is a collection of various writings of M. Vilar. Many of them were done in 1944, three years before the first Festival of Avignon and seven years before his appointment at the T.N.P. They are all related to practical and aesthetic problems of a theater director.

Villiers, André, *L'Art du comédien,* Presses Universitaires de France, 1953.

A brief but extremely lucid analysis of acting techniques. Half of the book concerns the stage actor and his preparation of a role, and the second half treats the technique of the movie actor.

Index

THE MERIDIAN

Twice yearly, in the spring and fall publishing seasons, Meridian Books take to newspaper format and issue *The Meridian,* a lively eight-page tabloid distributed free to thousands of subscribers. Its purpose, like that of any good house organ, is to acquaint readers with the present and future activities of the various imprints of the firm: Meridian Books, Meridian Giants, Living Age Books, Greenwich Editions, the Jewish Publication Society Series, Meridian Fiction, and Meridian Periodicals. The news is scattered in pre-publication reviews, selections from forthcoming books, guest features by authors, blurbs on projects vague and concrete—even in pictures. Among the standard features are the ever-popular "Tax Tips for the Teacher" and a complete list of all titles published by Meridian Books. For a free, unlimited subscription, write to:

The Meridian
12 East 22 Street
New York 10, New York

MERIDIAN BOOKS

12 East 22 Street, New York 10, New York